The Supreme Court's Impact on Public Education

E. Edmund Reutter, Jr.

PHI DELTA KAPPA

and

NATIONAL ORGANIZATION ON
LEGAL PROBLEMS OF EDUCATION

Cover design by

Nancy Rinehart

Library of Congress Catalog Card Number 81-060805

ISBN 0-87367-783-8 (hard cover edition)
ISBN 0-87367-784-6 (paper cover edition)

Printed in the United States of America

TABLE OF CONTENTS

PREFACE

The Phi Delta Kappa Commission on the Impact of Court Decisions on Education was created in 1976 and completed its work and made its final report in 1978. The first product of the Commission was *A Digest of Supreme Court Decisions Affecting Education*, edited by Perry A. Zirkel and published by Phi Delta Kappa in 1978. The *Digest* was updated by Zirkel with a supplement, which was published in 1982.

This volume, *The Supreme Court's Impact on Public Education*, is also an outgrowth of the work of the Commission. In 1977 Phi Delta Kappa and the National Organization on Legal Problems of Education (NOLPE) agreed to commission E. Edmund Reutter, Jr., one of the foremost authorities in school law, to analyze all the decisions of the United States Supreme Court that have some bearing on the operation of public schools. This volume is the result of Dr. Reutter's efforts to provide the most up-to-date and comprehensive analysis of the Supreme Court's decisions. We believe it makes an outstanding contribution to the literature of school law and serves as a reference work that is unparallelled in its scope and thoroughness.

Lowell C. Rose
Executive Secretary
Phi Delta Kappa

M. A. McGhehey
Executive Secretary
NOLPE

CHAPTER 1

Overview

This Constitution, and the Laws of the United States which shall be made in Pursuance thereof; . . . shall be the supreme Law of the Land; and the Judges in every State shall be bound thereby, any Thing in the Constitution or Laws of any State to the Contrary notwithstanding.[1]

The judicial Power of the United States, shall be vested in one supreme Court, and in such inferior Courts as the Congress may from time to time ordain and establish.[2]

The judicial Power shall extend to all Cases, in Law and Equity, arising under this Constitution, [and] the Laws of the United States, ...[3]

This volume presents an analysis and synthesis of the opinions of the Supreme Court explaining judgments that have directly decided education matters and those that have had substantial impact on public education policies and procedures even though the parties to the suits were not connected with public education.[4] The following chapters are structured thematically to highlight, in an integrated fashion, the main thrusts of the Supreme Court opinions. The cases within each area usually are presented in chronological order. This approach enhances the opportunity for the reader to observe the development of constitutional law in these major domains. Occasionally, closely related areas have developed simultaneously with points of law made in one directly impinging on another. Illustrations include the interrelationship of cases focused on financial aid for parochial schools with those focused on religious influences in public schools and those on conditions of teacher employment with those on discriminatory employment practices.

Education cases, of course, are not decided in isolation from cases in other walks of life involving related challenges to government action or inaction. There has been an abundance of Supreme Court decisions, for instance, in the realm of church-state relations, only a portion of which have involved education. The same phenomenon is evident in the area of race-state relations. However, schools, by the nature of the enterprise and the immediacy of the impact of educational policies on large numbers of persons of disparate backgrounds, have been the focus of a significiant share of Supreme Court opinions on social policy issues.

Since education is not mentioned in the Constitution, it is a state rather than a federal function by virtue of the tenth amendment.[5] Yet its operation must comport with the Constitution. Therefore, if a substantial federal issue is involved, the case may ultimately warrant Supreme Court action regardless of whether it originally proceeded through the courts of a state or those of the federal system.

The number of education cases decided by the Supreme Court has burgeoned in recent years. Partly, this has been a reflection of the general post-World War II accent on civil rights and liberties. Since the federal Constitution establishes many of these "freedoms" in general terms (for example, religion, speech, and assembly in the first amendment) and protects these and other "liberties" against government deprivation without "due process of law" through the fourteenth amendment, the Supreme Court inevitably must be involved as applications of these provisions in education settings are contested. In addition, state statutes may grant to individuals "property" rights which are protected from deprivation without due process. Various education rights are in this category. Further, many education cases are framed in terms of alleged "unequal protection" and thus may be brought under the fourteenth amendment's prohibition against a state's "deny[ing] to any person within its jurisdiction the equal protection of the laws."

The holdings of the Supreme Court do not provide a complete picture of the Court's impact in the sphere of any subject because opinions can be rendered only on questions properly presented in cases actually brought before the Court. Constitutional law is amplified and particularized by the decisions of lower courts which apply to new facts the principles enunciated by the Supreme Court in its opinions. To expedite the reader's pursuit of lower court extensions of points discussed in the Supreme Court cases, the points are footnoted to the *Supreme Court Reporter*, which permits ready access to the National Reporter System, in addition to the *United States Reports*.

The Supreme Court also influences education when it rejects a request that it review the decision of a lower court. Such a so-called "denial of [a writ of] certiorari" leaves the opinion of the state appellate court or the federal court of appeals as the controlling word on the issues raised and binding on all lower courts within the jurisdiction of the court that ruled and persuasive to courts in other jurisdictions. Sometimes the Supreme Court gives a reason for declining to review a case, such as "lack of a substantial federal question" in a petition involving a state court decision.

Only four to five percent of the cases on which review is sought are accepted by the Court. In a limited number of situations the Court must accept cases; for example, when a state court upholds a state statute against a claim of federal unconstitutionality. For most cases, however, review is discretionary with the Court. The Court has adopted some nonbinding guidelines for itself as to when it will review a case. These guidelines include as reviewable a case that creates a conflict between two federal courts of appeals and a case deciding a question of federal law so important that it should be settled at once for the whole nation. The granting of discretionary review requires the vote of four Justices.

The cases considered herein are those in which substantive issues were decided by the Court with full opinions. Not included are cases arising in the education domain involving only technical matters of law (such as standing to sue or mootness of an issue) and cases decided without opinions.

The discussion for each case is based on "the opinion of the Court," in which exposition of the precedent on a point of law is to be found. Although the vote is given for each case (primarily as a matter of interest, for the precedential value of a case is not dependent on the margin of the vote), concurring opinions in which Justices voting with the majority may express individual views and dissenting opinions of Justices who disagree with the majority decision are generally not discussed.

When feasible in this presentation, the words of the Court have been allowed to speak for themselves. Quotations generally are preferable to paraphrases not only for accuracy but also for flavor. The reader then can appreciate the precision, as well as the quality of writing, found in most Supreme Court opinions. Since the function of the Court in offering guidance through explicating the Constitution is even more important than deciding the specific questions presented in a given case, the Court's opinions are designed to be far-reaching in their scope and implications. As each holding establishes a precedent binding on all lower courts, and practically so on the Supreme Court itself in subsequent cases, the factual context of the question or questions presented becomes crucial. A change in a material fact may change the outcome of a subsequent case.

Cases taken to the Supreme Court usually have passed through at least two tiers of lower state or federal courts. They minimally involve strong emotional and financial commitments by some persons to a particular outcome. Those sympathetic to the view of the "losing side" in a Supreme Court case tend to grasp at elements of fact or comment presented in the opinion that could be a possible basis for pursuing their general goals in a slightly altered way. The "winning side" tends to overexpand the implications of the ruling in an effort to have it encompass a maximum number of other situations. Thus, those desiring truly to understand the law as expounded in an opinion and to conform to it in a responsible fashion must pay close attention to the opinion as a whole rather than to selected parts. They must also examine the place of the opinion in the pattern of cases decided previously by the Court.

A conscientious effort has been made in this treatise to present the cases in an objective fashion. Consideration is given to what the Court actually said, not to whether it rendered a "correct" or a "good" opinion. Such value judgments are left to the individual reader.

---

1. U.S. CONST. art. VI, cl. 2.
2. U.S. CONST. art. III, § 1.
3. U.S. CONST. art. III, § 2.
4. Coverage is through the 1981-1982 Term of the Supreme Court.
5. *See* Appendix B for texts of constitutional provisions referred to in this volume.

CHAPTER 2

Parent Rights in General

Child's Health

The first Supreme Court opinion to impinge on the question of the extent of parent rights in regard to education was rendered in 1922 in a case upholding the requirement that children be vaccinated before being permitted to attend "a public school or other place of education."[1] The unvaccinated child in the case had been refused admission to the public schools and to a private school. The Supreme Court said that a prior case[2] had settled that it was within the police power of a state to provide for compulsory vaccination. Here the regulation had been promulgated by the city of San Antonio, Texas, but the Court stated that authority to determine when vaccination was to be mandated could be delegated by the state to local authorities. The fact that the city had not made the ordinance applicable to all citizens did not constitute unequal protection. Further, it was held not necessary that there be an epidemic in order that the regulation be constitutionally enforceable.

Child's Knowledge

The first Supreme Court opinion to treat expressly the point of parent rights concerned the question of the constitutionality of a statute for the violation of which a private school teacher had been fined.[3]

Immediately following World War I, the state of Nebraska enacted a statute with two prohibitions. One was that "no person, individually or as a teacher, shall in any private, denominational, parochial or public school, teach any subject to any person in any language other than the English language."[4] The other was that "languages, other than the English language, may be taught as languages only after a pupil shall have attained and successfully passed the eighth grade. . . ."[5]

The appellant in the case (Meyer) had been convicted on a charge of teaching reading in the German language to a ten-year-old student in a nonpublic school. The Supreme Court of Nebraska had construed the statute as not covering "the so-called ancient or dead languages" such as Latin, Greek, and Hebrew, but it upheld the power of the state to proscribe the teaching of modern languages to the very young and the conviction of the teacher for doing so. The Nebraska court found that the legislature had reason to discourage the rearing of children with a foreign language as their mother tongue because of its effect on citizenship and held that the statute could be justified on grounds of public safety and the general welfare.

The Supreme Court of the United States phrased the question as "whether the statute as construed and applied unreasonably infringes the liberty guaranteed to [Meyer] by the Fourteenth Amendment."[6] In answering in the affirmative, the Court for the first time expounded on the substantive concept of "liberty" in the fourteenth amendment. The seven-member majority stated:

> While this Court has not attempted to define with exactness the liberty thus guaranteed, the term has received much consideration and some of the included things have been definitely stated. Without doubt, it denotes not merely freedom from bodily restraint but also the right of the individual to contract, to engage in any of the common occupations of life, to acquire useful knowledge, to marry, establish a home and bring up children, to worship God according to the dictates of his own conscience, and generally to enjoy those privileges long recognized at common law as essential to the orderly pursuit of happiness by free men.[7]

The Court observed that "[t]he American people have always regarded education and acquisition of knowledge as matters of supreme importance which should be diligently promoted."[8] Further, "corresponding to the right of control, it is the natural duty of the parent to give his children education suitable to their status in life,"[9] an obligation generally enforced by state compulsory education laws.

The Court then enunciated specifically that "liberty" covered the right of the teacher to teach a nonharmful subject and the right of parents to engage him therefor:

> Practically, education of the young is only possible in schools conducted by especially qualified persons who devote themselves thereto. The calling always has been regarded as useful and honorable, essential, indeed, to the public welfare. Mere knowledge of the German language cannot reasonably be regarded as harmful. Heretofore it has been commonly looked upon as helpful and desirable. [Meyer] taught this language in school as part of his occupation. His right thus to teach and the right of parents to engage him so to instruct their children, we think, are within the liberty of the amendment.[10]

The Court later in the opinion commented that "evidently the legislature has attempted materially to interfere with the calling of modern language teachers, with the opportunities of pupils to acquire knowledge, and with the power of parents to control the education of their own."[11] Of these three prongs, only the first was necessary to resolve the question at issue. The introduction and discussion of the parental rights issue was not essential, but was a clear indication of the Court's sympathy for parental concerns (although here there were no parental complainants). The reference to pupils' rights received no amplification elsewhere in the opinion.

The power of the state in educational matters was described by the Court for the first time in the following words: "That the State may do much, go very far, indeed, in order to improve the quality of its citizens, physically, mentally and morally, is clear; but the individual has certain fundamental rights which must be respected."[12]

The Court discussed some ideas of Plato and of the government of Sparta designed to develop ideal citizens and states and said that such relations between individuals and the state were barred by the Constitution of the United States. The Court further described the power of the state in educational matters as follows:

> The power of the State to compel attendance at some school and to make reasonable regulations for all schools, including a requirement that they shall give instructions in English, is not questioned. Nor has challenge been made of the State's power to prescribe a curriculum for institutions which it supports. Those matters are not within the present controversy. Our concern is with the prohibition approved by the Supreme Court [of Nebraska].[13]

The Court concluded its opinion by tying the case to a line of cases recent at the time wherein the Court had held that in order for the state to outlaw an occupation it was necessary to show substantial harm to the public derived from existence of the occupation. Otherwise, abuses incidental to the activity must be controlled by regulation short of abolition. The Court observed that "no emergency has arisen which renders knowledge by a child of some language other than English so clearly harmful as to justify its inhibition with the consequent infringement of rights long freely enjoyed."[14]

The wide-ranging opinion of the Court may have obscured the precise issue resolved. It was: Can a teacher be criminally penalized for teaching a modern foreign language in a private school? There was no holding about what subjects the state may or may not decide to offer in the public schools. A state was not required to offer a foreign language in its schools. Foreign language teachers were granted no right to employment by local public school boards. Neither parents nor students were given any specific rights by this case except the right, at their expense and by their arrangements, to learn something not hostile to the public welfare.

There is an implication in the opinion that a requirement that the basic medium of instruction in all full-time schools be English is constitutionally sound. There is also an intimation, to be repeated two years later in *Pierce v. Society of Sisters of the Holy Names of Jesus and Mary*,[15] that a requirement of attendance at a school (*i.e.*, no substitution of home instruction) would not be in violation of the Constitution. These points have not come squarely before the Court.

Four years later the Supreme Court unanimously invalidated an Hawaii statute because it too comprehensively controlled schools conducted in foreign languages for the purpose of teaching the languages.[16] Parents of Japanese ancestry contended that regulations adopted under the statute would in effect destroy the schools, which were conducted for one hour each day of the week. The detailed rules required permits for schools and teachers; specified prerequisites of age and achievement for students attending; and regulated what could be taught, textbooks that could be used, and hours when the schools could operate.

The Supreme Court stated:

> [T]he School Act and the measures adopted thereunder go far beyond mere regulation of privately supported schools, where children obtain instruction deemed valuable by their parents and which is not obviously in conflict with any public interest. They give affirmative direction concerning the intimate and essential details of such schools, intrust their control to public officers, and deny both owners and patrons reasonable choice and discretion in respect of teachers, curriculum and text-books. Enforcement of the act probably would destroy most, if not all, of them; and, certainly, it would deprive parents of their opportunity to procure for their children instruction which they think important and we cannot say is harmful.[17]

Citing *Meyer* and *Pierce*, the Court said, "The general doctrine touching rights guaranteed by the Fourteenth Amendment to owners, parents and children in respect of attendance upon schools has been announced in recent opinions."[18] It stated that the due process clause of the fifth amendment places similar restrictions on the federal government, which was involved because Hawaii at the time was a territory.

The cornerstone case for parent rights was *Pierce*, decided in 1925.[19] As with *Meyer*, this case procedurally arose with parent rights as a subordinate element. At issue was the constitutionality of a statute that would have had the effect of damaging an enterprise that was not harmful to society, namely the operation of all private schools. Such schools were imperiled by an Oregon statute, adopted through the process of voter initiative, that required all "normal" children between the ages of eight and sixteen, who had not completed the eighth grade, to attend a public school.

The statute was challenged, not by parents, but by operators of two private schools. One of the schools was under religious auspices, the other was a proprietary military academy. The operators of the schools asserted that enforcement of the statute would seriously impair, if not destroy, their "business" and greatly diminish the value of their property. The religious complainant, the Society of the Sisters of the Holy Names of Jesus and Mary, was organized as an Oregon corporation for the secular and religious education and care of children, and operated schools through the junior college level; the Hill Military Academy was a corporation organized for profit in operating educational facilities for males between the ages of five and twenty-one.

The Supreme Court, in unanimously declaring the statute unconstitutional, closely followed the reasoning of the *Meyer* case. It declared:

> The inevitable practical result of enforcing the Act under consideration would be destruction of appellees' primary schools, and perhaps all other private primary schools for normal children within the State of Oregon. These parties are engaged in a kind of undertaking not inherently harmful, but long regarded as useful and meritorious. Certainly there is nothing in the present records to indicate that they have failed to discharge their obligations to patrons, students or the State. And there are no peculiar circumstances or present emergencies which demand extraordinary measures relative to primary education.
>
> Under the doctrine of [*Meyer*] we think it entirely plain that the Act of 1922 unreasonably interferes with the liberty of parents and guardians to direct the upbringing and education of children under their control. As often heretofore pointed out, rights guaranteed by the Constitution may not be abridged by legislation which has no reasonable relation to some purpose within the competency of the State. The fundamental theory of liberty upon which all governments in this Union repose excludes any general power of the State to standardize its children by forcing them to accept instruction from public teachers only. The child is not the mere creature of the State; those who nurture him and direct his destiny have the right, coupled with the high duty, to recognize and prepare him for additional obligations.[20]

The preceding statements about parental rights in the education of their children have come to be widely quoted. Frequently there has been a temptation for some to try to extend the words beyond their meaning in the *Pierce* case, particularly in regard to questions of financial aid to private schools or their students and of curricular requirements within public schools. Almost a half century after this case, the Court was constrained to point out that "*Pierce* 'held simply that while a State may posit [educational] standards, it may not pre-empt the educational process by requiring children to attend public schools.' ... It is one thing to say that a State may not prohibit the maintenance of private schools and quite another to say that such schools must, as a matter of equal protection, receive state aid."[21]

In *Pierce*, the Court presented one of its most seminal paragraphs regarding the power of the state in educational matters:

> No question is raised concerning the power of the State reasonably to regulate all schools, to inspect, supervise and examine them, their teachers and pupils; to require that all children of proper age attend some school, that teachers shall be of good moral character and patriotic disposition, that certain studies plainly essential to good citizenship must be taught, and that nothing be taught which is manifestly inimical to the public welfare.[22]

Child's Associates

The most extensive discussion by the Supreme Court of the tension between parent rights and state rights in regard to education was presented in 1972 in a case involving members of the Amish faith who refused to allow their children to attend public school beyond the eighth grade and the age of fourteen.[23] Although technically freedom of religion rights were at stake and the case was decided on that issue, the Court was obliged to address parent rights in general. The case had been widely (and often misleadingly) publicized as one that would, if decided in favor of the Amish, strengthen existing private schools and facilitate the creation of new private arrangements for implementing various approaches to the education process outside the public school structure.

The state of Wisconsin had prosecuted and convicted Amish parents for violating the state's compulsory education law, which required attendance until the age of sixteen. The State Superintendent of Public Instruction had rejected a proposal to determine administratively that the Amish could satisfy the law by establishing their own vocational training plan, as had been done in some other states. His reasoning was that it would not afford Amish children an education substantially equivalent to that offered in the schools in that area. After the Supreme

Court of Wisconsin had ruled in favor of the Amish, the state carried the case to the United States Supreme Court. The Court held that Wisconsin's statute, as applied to the Amish, violated the free exercise of religion provision of the first amendment.

The reasoning of the Court supporting that holding is treated in Chapter 6. Here, the statements of the Court regarding parent and state rights in general are pertinent.

The state had argued that it was exercising its inherent powers as *parens patriae* to extend the benefit of a secondary education to the Amish child regardless of parental wishes. Reliance for the view was placed on a 1944 case in which the Supreme Court had sustained the state's right to regulate or prohibit child labor.[24] In that case, the child was selling religious pamphlets, an act characterized by the parent as a religious duty. The Court distinguished the present case by noting that here there was no evidence of any potential harm to the child by being taken from public school after the eighth grade and placed in an environment of more direct parental supervision in a form of vocational learning-by-doing on a farm. Further, unlike cases in which compulsory vaccination had been upheld against religious claims[25] and a ban on religion-sanctioned polygamy had been sustained,[26] the excusal constituted no substantial threat to public health or welfare.

The Court, referring to its statements in *Pierce* that parents have "the right, coupled with the high duty, to recognize and prepare [their child] for additional obligations,"[27] said that "additional obligations" must be read to include "the inculcation of moral standards, religious beliefs and elements of good citizenship."[28] However, the Court added that *Pierce* "recognized that where nothing more than the general interest of the parent in the nurture and education of his children is involved, it is beyond dispute that the State acts 'reasonably' and constitutionally in requiring education to age 16 in some public or private school meeting the standards prescribed by the State."[29]

Parent interests and rights were referred to twice in the opinion as being "traditional,"[30] and the Court stated that "the values of parental direction of the religious upbringing and education of their children in their early and formative years have a high place in our society."[31] However, the Court also noted that "a State [has] a high responsibility for education of its citizens, . . . [and] [p]roviding public schools ranks at the very apex of the function of a State."[32] Thus, "[a]way of life, however virtuous and admirable, may not be interposed as a barrier to reasonable state regulation of education if it is based on purely secular considerations."[33]

This important caveat as to the narrowness of the present holding was restated in the following words: "It cannot be over-emphasized that we are not dealing with a way of life and mode of education by a group claiming to have recently discovered some 'progressive' or more enlightened process for rearing children for modern life."[34] The Court further stated, "Nothing we hold is intended to undermine the general applicability of the State's compulsory school-attendance statutes."[35] The Amish not only possessed a three-century old *religious* base that evidence showed would be impaired, but they demonstrated that their children ages fourteen to sixteen were placed in a vocationally oriented program of instruction. They further showed that the Amish were no burden to the state in that criminal and welfare cases were nonexistent in the Amish community.

In a 1976 case involving racially discriminatory admissions policies in private schools,[36] the Court, by a vote of seven-to-two, held that constitutional rights of parents affecting the education of their children did not supersede an 1866 federal statute granting to all persons "the same right in every State and Territory to make and enforce contracts . . . as is enjoyed by white citizens."[37] The statute had been enacted under the thirteenth amendment as legislation designed to eliminate "the badges and the incidents" of slavery. In 1968, the Court had held that the statute prohibited private acts of racial discrimination, specifically in the sale or rental of real or personal property.[38] As the students in the present case were refused admission to private schools on the basis of race (the schools would not contract with the black parents because of their race), the statute was clearly applicable under the precedent of the 1968 case.[39] The Court thus was required to determine whether the statute, as applied, violated general constitutionally protected rights of free association and privacy or a parent's right to direct the education of his or her children. No violation was found.

The Court observed that from the first amendment right to engage in association for the advancement of beliefs and ideas,

> it may be assumed that parents have a First Amendment right to send their children to educational institutions that promote the belief that racial segregation is desirable, and that the children have an equal right to attend such institutions. But it does not follow that the *practice* of excluding racial minorities from such institutions is also protected by the same principle.[40]

The Court referred to its statement in *Norwood*[41] that the Constitution did not afford invidious private discrimination any affirmative protection, and noted that although such acts were not per se constitutionally barred, they could be subject to remedial legislation under the thirteenth amendment. It further noted that discontinuance of the discriminatory admissions policies would in no way inhibit the teaching of any ideas or dogma in the schools.

The Court then offered the following review of its cases in support of its conclusion that "[i]t is clear that the present application of § 1981 infringes no parental rights recognized"[42] in prior cases:

> In *Meyer v. Nebraska* the Court held that the liberty protected by the Due Process Clause of the Fourteenth Amendment includes . . . the right to send one's children to a private school that offers specialized training—in that case, instruction in the German language. In *Pierce v. Society of Sisters* the Court applied "the doctrine of *Meyer v. Nebraska*" to hold unconstitutional an Oregon law requiring the parent, guardian, or other person having custody of a child between eight and 16 years of age to send that child to public school on pain of criminal liability. The Court thought it "entirely plain that the [statute] unreasonably interferes with the liberty of parents and guardians to direct the upbringing and education of children under their control." In *Wisconsin v. Yoder* the Court stressed the limited scope of *Pierce*, pointing out that it lent "no support to the contention that parents may replace state educational requirements with their own idiosyncratic views of what knowledge a child needs to be a productive and happy member of society" but rather "held simply that while a State may posit [educational] standards, it may not pre-empt the educational process by requiring children to attend public schools." And in *Norwood v. Harrison* the Court once again stressed the "limited scope of *Pierce*," which simply "affirmed the right of private schools to exist and to operate. . . ."[43]

In a separate treatment of the right of privacy (which in a footnote the Court suggested might be a variation of "the *Meyer-Pierce-Yoder* 'parental' right"[44]), the Court emphasized that "it does not follow that because government is largely or even entirely precluded from regulating the child-bearing decision, it is similarly restricted by the Constitution from regulating the implementation of parental decisions concerning a child's education."[45] The Court said it had repeatedly stressed that states could reasonably regulate the private school education that parents had a constitutional right to choose as an alternative to public schools. It recalled that "the Court in *Pierce* expressly acknowledged 'the power of the State reasonably to regulate all schools, to inspect, supervise and examine them, their teachers and pupils.'"[46]

---

1. Zucht v. King, 260 U.S. 174, 43 S. Ct. 24 (1922).
2. Jacobson v. Commonwealth of Mass., 197 U.S. 11, 25 S. Ct. 358 (1905).
3. Meyer v. Nebraska, 262 U.S. 390, 43 S. Ct. 625 (1923).
4. 1919 Neb. Laws c.249.

5. *Id.*
6. Meyer v. Nebraska, 262 U.S. at 399, 43 S. Ct. at 626.
7. *Id.*
8. 262 U.S. at 400, 43 S. Ct. at 627.
9. *Id.*
10. *Id.*
11. *Id.*
12. 262 U.S. at 401, 43 S. Ct. at 627.
13. *Id.* at 402, 43 S. Ct. at 628.
14. *Id.*
15. 268 U.S. at 5 10, 45 S. Ct. 571 (1925).
16. Farrington v. Tokushige, 273 U.S. 284, 47 S. Ct. 406 (1927).
17. 273 U.S. at 298, 47 S. Ct. at 408-409.
18. 273 U.S. at 298-299, 47 S. Ct. at 409.
19. Pierce v. Society of Sisters of the Holy Names of Jesus and Mary, 268 U.S. 510, 45 S. Ct. 571 (1925).
20. 268 U.S. at 534-535, 45 S. Ct. at 573.
21. Norwood v. Harrison, 413 U.S. 455, 461-462, 93 S. Ct. 2804, 2809 (1973).
22. Pierce, 268 U.S. at 534, 45 S. Ct. at 573.
23. Wisconsin v. Yoder, 406 U.S. 205, 92 S. Ct. 1526 (1972).
24. Prince v. Massachusetts, 321 U.S. 158, 64 S. Ct. 438 (1944).
25. Zucht v. King, 260 U.S. 174, 43 S. Ct. 24 (1922); Jacobson v. Commonwealth of Mass., 197 U.S. 11, 25 S. Ct. 358 (1905).
26. Reynolds v. United States, 98 U.S. 145, 25 L.Ed. 244 (1878).
27. Pierce, 268 U.S. at 535, 45 S. Ct. at 573.
28. Wisconsin v. Yoder, 406 U.S. at 233, 92 S. Ct. at 1542.
29. *Id.*
30. *Id.* at 214 and 232, 92 S. Ct. at 1532 and 1541.
31. *Id.* at 213-214, 92 S. Ct. at 1532.
32. *Id.* at 213, 92 S. Ct. at 1532.
33. *Id.* at 215, 92 S. Ct. at 1533.
34. *Id.* at 235, 92 S. Ct. at 1543.
35. *Id.* at 236, 92 S. Ct. at 1543.
36. Runyon v. McCrary, 427 U.S. 160, 96 S. Ct. 2586 (1976).
37. 42 U.S.C. § 1981 (1976).
38. Jones v. Alfred H. Mayer Co., 392 U.S. 409, 88 S. Ct. 2186 (1968).
39. Two Justices (Powell and Stevens), in separate concurring opinions, said they felt bound by *Jones* even though they were not in agreement with it.
40. Runyon v. McCrary, 427 U.S. at 176, 96 S. Ct. at 2597.
41. Norwood v. Harrison, 413 U.S. 455, 93 S. Ct. 2804 (1973).
42. Runyon v. McCrary, 427 U.S. at 177, 96 S. Ct. at 2598.
43. *Id.* at 176-177, 96 S. Ct. at 2597-2598.
44. *Id.* at 178 n.15, 96 S. Ct. at 2598 n.15.
45. *Id.* at 178, 96 S. Ct. at 2598.
46. *Id.*

CHAPTER 3

Financial Aid for
Secular Private Schools

The first Supreme Court decision involving financial assistance to private schools or their students was written in 1930.[1] The legislature of Louisiana had enacted a statute providing that the proceeds of the severance tax, after constitutional appropriations were covered, was to be devoted "first, to supplying school books to the school children of the State."[2] The state board of education was directed to provide "school books for school children free of cost to such children."[3] The suit sought to restrain the state board from expending any funds for books for children attending nonpublic schools on the principal ground that such an expenditure constituted a taking of private property (money paid in taxes) for a private purpose, an act allegedly barred by the due process clause of the fourteenth amendment.

The Supreme Court unanimously affirmed the decision of the Supreme Court of Louisiana, which had found the arrangement to be constitutional. The Court's opinion was brief, much of it being quoted from the opinion of the state court. That court had sustained the legislation as implemented by the state board to include all children in all types of schools. In the opinion, a distinction was made between aid to a private school and aid to students attending the school, the former being a violation of the due process clause of the fourteenth amendment and the latter being constitutionally permissible. It was held that the school children and the state, not the schools, were the beneficiaries of this act. The Louisiana court expressly had construed the statute to mean that private school students would receive the same books as public school students so that no books would be adapted to religious instruction. The Louisiana court had noted that the books were lent, rather than given, to the students, but the Supreme Court observed that this point was not of importance in relation to the federal question.

The reasoning of the Supreme Court of Louisiana, quoted with approval by the United States Supreme Court, follows:

> "One may scan the acts in vain to ascertain where any money is appropriated for the purchase of school books for the use of any church, private, sectarian or even public school. The appropriations were made for the specific purpose of purchasing

school books for the use of the school children of the state, free of cost to them. It was for their benefit and the resulting benefit to the state that the appropriations were made. True, these children attend some school, public or private, the latter, sectarian or nonsectarian, and that the books are to be furnished them for their use, free of cost, whichever they attend. The schools, however, are not the beneficiaries of these appropriations. They obtain nothing from them, nor are they relieved of a single obligation because of them. The school children and the state alone are the beneficiaries. It is also true that the sectarian schools, which some of the children attend, instruct their pupils in religion, and books are used for that purpose, but one may search diligently the acts, though without result, in an effort to find anything to the effect that it is the purpose of the state to furnish religious books for the use of such children. . . . What the statutes contemplate is that the same books that are furnished children attending public schools shall be furnished children attending private schools. This is the only practical way of interpreting and executing the statutes, and this is what the state board of education is doing. Among these books, naturally, none is to be expected, adapted to religious instruction."[4]

The conclusion of the United States Supreme Court was:

Viewing the statute as having the effect thus attributed to it, we cannot doubt that the taxing power of the State is exerted for a public purpose. The legislation does not segregate private schools, or their pupils, as its beneficiaries or attempt to interfere with any matters of exclusively private concern. Its interest is education, broadly; its method, comprehensive. Individual interests are aided only as the common interest is safeguarded.[5]

This case is the genesis of the "child benefit" theory, which ever since has played an important role as a criterion by which permissible aid to private (and especially sectarian) education may be distinguished from constitutionally forbidden assistance. Obviously it is not an objective criterion, but it constituted a start toward developing a standard that was to become more and more refined, though never free of dispute, in subsequent cases.

It must be emphasized that in *Cochran*, the first amendment prohibition against "an establishment of religion" was not argued. The Supreme Court had not yet interpreted fourteenth amendment prohibitions against actions of states as specifically including infringements of the rights guaranteed by the first amendment against enroachment by the federal government. That holding lay a decade away;[6] its application to an education case involving public funds was seventeen years in the future;[7] and its application to textbooks lay thirty-eight years ahead.[8]

The Supreme Court of Louisiana seems quite certainly to have recognized the religion issue by its specific construction that "school books" meant the "same books that are furnished children attending public schools" and its further comment that "naturally" the books would not be adapted to religious instruction. The United States Supreme Court's quotation of this part of the Louisiana court's opinion implies a like sensitivity on its part.

Only one subsequent aid-to-private-secular-schools case has been decided by the Supreme Court with a full opinion.[9] That case too involved textbooks. The question was whether books could be furnished to children in private schools that refused to admit black students.

The enrollment in private schools in Mississippi had increased twenty-fold between 1963 and 1970. Many of the private schools were established or enlarged simultaneously with major events in the desegregation of public schools. Mississippi, since 1940, had had a textbook arrangement similar to that of Louisiana. The inclusion in the program of children enrolled in the all-white academies was challenged as state aid to racially segregated education and an impediment to the process of fully desegregating public schools.

The Supreme Court, in a unanimous decision, held that books must not be furnished by the state to students attending schools with racially discriminatory admissions policies. The Court said:

> [T]he constitutional infirmity of the Mississippi textbook program is that it significantly aids the organization and continuation of a separate system of private schools which ... may discriminate if they so desire. A State's constitutional obligation requires it to steer clear not only of operating the old dual system of racially segregated schools but also of giving significant aid to institutions that practice racial or other invidious discrimination.[10]

The Court commented that it had consistently affirmed (without opinions) lower court decisions enjoining tuition grants by states to students attending racially discriminatory private schools and that a textbook lending program was not legally different. It said:

> Free textbooks, like tuition grants directed to private school students, are a form of financial assistance inuring to the benefit of the private schools themselves. An inescapable educational cost for students in both public and private schools is the expense of providing all necessary learning materials.

When, as here, that necessary expense is borne by the State, the economic consequence is to give aid to the enterprise; if the school engages in discriminatory practices the State by tangible aid in the form of textbooks thereby gives support to such discrimination.[11]

The Court said that it was distinguishing textbooks, which are only provided in connection with schools and which can be purchased on the open market, from generalized services such as electricity or fire protection, which are "necessities of life" not readily available from sources entirely independent of the state. The latter constitutionally can be provided to private entities that racially discriminate, in common with all entities, under a decision of the year before holding that a social organization could not be refused a liquor permit on the ground that it did not admit blacks to membership.[12]

Between the times of *Cochran* and *Norwood*, the Court had extended the "child benefit" theory of *Cochran*[13] and thus was required to indicate why the theory did not require a different result in *Norwood*. The Court said that when it had stated that furnishing textbooks was of direct financial benefit to parents and children, not to schools, it was "in the sense that parents and children—not schools—would in most instances be required to procure their textbooks if the State did not. . . . [T]he Court has never denied that 'free books make it more likely that some children choose to attend a [private] school.'"[14] The Court recognized that it had permitted "indirect" aids like textbooks and transportation to sectarian school students under the first amendment, but differentiated the present situation as follows:

> The leeway for indirect aid to sectarian schools has no place in defining the permissible scope of state aid to private racially discriminatory schools. "State support of segregated schools through any arrangement, management, funds or property cannot be squared with the [Fourteenth] Amendment's command that no State shall deny to any person within its jurisdiction the equal protection of the laws.[15]

The Court said that, within first amendment bounds, the state may assist sectarian schools in their secular functions because the state has a substantial interest in the quality of education provided in private schools. However, in the present case, "the legitimate educational function cannot be isolated from [alleged] discriminatory practices."[16] Furthermore, the Court added:

> [A]lthough the Constitution does not proscribe private bias, it places no value on discrimination as it does on the values inherent in the Free Exercise Clause. Invidious private discrimination may be characterized as a form of exercising freedom of association protected by the First Amendment, but

it has never been accorded affirmative constitutional protections. And even some private discrimination is subject to special remedial legislation in certain circumstances under Sec. 2 of the Thirteenth Amendment. . . . However narrow may be the channel of permissible state aid to sectarian schools . . . , it permits a greater degree of state assistance than may be given to private schools which engage in discriminatory practices that would be unlawful in a public school system.[17]

Since not all private schools in Mississippi could be assumed to have discriminatory admissions policies, the trial court was directed to require state officials to establish a certification procedure under which any school seeking textbooks for its students could apply on behalf of the students by supplying information that would establish the fact of nondiscriminatory admissions policies. The procedure would be subject to judicial review.

It is to be observed that in this situation there was no improper motive in establishing the textbook arrangement. The system was not, like the tuition grants referred to by the Court, established after desegregation was mandated. However, the constitutional duty to desegregate required that all state actions be subject to judicial scrutiny as to their effect on the process of vindicating constitutional rights of black students that had been violated by the dual school system. The narrow issue was whether a state could provide tangible assistance to students attending private schools that admitted only whites at the time the state was undertaking a constitutional duty to correct its former violations of rights of blacks in the area of education.

---

1. Cochran v. Louisiana State Bd. of Educ., 281 U.S. 370, 50 S. Ct. 335 (1930).
2. 1928 La. Acts No. 100.
3. *Id.*
4. Cochran, 281 U.S. at 374-375, 50 S. Ct. at 335.
5. *Id.* at 375, 50 S. Ct. at 336.
6. Cantwell v. Connecticut, 310 U.S. 296, 60 S. Ct. 900 (1940). In this case, the Court established the right of members of a religious sect to propagate their religious views and to solicit funds without obtaining a license from civil authorities.
7. Everson v. Board of Educ., 330 U.S. 1, 67 S. Ct. 504 (1947). Discussed *infra*, chapter 4.
8. Board of Educ. of Cent. School Dist. No. 1 v. Allen, 392 U.S. 236, 88 S. Ct. 1923 (1968). Discussed *infra*, chapter 4.
9. Norwood v. Harrison, 413 U.S. 455, 93 S. Ct. 2804 (1973). In *Everson*, n.7 *supra*, the Court had said that, since education of a general nature clearly serves a public purpose, legislation facilitating secular education does not violate the fourteenth amendment's prohibition against use of public funds for private purposes.
10. Norwood v. Harrison, 413 U.S. at 467, 93 S. Ct. at 2812.
11. *Id.* at 463-465, 93 S. Ct. at 2810.
12. Moose Lodge No. 107 v. Irvis, 407 U.S. 163, 92 S. Ct. 1965 (1972).
13. Especially in *Everson*, n.7 *supra*, and in *Allen*, n.8 *supra*.
14. Norwood v. Harrison, 413 U.S. at 464 n.7, 93 S. Ct. at 2810 n.7.
15. *Id.*
16. *Id.* at 469, 93 S. Ct. at 2812.
17. *Id.* at 469-470, 93 S. Ct. at 2813.

CHAPTER 4

Financial Aid for Parochial Schools: Evolution of the Constitutional Criteria

Transportation to and from School

It was not until 1947 that the Supreme Court was required to elucidate the meaning of the establishment of religion clause of the first amendment in an education context.[1] The precise question was whether the clause was violated by a New Jersey statute that required local school boards that provide transportation for children attending public schools to supply the same transportation, along the established routes, to children attending nonprofit, private schools. A taxpayer challenged the resolution of a local board that implemented the statute by reimbursing parents of children in public and Catholic parochial schools for expenditures for bus transportation to and from school on public transit buses. (There was no challenge to the statutory exclusion of the benefit to children attending for-profit private schools nor to the fact that the board resolution specified only public and Catholic school parents as beneficiaries.)

The arrangement was attacked also on the fourteenth amendment ground of deprivation of property without due process in that the state allegedly was taking the private property of some by taxation and bestowing it upon others for use in a private purpose. The Court rejected this argument. It found a public purpose to be involved because the legislation was intended to facilitate the opportunity of children to get a secular education free from risks of traffic and other hazards. That the law coincided with the personal desires of some individuals was deemed an inadequate reason for the Court to say the legislature had acted improperly in appraising a public need. The Court observed that legislation for the public welfare was a primary reason for the existence of states. It commented that subsidies and loans to individuals such as farmers and home owners and to privately owned transportation systems and other businesses had been "commonplace practices" in United States history.

The profound significance of the case lies in the first amendment aspect, the discussion of the meaning of a "law respecting an establishment of religion." It was in 1940 that the Court had stated that the concept of "liberty" embodied in the fourteenth amendment included the liberties guaranteed by the first amendment.[2] Thus, state legislatures, as well as Congress, were restricted in the area of religion. Although the vote in the present case was five-to-four to uphold the statute, the disagreement centered not on the meaning of the constitutional provision but on its application to the facts at hand. Indeed, even though the majority ruled in favor of the parochial school interests, its interpretation of the establishment clause was not what was argued by the parochial schools. The opinion of the Court traced the history of the concept behind the first words of the first amendment and concluded as follows:

> The "establishment of religion" clause of the First Amendment means at least this: Neither a state nor the Federal Government can set up a church. Neither can pass laws which aid one religion, aid all religions, or prefer one religion over another. Neither can force nor influence a person to go to or to remain away from church against his will or force him to profess a belief or disbelief in any religion. No person can be punished for entertaining or professing religious beliefs or disbeliefs, for church attendance or non-attendance. No tax in any amount, large or small, can be levied to support any religious activities or institutions, whatever they may be called, or whatever form they may adopt to teach or practice religion. Neither a state nor the Federal Government can, openly or secretly, participate in the affairs of any religious organizations or groups and vice versa. In the words of Jefferson, the clause against establishment of religion by law was intended to erect "a wall of separation between Church and State."[3]

It was the bar on aid to *all* religions that disturbed advocates of aid to parochial schools. This interpretation was to become a key pillar in the reasoning supporting subsequent establishment clause decisions. That it appeared in a majority opinion *upholding* an arguable aid prompted Justice Jackson, one of the four Justices who would have invalidated the statute, to comment that the disposition of the case by the majority reminded him of Byron's Julia, who, "whispering 'I will ne'er consent,'—consented."[4] A dissenting opinion, subscribed to by four Justices, agreed with the majority that the amendment barred aid to all religions as well as preference for any one or more.[5]

The opinion of the Court said that a state could restrict transportation to those attending public schools, but if it were furnished to non-public school students, it was to be considered analogous to general welfare services such as police protection and sewage disposal. Although these services *might* be considered aids to parents sending their children to parochial schools, cutting off church schools from these services, so separate and so indisputably marked off from the religious functioning, . . . is obviously not the purpose of the First Amendment. That Amendment requires the state to be a neutral in its relations with groups of religious believers and non-believers; it does not require the state to be their adversary. State power is no more to be used so as to handicap religions, than it is to favor them.[6]

The opinion concluded with these words:

It appears that these parochial schools meet New Jersey's requirements. The State contributes no money to the schools. It does not support them. Its legislation, as applied, does no more than provide a general program to help parents get their children, regardless of their religion, safely and expeditiously to and from accredited schools.

The First Amendment has erected a wall between church and state. That wall must be kept high and impregnable. We could not approve the slightest breach. New Jersey has not breached it here.[7]

It is interesting to note that fifteen years later, in a concurring opinion, Justice Douglas (whose "fifth vote" was necessary in *Everson* to uphold the busing statute) stated that in retrospect he agreed with the four dissenters.[8]

Textbooks

The next case to deal with the issue of establishment of religion through direct use of public funds in relation to parochial schools was decided in 1968.[9] Intervening cases had treated the establishment clause in the context of religious influences in the public schools and had amplified in general terms the *Everson* discussion of the clause.[10] At issue was the constitutionality of a New York statute requiring each local school board to purchase textbooks and lend them, without charge, to all children residing in the district who were enrolled in grades seven to twelve of public or private schools that complied with the compulsory education law. The books loaned were to be "'textbooks which are designated for use in any public, elementary or secondary schools of the state or are approved by any boards of education, ...' "[11]

With one important factual difference this case was a reprise of the *Cochran* case of 1930. The difference was that here the textbooks were not limited to those actually used in public schools. Legally the basis of attack was different; it was the establishment clause, which had not been argued in *Cochran.* The Court's majority of six attached no significance to the difference in facts. The opinion did, however, emphasize that "religious books" could not be loaned under the law as construed by the Court of Appeals of New York. The Supreme Court said:

> Absent evidence we cannot assume that school authorities, who constantly face the same problem in selecting textbooks for use in the public schools, are unable to distinguish between secular and religious books or that they will not honestly discharge their duties under the law. In judging the validity of the statute on this record we must proceed on the assumption that books loaned to students are books that are not unsuitable for use in the public schools because of religious content.[12]

Quoting the *Everson* statement that the establishment clause forbids "laws which aid one religion, aid all religions, or prefer one religion over another,"[13] the Court ruled that the furnishing of textbooks was similar to the furnishing of transportation and thus was not an aid to religion but rather an assistance in the accomplishment of the legitimate state objective of secular education of all children. The "child benefit" rationale of *Cochran* was expressed here in the following words:

> The express purpose of [the statute] was stated by the New York Legislature to be furtherance of the educational opportunities available to the young. Appellants have shown us nothing about the necessary effects of the statute that is contrary to its stated purpose. The law merely makes available to all children the benefits of a general program to lend school books free of charge. Books are furnished at the request of the pupil and ownership remains, at least technically, in the State. Thus no funds or books are furnished to parochial schools, and the financial benefit is to parents and children, not to schools. Perhaps free books make it more likely that some children choose to attend a sectarian school, but that was true of the state-paid bus fares in *Everson* and does not alone demonstrate an unconstitutional degree of support for a religious institution.[14]

To the argument that textbooks, particularly those selected by private schools for their students, bore a different relationship to the education process than did transportation, fire protection, or sewage disposal, the Court responded:

> Of course books are different from buses. Most bus rides have no inherent religious significance, while religious books are common. However, the language of [the statute] does not

authorize the loan of religious books, and the State claims no right to distribute religious literature. Although the books loaned are those required by the parochial school for use in specific courses, each book loaned must be approved by the public school authorities; only secular books may receive approval. . . .

The major reason offered by appellants for distinguishing free textbooks from free bus fares is that books, but not buses, are critical to the teaching process, and in a sectarian school that process is employed to teach religion. However, this Court has long recognized that religious schools pursue two goals, religious instruction and secular education.[15]

Concerning the general role of nonpublic schools in relation to a state's interest in the secular education of its youth, the Court said:

Underlying [the cases of *Pierce* and *Cochran*], and underlying also the legislative judgments that have preceded the court decisions, has been a recognition that private education has played and is playing a significant and valuable role in raising national levels of knowledge, competence, and experience. Americans care about the quality of the secular education available to their children. They have considered high quality education to be an indispensable ingredient for achieving the kind of nation, and the kind of citizenry, that they have desired to create. Considering this attitude, the continued willingness to rely on private school systems, including parochial systems, strongly suggests that a wide segment of informed opinion, legislative and otherwise, has found that those schools do an acceptable job of providing secular education to their students. This judgment is further evidence that parochial schools are performing, in addition to their sectarian function, the task of secular education.[16]

Thus was introduced the secular/sectarian distinction which was capitalized upon in much of the rash of "parochiaid" legislation (proposed or enacted) after 1968. "Parochiaid" has no precise definition but is taken to refer generically to plans aimed at channeling public funds to the support of education carried on under religious auspices but complying with minimum compulsory education requirements set by the state. Pressures for such aid had been mounting steadily since World War II and were becoming especially heavy in the late 1960's.

In the *Allen* case, the statute was attacked "on its face," without any evidence as to what its effects actually would be. Indeed, the Court mentioned four times in the opinion that it was deciding the case on the record before it, which it characterized as meager. No books previously used in parochial schools were put into evidence; nor was there evidence of books which would be requested. Thus the issue of indoctrination through inclusions and exclusions from textbooks (a problem obviated in *Cochran* by the edict of the Louisiana court that the books must be the same ones used in public schools) was addressed only by the Court's saying it was unable to hold, based solely on judicial notice, that secular and religious training would be unconstitutionally intertwined.

Although *Everson* was the precedent that *Allen* was said to follow, both Justice Black, who wrote the *Everson* opinion, and Justice Douglas, the only other Justice who had been on the Court at the time of *Everson*, dissented in *Allen*.

Secular Services and Salary Supplements

Subsequent to *Allen*, many states plunged into varying forms of "parochiaid." "Purchase of secular services" was the rubric adopted by several states. The first statute of this type to be judicially challenged under the establishment clause was one in Pennsylvania authorizing the state superintendent of education to "purchase" specified "secular educational services" from nonpublic schools. The state directly reimbursed the schools for their actual expenditures for teachers' salaries, textbooks, and instructional materials. The textbooks and materials had to be approved by the state superintendent and were restricted to the areas of mathematics, modern foreign languages, physical science, and physical education.

A Rhode Island statute authorized state officials to provide supplements for the salaries of teachers of secular subjects in nonpublic elementary schools by paying directly to such a teacher an amount not to exceed fifteen percent of his or her current salary. Restrictions were placed on the maximum amount of salary and the qualifications of the teacher and on per pupil expenditures in the schools. Eligible teachers were required to teach only those subjects offered in the public schools and to use only materials that were used in the public schools.

In 1971, the Supreme Court consolidated challenges to these statutes and, with only one dissent, found both statutes unconstitutional.[17] For the first time, the Court emphasized the word "respecting" in the establishment clause. It said:

> A law may be one "respecting" the forbidden objective while falling short of its total realization. A law "respecting" the proscribed result, that is, the establishment of religion, is not always easily identifiable as one violative of the Clause. A given law might not *establish* a state religion but nevertheless be one "respecting" that end in the sense of being a step that could lead to such establishment and hence offend the First Amendment.[18]

Quoting from its opinion in *Walz v. Tax Commission*,[19] a nonschool case decided a year before, the Court identified "the three main evils against which the Establishment Clause was intended to afford protection" to be "sponsorship, financial support, and active involvement of the sovereign in religious activity."[20] The 1970 *Walz* decision had upheld the constitutionality of including church property used solely for religious purposes in a broad class of property of nonprofit corporations (such as hospitals, libraries, and educational institutions) that was exempted from payment of local property taxes. The Court considered that situation to be acceptable because the state reasonably could determine it to be in the public interest to encourage the operation of such social welfare organizations, and the inclusion of churches was not intended to benefit them nor did it have an effect of giving them more than indirect aid. This policy of all fifty states is firmly rooted in history predating the Constitution, and the Court found no resultant harmful effects. Moreover, the Court suggested that the alternative of taxing churches would lead to more government involvement with them because of the need to set valuations on property and the possibility of tax liens and foreclosures. The Court emphasized the perils both to government and to religion if "involvements" and "entanglements" replaced "insulation" and "separation." It said that the religion clauses prohibited "excessive government entanglement with religion."[21]

That semantic formulation was elevated in the *Lemon* case to the status of an independent criterion, joining two others set forth first in *School District of Abington Township, Pennsylvania v. Schempp*.[22]

> Every analysis in this area must begin with consideration of the cumulative criteria developed by the Court over many years. Three such tests may be gleaned from our cases. First, the statute must have a secular legislative purpose; second, its principal or primary effect must be one that neither advances nor inhibits religion; finally, the statute must not foster "an excessive government entanglement with religion."[23]

The Court explained its approach to the question of entanglement as follows:

> In order to determine whether the government entanglement with religion is excessive, we must examine the character and purposes of the institutions which are benefited, the nature of the aid that the State provides, and the resulting relationship between the government and the religious authority.[24]

The Court observed that parochial schools constitute an integral part of the religious mission of the church. They are vehicles for the transmission of the faith to the young. The "substantial religious character of these church-related schools gives rise to entangling church-state relationships of the kind the Religion Clauses sought to avoid"[25] because of the need for the state to be certain that state funds support only secular education.

In elaboration, the Court said:

> Our decisions from *Everson* to *Allen* have permitted the States to provide church-related schools with secular, neutral, or nonideological services, facilities, or materials. Bus transportation, school lunches, public health services, and secular textbooks supplied in common to all students were not thought to offend the Establishment Clause....
>
> ... We cannot, however, refuse here to recognize that teachers have a substantially different ideological character from books. In terms of potential for involving some aspect of faith or morals in secular subjects, a textbook's content is ascertainable, but a teacher's handling of a subject is not. We cannot ignore the danger that a teacher under religious control and discipline poses to the separation of the religious from the purely secular aspects of precollege education. The conflict of functions inheres in the situation.
>
> . . . .
>
> A comprehensive, discriminating, and continuing state surveillance will inevitably be required to ensure that ... the First Amendment ... [is] respected. Unlike a book, a teacher cannot be inspected once so as to determine the extent and intent of his or her personal beliefs and subjective acceptance of the limitations imposed by the First Amendment. These prophylactic contacts will involve excessive and enduring entanglement between state and church.[26]

The Court also gave attention to future consequences if it approved such statutes. It commented that the history of government grants of continuing cash subsidies indicated that the programs had almost always been accompanied by varying measures of control and surveillance. The Court found no reason to believe the same would not happen in connection with the arrangements it was considering. "In particular the government's post-audit power to inspect and evaluate a church-related school's financial records and to determine which expenditures are religious and which are secular creates an intimate and continuing relationship between church and state."[27]

Also articulated as an aspect of entanglement was a "political-divisiveness" element. The Court discussed it as follows:

Ordinarily political debate and division, however vigorous or even partisan, are normal and healthy manifestations of our democratic system of government, but political division along religious lines was one of the principal evils against which the First Amendment was intended to protect. The potential divisiveness of such conflict is a threat to the normal political process.... The history of many countries attests to the hazards of religion's intruding into the political arena or of political power intruding into the legitimate and free exercise of religious belief.[28]

The Court concluded that the "potential for political divisiveness related to religious belief and practice is aggravated in these two statutory programs by the need for continuing annual appropriations and the likelihood of larger and larger demands as costs and populations grow."[29]

This case was a pivotal one in the area of public funds in relation to religion-based education. The vote was eight-to-one. The opinion, written by Chief Justice Burger, was endorsed on substantive points by all the Justices except Justice White. The delineation of the three tests to be applied in deciding establishment clause cases was set out in a formulation consistently referred to thereafter by the Court.

Higher Education

On the same day it released the preceding opinion, the Court upheld all provisions but one of the Higher Education Facilities Act of 1963 against a first amendment challenge.[30] The Act, providing federal funds for "academic facilities" to institutions of higher education, was challenged insofar as funds were made available to certain colleges "sponsored" by religious organizations. The Act prohibited use of the buildings for religious instruction or worship for twenty years. All Justices agreed that the twenty-year limitation was unconstitutional in that the buildings must never be used for sectarian purposes. On the basic sections of the Act, however, the Court's vote for constitutionality was five-to-four.

No opinion was accepted by a majority of the Justices. The four Justices who distinguished this case from *Lemon* did so on the grounds that indoctrination was not a substantial purpose or activity of church-related colleges, college students were not as impressionable as those in graded schools, the aid was nonideological in nature, and excessive entanglement was avoided because the grants for buildings were one-time and single-purpose grants. This reasoning was essentially accepted by a six-Justice majority in 1973 when the Court upheld the constitutionality of the issuance of revenue bonds by South Carolina for facilities at church-related colleges.[31]

1. Everson v. Board of Educ., 330 U.S. 1, 67 S. Ct. 504 (1947).
2. *See* chapter 3 n.6 *supra*.
3. Everson, 330 U.S. at 15-16, 67 S. Ct. at 511-512.
4. *Id.* at 19, 67 S. Ct. at 513.
5. *Id.* at 18, 67 S. Ct. at 513.
6. *Id.*, 67 S. Ct. at 512-513.
7. *Id.*, 67 S. Ct. at 513.
8. Engel v. Vitale, 370 U.S. 421, 443-444, 82 S. Ct. 1261, 1273-1274 (1962).
9. Board of Educ. of Cent. School Dist. No. 1 v. Allen, 392 U.S. 236, 88 S. Ct. 1923 (1968) [hereinafter cited as Allen].
10. *See* chapter 6.
11. Allen, 392 U.S. at 239, 88 S. Ct at 1924.
12. *Id.* at 245, 88 S. Ct. at 1927.
13. Everson, 330 U.S. at 15, 67 S. Ct. at 511.
14. Allen, 392 U.S. at 243, 88 S. Ct. at 1926-1927.
15. *Id.* at 245, 88 S. Ct. at 1927.
16. *Id.* at 247-248, 88 S. Ct. at 1928-1929.
17. Lemon v. Kurtzman and Earley v. DiCenso, 403 U.S. 602, 91 S. Ct. 2105 (1971).
18. *Id.* at 612, 91 S. Ct. at 2111.
19. 397 U.S. 664, 90 S. Ct. 1409 (1970).
20. Lemon v. Kurtzman, 403 U.S. at 612, 91 S. Ct. at 2111.
21. Walz v. Tax Comm'n, 397 U.S. at 674, 90 S. Ct. at 1414.
22. 374 U.S. 203, 83 S. Ct. 1560 (1963). Discussed *infra*, chapter 6 pp. 43-46.
23. Lemon v. Kurtzman, 403 U.S. at 612, 91 S. Ct. at 2111.
24. *Id.* at 615, 91 S. Ct. at 2112.
25. *Id.* at 616, 91 S. Ct. at 2113.
26. *Id.* at 616-619, 91 S. Ct. at 2113-2114.
27. *Id.* at 621-622, 91 S. Ct. at 2115.
28. *Id.* at 622-623, 91 S. Ct. at 2116.
29. *Id.*
30. Tilton v. Richardson, 403 U.S. 672, 91 S. Ct. 2091 (1971).
31. Hunt v. McNair, 413 U.S. 734, 93 S. Ct. 2868 (1973).

CHAPTER 5

Financial Aid for Parochial Schools: Continuing Application of the Constitutional Criteria

The 1973 Trilogy of Cases

Three days less than two years after *Lemon*, the Supreme Court decided three cases involving four distinct approaches to aid for parochial schools. All four were held to be unconstitutional. In no instance were there more than three dissenting Justices.

The most extensive of the 1973 opinions involved a New York statute that established three financial aid programs for nonpublic graded schools.[1] The Court observed that "the controlling constitutional standards have become firmly rooted and the broad contours of our inquiry are now well defined. Our task, therefore, is to assess New York's several forms of aid in the light of principles already delineated."[2] The Court further noted that the existence of guiding principles at this stage of the Court's history did not render the assignment an easy one.

Maintenance and Repair of Buildings

One type of aid was for "maintenance and repair" of nonpublic schools serving a high concentration of pupils from low-income families. No restriction of the payments to the upkeep of facilities used exclusively for secular purposes was incorporated in the plan. Thus, said the Court, there is a primary effect that advances religion. The setting in the statute of a dollar-limit on expenditures did not insure that the money would not be expended to advance the religious mission of the parochial schools. The Court stated that it was clear that the government may not erect buildings in which religious activities take place. Therefore, it may not maintain such buildings or renovate them when they fall into disrepair.

Tuition Reimbursement for Low Income Parents

A second type of aid was a partial "tuition reimbursement" to parents in low-income brackets whose children attended nonpublic schools. This, too, failed the "effect" test, for the effect was to subsidize educational costs in parochial schools. That the grants were to parents, rather than schools, did not change the end result: the parent received from the government money he had paid to the school. Since the money would be used by parents for tuition with no attempt made to separate secular from sectarian uses, the effect of the aid was "unmistakably to provide desired financial support for nonpublic sectarian institutions."[3]

The argument was advanced by defenders of the legislation that the parent was not simply a conduit because he was free to spend the money he received in any manner. Since the parent had already paid the tuition, reimbursement payment provided by the statute might not end up in the hands of a religious school. The Court rejected this strained logic by stating that if the grants were offered as an incentive to parents to send their children to sectarian schools by making unrestricted cash payments to them, the establishment clause would be violated whether or not the actual dollars given eventually found their way into the sectarian institutions. "Whether the grant is labeled a reimbursement, a reward, or a subsidy, its substantive impact is still the same."[4]

Other arguments rejected by the Court included the argument that since the amount of money paid for reimbursement would cover a percentage of cost less than the percentage of school time devoted to teaching secular courses, the arrangement would not be advancing religion, and the argument that since the New York statute provided the subsidy only to low-income parents, it had a legitimate result of aiding them in the free exercise of their religion.

Income Tax Benefits

Another section of the statute provided a third type of aid through the device of income tax benefits. Parents of children attending nonpublic schools were permitted to subtract a specified amount from their adjusted gross income (provided they did not receive a tuition reimbursement under the other part of the statute). Regarding this provision, the Court observed:

> In practical terms there would appear to be little difference, for purposes of determining whether such aid has the effect of advancing religion, between the tax benefit . . . and the tuition grant. . . . The qualifying parent under either program receives the same form of encouragement and reward for sending his children to nonpublic schools. The only difference is that one parent receives an actual cash payment while the other is allowed to reduce by an arbitrary amount the sum he would otherwise be obliged to pay over to the State.[5]

An attempt to analogize the tax benefits here to those permitted in *Walz* for property used for religious purposes was unsuccessful. An important element of the *Walz* decision had been a recognition that the concept of exempting church property was deeply embedded in the fabric of our national life predating the American Revolution and postdating the adoption of the first amendment. As to tax benefits to parents of nonpublic school students, the Court found no historical precedent for New York's tax relief program. The Court added, however, that historical acceptance, without more, would not suffice to support a legislative scheme, and furthermore, that such did not suffice in the church property tax-exemption case, where the reason underlying that history had been the controlling factor.

Although the Court based its holdings of unconstitutionality of the three plans on the findings that each had the impermissible effect of advancing religion, it said that "the importance of the competing societal interests implicated here prompts us to make the further observation that, apart from any specific entanglement of the State in particular religious programs, assistance of the sort here involved carries grave potential for entanglement in the broader sense of continuing political strife over aid to religion."[6]

Costs of Unrestricted Testing

In a second case from New York, the Court used essentially the same reasoning to invalidate a statute under which nonpublic schools were to be reimbursed for expenses incurred while complying with state requirements pertaining to the administration and reporting of results of tests and the compilation of other records.[7] The use of the funds was not restricted in any way, and teacher-prepared tests were covered because they were required in all schools by state regulations. The Court observed:

> [D]espite the obviously integral role of such testing in the total teaching process, no attempt is made under the statute, and no means are available, to assure that internally prepared tests are free of religious instruction.
>
> We cannot ignore the substantial risk that these examinations, prepared by teachers under the authority of religious institutions, will be drafted with an eye, unconsciously or otherwise, to inculcate students in the religious precepts of the sponsoring church.[8]

In this case, the Court expressly rejected the "mandated services" contention that the state can pay for whatever it requires private schools to do. Such a position could not be squared with the establishment clause.

The Court offered an example: a state might properly require minimum lighting or sanitary facilities for all school buildings but it would be barred from providing support for those facilities in church-sponsored schools. The Court restated that the "essential inquiry" in each case is the three-pronged one set out in *Lemon*: purpose, effect, entanglement.

Tuition Reimbursements for All Parents

In the third case in the 1973 triology, the Court invalidated a "tuition reimbursement" statute that had been enacted in Pennsylvania following the voiding in *Lemon* of that state's "purchase of secular services" legislation.[9] Constitutionally, there were no significant differences between the Pennsylvania statute and the New York provision struck down in *Nyquist*. The Court summarized the constitutional defects of making payments to parents of children in parochial schools as follows:

> The State has singled out a class of its citizens for a special economic benefit. Whether that benefit be viewed as a simple tuition subsidy, as an incentive to parents to send their children to sectarian schools, or as a reward for having done so, at bottom its intended consequence is to preserve and support religion-oriented institutions. We think it plain that this is quite unlike the sort of "indirect" and "incidental" benefits that flowed to sectarian schools from programs aiding *all* parents by supplying bus transportation and secular textbooks for their children. Such benefits were carefully restricted to the purely secular side of church-affiliated institutions and provided no special aid for those who had chosen to support religious schools.[10]

The Court also addressed the argument that if any aid went to parents of children attending nonsectarian private schools, the equal protection clause of the fourteenth amendment would require such assistance to parents of children attending sectarian schools. The Court said:

> The argument is thoroughly spurious. . . . [V]alid aid to non-public, nonsectarian schools would provide no lever for aid to their sectarian counterparts. The Equal Protection Clause has never been regarded as a bludgeon with which to compel a State to violate other provisions of the Constitution.[11]

Recognizing the difficulty of developing arrangements for getting public funds to assist in the financing of parochial schools without running afoul of either the "primary effect" test on the one hand or the "entanglement" test on the other, the Court stated, "But if novel forms of aid have not readily been sustained by this Court, the 'fault' lies not with the doctrines which are said to create a paradox but rather with the Establishment Clause itself: . . . [with which] we are not free to tamper. . . ."[12]

The 1975 and 1977 Cases

The increasing rash of legislation designed to use public funds to facilitate parochial elementary and secondary education led to additional Supreme Court opinions on the topic in a Pennsylvania case in 1975[13] and an Ohio case in 1977.[14] In each, the Court repeated the principles developed in the earlier cases and applied them to newly developed arrangements. On only one specific was the decision by a margin of fewer than three votes. However, a college-level case was decided in 1976 on a five-to-four vote upholding a Maryland statute providing annual grants for nonsectarian purposes to all colleges, including those affiliated with churches.[15] There was no opinion of the Court in the Maryland case.

Auxiliary Services

In 1975, a majority of six Justices held a Pennsylvania statute providing "auxiliary services" to nonpublic schools invalid for violating the "excessive entanglement" test. These services included:

> guidance, counseling and testing services; psychological services; services for exceptional children; remedial and therapeutic services; speech and hearing services; services for the improvement of the educationally disadvantaged (such as, but not limited to, teaching English as a second language), and such other secular, neutral, non-ideological services as are of benefit to nonpublic school children and are presently or hereafter provided for public school children of the Commonwealth.[16]

Personnel for teaching and other activities were to be supplied by public school authorities. The Court held that the arrangement was proscribed by *Lemon*. The fact that state funding for teachers was only for remedial and exceptional students was not material.

> Whether the subject is "remedial reading," "advanced reading," or simply "reading," a teacher remains a teacher, and the danger that religious doctrine will become intertwined with secular instruction persists. . . . And a state-subsidized guidance counselor is surely as likely as a state-subsidized chemistry teacher to fail on occasion to separate religious instruction and the advancement of religious beliefs from his secular educational responsibilities.[17]

The fact that the teachers and counselors providing the auxiliary services were employed by the public schools rather than the church-related schools in which they worked would not substantially eliminate the need for the continuing surveillance that is barred by the establishment clause. The Court observed in a footnote, however, that "authorization of 'speech and hearing services,' at least to the extent such services are diagnostic, seems to fall within that class of general welfare services for children that may be provided by the State regardless of the incidental benefit that accrues to church-related schools."[18]

Diagnostic and Therapeutic Services

Two years later, the Court expressly held that such diagnostic services could be performed within parochial schools by public employees, stating:

> The reason for considering diagnostic services to be different from teaching or counseling is readily apparent. First, diagnostic services, unlike teaching or counseling, have little or no educational content and are not closely associated with the educational mission of the nonpublic school. Accordingly, any pressure on the public diagnostician to allow the intrusion of sectarian views is greatly reduced. Second, the diagnostician has only limited contact with the child, and that contact involves chiefly the use of objective and professional testing methods to detect students in need of treatment. The nature of the relationship between the diagnostician and the pupil does not provide the same opportunity for the transmission of sectarian views as attends the relationship between teacher and student or that between counselor and student.[19]

In *Wolman v. Walter,* the Court sharply distinguished therapeutic, guidance, and remedial services from diagnostic ones. Although diagnostic services may be performed within a church-related school, therapeutic services must not be offered there. The latter may be provided under the concept of a general benefit to all children, but must be offered in circumstances reflecting religious neutrality, which would include a site not part of a parochial school. The Court reasoned:

> We recognize that, unlike the diagnostician, the therapist may establish a relationship with the pupil in which there might be opportunities to transmit ideological views. In *Meek* the Court acknowledged the danger that publicly employed personnel who provide services analogous to those at issue here might transmit religious instruction and advance religious

beliefs in their activities.... The danger existed there not because the public employee was likely deliberately to subvert his task to the service of religion, but rather because the pressures of the environment might alter his behavior from its normal course. So long as these types of services are offered at truly religiously neutral locations, the danger perceived in *Meek* does not arise.

The fact that a unit on a neutral site on occasion may serve only sectarian pupils does not provoke the same concerns that troubled the Court in *Meek*. The influence on a therapist's behavior that is exerted by the fact that he serves a sectarian pupil is qualitatively different from the influence of the pervasive atmosphere of a religious institution. The dangers perceived in *Meek* arose from the nature of the institution, not from the nature of the pupils.[20]

Instructional Materials and Equipment

In both *Meek* and *Wolman* the Court disapproved of the furnishing of instructional materials and equipment on loan to parochial schools. The only arguable difference between the two plans was that in the first, the loans were directly to the schools, and in the second, they were to the pupils or parents. The Court said that it "would exalt form over substance."[21] if the distinction were the basis for different holdings. The Court, in *Meek*, had held that the Pennsylvania plan for furnishing such items as projectors, recorders, laboratory equipment, maps, films, and video tapes had an impermissible primary effect of advancing religion. It said that "the massive aid provided the church-related nonpublic schools ... is neither indirect or incidental."[22] Although the items intrinsically were nonideological, "faced with the substantial amounts of direct support authorized by [the Act], it would simply ignore reality to attempt to separate secular educational functions from the predominantly religious role performed"[23] by the schools. This marked the first time the Court had so emphasized the amount of money involved in an aid scheme.

In both cases, the Court reaffirmed its precedent on the furnishing of secular textbooks to parochial school students (although a total of four Justices, three active on the Court in each case, indicated in one or both that they believed that *Board of Education of Central School District No. 1 v. Allen* should be overruled).

Transportation for Field Trips

The closest vote on a matter decided in the 1975 *Meek* case was five-to-four against the constitutionality of furnishing transportation for field trips to children in church-related schools on the same basis as to children in public schools. The Court said that, unlike the transportation to and from school approved in *Everson*, field trips are an integral part of the education experience made meaningful by the individual teacher. The timing and places to be visited lie in the discretion of the sectarian authorities. Thus, there is a forbidden direct aid to sectarian education. Moreover, surveillance would be required to assure secular use of field trip funds, leading to excessive entanglement between state and church.

Standardized Testing

Also challenged in *Wolman* was the furnishing to parochial schools' of such standardized tests and scoring services as are in use in the public schools of the state. There was no authorization of any payment to the schools or personnel for costs of administering the tests. Only the tests themselves and grading services were furnished. The Court said that the tests were for the legitimate secular purpose of ensuring that minimum standards were met. Since the tests were standardized, they could not be used for the inculcation of religious precepts, as could the teacher-prepared tests ruled out in *Levitt*. Hence, this arrangement passed constitutional muster.

The 1980 Case

Almost immediately after the *Levitt* decision, the New York legislature enacted a new statute providing for payments to nonpublic schools of actual costs incurred as a result of compliance with certain state-mandated requirements, including the supplying to the state of specific data regarding enrollments and attendance and the administering of state-prepared examinations. The Supreme Court upheld the constitutionality of this statute in 1980 by a five-to-four vote.[24]

The New York statute differed from the Ohio one in *Wolman* in that reimbursements to the schools were to be provided in New York, whereas the testing and scoring services were to be furnished by state personnel in Ohio. However, the Court found that the difference was not of constitutional dimensions. It noted that the tests were prepared by the state and that grading procedures could not be utilized to further the religious mission of the schools. An additional observation was that the statute provided safeguards to assure that there would be no excessive reimbursements. The procedures for reimbursements called for the keeping by parochial schools of separate accounts for the clearly identifiable costs of the scoring of tests and the preparation of the other reports covered by the statute. As the costs should vary little from school to school, claims could be checked against costs in public schools. The direct "entanglement" involved was held not to be excessive, and because only actual costs were covered, there would be no "religious battles over legislative appropriations."[25]

The five-Justice majority terminated its reasoning with the following paragraph:

> This is not to say that this case, any more than past cases, will furnish a litmus-paper test to distinguish permissible from impermissible aid to religiously oriented schools. But Establishment Clause cases are not easy; they stir deep feelings; and we are divided among ourselves, perhaps reflecting the different views on this subject of the people of this country. What is certain is that our decisions have tended to avoid categorical imperatives and absolutist approaches at either end of the range of possible outcomes. This course sacrifices clarity and predictability for flexibility, but this promises to be the case until the continuing interaction between the courts and the States—the former charged with interpreting and upholding the Constitution and the latter seeking to provide education for their youth—produces a single, more encompassing construction of the Establishment Clause.[26]

---

1. Committee for Pub. Educ. and Religious Liberty v. Nyquist, 413 U.S. 756, 93 S. Ct. 2955 (1973) [hereinafter cited as Nyquist].
2. *Id.* at 761, 93 S. Ct. at 2959.
3. *Id.* at 783, 3 S. Ct. at 2971.
4. *Id.* at 786, 93 S. Ct. at 2972.
5. *Id.* at 790-791, 93 S. Ct. at 2974.
6. *Id.* at 794, 93 S. Ct. at 2976.
7. Levitt v. Committee for Pub. Educ. and Religious Liberty, 413 U.S. 472, 93 S. Ct. 2814 (1973).
8. *Id.* at 480, 93 S. Ct. at 2819.
9. Sloan v. Lemon, 413 U.S. 825, 93 S. Ct. 2982 (1973).
10. *Id.* at 832, 93 S. Ct. at 2986-2987.
11. *Id.* at 834, 93 S. Ct. at 2987-2988.
12. *Id.* at 835, 93 S. Ct. at 2988.
13. Meek v. Pittenger, 421 U.S. 349, 95 S. Ct. 1753 (1975).
14. Wolman v. Walter, 433 U.S. 229, 97 S. Ct. 2593 (1977).
15. Roemer v. Board of Pub. Works, 426 U.S. 736, 96 S. Ct. 2337 (1976).
16. Meek v. Pittenger, 421 U.S. at 353 n.2, 95 S. Ct. at 1757 n.2.
17. *Id.* at 370-371, 95 S. Ct. at 1766.
18. *Id.* n.21.
19. Wolman v. Walter, 433 U.S. at 244, 97 S. Ct. at 2603.
20. *Id.* at 247-248, 97 S. Ct. at 2605.
21. *Id.* at 250, 97 S. Ct. at 2606.
22. Meek v. Pittenger, 421 U.S. at 365, 95 S. Ct. at 1763.
23. *Id.*
24. Committee for Pub. Educ. and Religious Liberty v. Regan, 444 U.S. 646, 100 S. Ct. 840 (1980).
25. *Id.* at 661 n.8, 100 S. Ct. at 850 n.8.
26. *Id.* at 662, 100 S. Ct. at 851.

CHAPTER 6

Religious Influences in Public Schools

The Establishment Clause

Released Time for Religious Instruction

The first Supreme Court decision interpreting the establishment clause of the first amendment in the setting of activity in the public schools came thirteen months after *Everson* (the case that had upheld the constitutionality of providing transportation for children to parochial schools).[1] The issue was the constitutionality of an arrangement whereby those students whose parents signed "request cards" were allowed to attend classes in religious instruction during the regular school day within the public school building.

The plan was promoted in Champaign, Illinois, by a voluntary interfaith association called the Champaign Council on Religious Education, which was comprised of members of the Jewish, Roman Catholic, and Protestant faiths. Cards furnished by the council were distributed by the public school teachers to the children in grades four through nine. Children whose parents signed the cards were given thirty or forty-five minutes-a-week of instruction in the religion selected. The classes were conducted in the regular classrooms. Students who did not take the religious instruction were required to leave the classrooms and go elsewhere in the building for pursuit of secular studies. The teachers of religion were employed at no expense to the school district, but the instructors were subject to the approval and supervision of the superintendent of schools. Attendance at the religious classes was required and accounted for in the same manner as for other classes.

The Court, by a vote of eight-to-one, found that this "released time" arrangement fell "squarely under the ban of the first amendment (made applicable to the States by the fourteenth) as we interpreted it in *Everson*. . . ."[2] The Court quoted the key paragraph from *Everson* explicating the establishment clause[3] and observed that the dissenters in *Everson* also subscribed to that interpretation of the establishment clause even though they had disagreed with the application of it to the *Everson* facts. The eight-Justice majority expressly reaffirmed the interpretation that the clause prohibited impartial governmental assistance to *all* religions and was not restricted to preference of one or more religions over others.

On the facts of the *McCollum* case, the Court said:

> The . . . facts . . . show the use of tax-supported property for religious instruction and the close cooperation between the school authorities and the religious council in promoting religious education. The operation of the state's compulsory education system thus assists and is integrated with the program of religious instruction carried on by separate religious sects. Pupils compelled by law to go to school for secular education are released in part from their legal duty upon the condition that they attend the religious classes. This is beyond all question a utilization of the tax-established and tax-supported public school system to aid religious groups to spread their faith.[4]

The Court concluded:

> Here not only are the state's tax-supported public school buildings used for the dissemination of religious doctrines. The State also affords sectarian groups an invaluable aid in that it helps to provide pupils for their religious classes through use of the state's compulsory public school machinery. This is not separation of Church and State.[5]

Four years later, the Court decided another released-time-for-religious-instruction case, this time upholding the plan.[6] The arrangement was that children whose parents so requested (on forms supplied by participating religious organizations) were excused from public school attendance for one hour a week in order to receive religious training away from the school premises. The state of New York mandated the general program with local school boards to work out the details. Students not released stayed in school. Reports on absences from the religious instruction were made to school authorities.

Distinguishing *Zorach* from *McCollum*, the Court's majority of six emphasized that the program in *Zorach* involved neither religious instruction in public school classrooms nor the expenditure of public funds. The opinion rejected the argument that the case was governed by *McCollum* since the weight and influence of the school system was placed behind a program for religious instruction, primarily by the school's "keeping tab" on students who were released and by halting classroom activities while released students were away with teachers not allowed to take up new work during the period. The Court said:

> It takes obtuse reasoning to inject any issue of the "free exercise" of religion into the present case. No one is forced to go to the religious classroom and no religious exercise or instruction is brought to the classrooms of the public schools. A student need not take religious instruction. He is left to his own desires as to the manner or time of his religious devotions, if any.

There is a suggestion that the system involves the use of coercion to get public school students into religious classrooms. There is no evidence in the record before us that supports that conclusion. (Nor is there any indication that the public schools enforce attendance at religious schools by punishing absentees from the released time programs for truancy.) The present record indeed tells us that the school authorities are neutral in this regard and do no more than release students whose parents so request. If in fact coercion were used, if it were established that any one or more teachers were using their office to persuade or force students to take the religious instruction, a wholly different case would be presented. Hence we put aside that claim of coercion both as respects the "free exercise" of religion and "an establishment of religion" within the meaning of the First Amendment.[7]

Although "[t]here cannot be the slightest doubt that the first amendment reflects the philosophy that Church and State should be separated"[8] and that there can be no exception within the scope of first amendment coverage, the Court said that coverage does not extend to all contacts. If it did, the two entities would be hostile to each other, leading to possible situations whereby municipalities could not give police or fire protection, churches could not be required to pay property taxes, and Thanksgiving Day proclamations and "so help me, God" in courtroom oaths would have to be halted. The Court continued:

We would have to press the concept of separation of Church and State to these extremes to condemn the present law on constitutional grounds. The nullification of this law would have wide and profound effects. A Catholic student applies to his teacher for permission to leave the school during hours on a Holy Day of Obligation to attend a mass. A Jewish student asks his teacher for permission to be excused for Yom Kippur. A Protestant wants the afternoon off for a family baptismal ceremony. In each case the teacher requires parental consent in writing. In each case the teacher, in order to make sure the student is not a truant, goes further and requires a report from the priest, the rabbi, or the minister. The teacher in other words cooperates in a religious program to the extent of making it possible for her students to participate in it. Whether she does it occasionally for a few students, regularly for one, or pursuant to a systematized program designed to further the religious needs of all the students does not alter the character of the act.

We are a religious people whose institutions presuppose a Supreme Being. . . . When the state encourages religious instruction or cooperates with religious authorities by adjusting the schedule of public events to sectarian needs, it follows the best of our traditions. For it then respects the religious nature of our people and accommodates the public service to their spiritual needs.[9]

The Court said that "[t]he problem, like many problems in constitutional law, is one of degree."[10] It also observed that "this program may be unwise and improvident from an educational or a community viewpoint."[11] However, the Court emphasized that its function was to decide only the constitutional issue. Finally, the Court stated that it *was* following *McCollum*, but not expanding it to what would be a "philosophy of hostility to religion."[12]

Non-denominational Prayer

It was a decade later that the Supreme Court again decided a case concerning religion in the public schools.[13] The question was whether the Constitution permits saying the following prayer aloud each day in public school classrooms: "Almighty God, we acknowledge our dependence upon Thee, and we beg Thy blessings upon us, our parents, our teachers and our country."

This procedure was adopted by a local school board on the recommendation of the New York Board of Regents (state board of education). The latter body had composed the prayer and published it as a part of a "Statement on Moral and Spiritual Training in the Schools." New York courts had sustained the use of the prayer as long as no student was compelled to join in the exercise.

That use of prayer is a religious activity was not denied, but school authorities sought to justify this prayer because it was "non-denominational" and based on "our spiritual heritage." The Court, by a six-to-one vote, held that the program violated the establishment clause because that provision "must at least mean that in this country it is no part of the business of government to compose official prayers for any group of the American people to recite as part of a religious program carried on by government."[14]

The Court extensively reviewed the historical basis for the religion clauses of the first amendment, with special attention to the role of governmentally supported prayers, and concluded:

The First Amendment was added to the Constitution to stand as a guarantee that neither the power nor the prestige of the Federal Government would be used to control, support or influence the kinds of prayer the American people can say—that the people's religions must not be subjected to the pressures of government for change each time a new political administration is elected to office. Under that Amendment's prohibition against governmental establishment of religion, as reinforced by the provisions of the Fourteenth Amendment, government in this country, be it state or federal, is without power to prescribe by law any particular form of prayer which is to be used as an official prayer in carrying on any program of governmentally sponsored religious activity.[15]

The Court expanded its reasoning as follows:

Neither the fact that the prayer may be denominationally neutral, nor the fact that its observance on the part of the students is voluntary can serve to free it from the limitations of the Establishment Clause.... The Establishment Clause, unlike the Free Exercise Clause, does not depend upon any showing of direct governmental compulsion and is violated by the enactment of laws which establish an official religion whether those laws operate directly to coerce nonobserving individuals or not.... [The] first and most immediate purpose [of the Establishment Clause] rested on the belief that a union of government and religion tends to destroy government and to degrade religion.[16]

The Court pointedly observed that it was "neither sacrilegious nor antireligious to say that each separate government in this country should stay out of the business of writing or sanctioning official prayers and leave that purely religious function to the people themselves and to those the people choose to look to for religious guidance."[17]

Amidst the intensely emotional public reaction that followed this decision, a footnote that was responsive to many of the incorrect statements being made concerning what the Court actually had held was largely overlooked. It stated:

There is of course nothing in the decision reached here that is inconsistent with the fact that school children and others are officially encouraged to express love for our country by reciting historical documents such as the Declaration of Independence which contain references to the Deity or by singing officially espoused anthems which include the composer's professions of faith in a Supreme Being, or with the fact that there are many manifestations in our public life of belief in God. Such patriotic or ceremonial occasions bear no true resemblance to the unquestioned religious exercise that the State of New York has sponsored in this instance.[18]

Bible-reading and Lord's Prayer

Almost exactly twelve months after the *Engel* decision, the Court issued another opinion, which to many appeared unnecessary because

Engel seemed to have settled the matter of whether the recitation of the Lord's Prayer or the reading of verses from the Holy Bible at the opening of the school day were prohibited by the establishment clause.[19] Again, with only one dissent, the Court answered in the affirmative. This time, the case was decided by a full complement of Justices. This fact may have been one reason for deciding a case which was so similar to one decided just a year before by seven Justices. Another reason may have been to respond to the widespread charges that the Court's rationale in *Engel* was without a firm constitutional basis. *Engel* had not cited prior cases, only history and principles. Still another reason may have been that some Justices desired to write concurring opinions illuminating their personal views on the volatile subject of religious influence in governmental enterprises. In *Engel*, there had been only one concurring opinion, that of Justice Douglas, who, as previously observed, indicated that he had come to believe that *Everson* had been wrongly decided. In the present case, there were three concurring opinions involving four Justices; thus, with the opinion of the Court and the one-Justice dissent, only three Justices did not individually express themselves.

Actually, two cases were consolidated in the *Abington* opinion. One was from Abington Township, Pennsylvania, where the challenged rule provided that "at least ten verses from the Holy Bible shall be read, without comment, at the opening of each public school on each school day." Children whose parents requested it were excused from attending the reading. The other case, from Baltimore, Maryland, involved reading a chapter in the Bible "and/or the use of the Lord's Prayer," with excusal of those students whose parents objected.[20] Clearly, both documents were religious in nature and more narrowly sectarian than the "non-denominational" prayer in *Engel*.

The opinion of the Court reviewed its prior decisions holding that the strictures of the first amendment were applied to state governments by the fourteenth amendment and that the Court had "rejected unequivocally" the contention that the establishment clause forbids only governmental preference of one religion over another (aid to *all* religions is barred). It said that, although "none of the parties to either of these cases has questioned these basic conclusions of the Court, . . . others continue to question their history, logic and efficacy. Such contentions, in the light of the consistent interpretation in cases of this Court [some not concerned with education], seem entirely untenable and of value only as academic exercises."[21]

After overviewing the purpose of the establishment clause primarily by quotations and paraphrases from prior opinions, the Court summarized:

The wholesome "neutrality" of which this Court's cases speak thus stems from a recognition of the teachings of history that powerful sects or groups might bring about a fusion of governmental and religious functions or a concert or dependency of one upon the other to the end that official support of the State or Federal Government would be placed behind the tenets of one or of all orthodoxies. This the Establishment Clause prohibits.[22]

The Court then enunciated the following test to be applied in examining establishment clause cases:

The test may be stated as follows: what are the purpose and the primary effect of the enactment? If either is the advancement or inhibition of religion then the enactment exceeds the scope of legislative power as circumscribed by the Constitution. That is to say that to withstand the strictures of the Establishment Clause there must be a secular legislative purpose and a primary effect that neither advances nor inhibits religion.[23]

Reading of the Bible and reciting the Lord's Prayer as part of opening exercises failed the test.

As the exercises were prescribed as part of the curricular activities of students who were required by law to attend school, were held in school buildings, and were supervised by teachers, the arrangement differed from the "accommodation" of religion approved in the *Zorach* off-premises, released-time case. In the Pennsylvania case there was a specific finding by the lower court that the Bible-reading activity was religious in nature; in the Maryland case concerning the Lord's Prayer, there was no such finding, and the state argued that the activity had secular purposes such as "promotion of moral values, the contradiction to the materialistic trends of our times, the perpetuation of our institutions and the teaching of literature."[24] Pointing out that in the legal posture of the case, the state technically had admitted the religious character of the exercise, the Court nevertheless added:

But even if its purpose is not strictly religious, it is sought to be accomplished through readings, without comment, from the Bible. Surely the place of the Bible as an instrument of religion cannot be gainsaid, and the State's recognition of the pervading religious character of the ceremony is evident from the rule's specific permission of the alternative use of the Catholic Douay version as well as the recent amendment permitting nonattendance at the exercises. None of these factors is consistent with the contention that the Bible is here used either as an instrument for nonreligious moral inspiration or as a reference for the teaching of secular subjects.[25]

Indicating that its holding was not hostile to religion in general nor to the Bible per se, the Court continued:

> [I]t might well be said that one's education is not complete without a study of comparative religion or the history of religion and its relationship to the advancement of civilization. It certainly may be said that the Bible is worthy of study for its literary and historic qualities. Nothing we have said here indicates that such study of the Bible or of religion, when presented objectively as part of a secular program of education, may not be effected consistent with the First Amendment. But the exercises here do not fall into those categories. They are religious exercises, required by the States in violation of the command of the First Amendment that the Government maintain strict neutrality, neither aiding nor opposing religion.[26]

Prohibition of Teaching Evolution

The first education case decided by the Supreme Court in which the purpose of challenged legislation was found to conflict with the establishment clause was decided in 1968.[27] The question was the constitutionality of an Arkansas statute enacted by initiative forty years earlier that made it unlawful for a teacher in any school or college receiving state funds "to teach the theory or doctrine that mankind ascended or descended from a lower order of animals" or "to adopt or use in any such institution a textbook that teaches" this theory. Violation not only could lead to dismissal of a teacher, but also was made a criminal offense. Only three states had such statutes on the books at the time of *Epperson v. Arkansas.*

No attempts had ever been made to enforce the Arkansas law, which was patterned after the Tennessee statute that had been the subject of the celebrated "Scopes monkey trial" in 1927. In the *Scopes* case, the statute had been upheld, but the state supreme court, on a technicality, reversed Scopes' conviction, voided his fine, and suggested that no further efforts be made to enforce the provision.[28] In the present situation, the issue was drawn when a biology teacher who was to teach from a new book having a chapter on Darwin's theory sought an injunction against possible enforcement of the statute.

The Supreme Court unanimously found that the statute was unconstitutional. The basis of the holding was violation of the establishment clause. The Court said that regardless of what "teach" embraced, "[t]he overriding fact is that Arkansas' law selects from the body of knowledge a particular segment which it proscribes for the sole reason that it is deemed to conflict with a particular religious doctrine; that is, with a particular interpretation of the Book of Genesis by a particular religious group."[29]

The Court further stated:

> There is and can be no doubt that the First Amendment does not permit the State to require that teaching and learning must be tailored to the principles or prohibitions of any religious sect or dogma.
>
> . . . .
>
> In the present case, there can be no doubt that Arkansas has sought to prevent its teachers from discussing the theory of evolution because it is contrary to the belief of some that the Book of Genesis must be the exclusive source of doctrine as to the origin of man. No suggestion has been made that Arkansas' law may be justified by considerations of state policy other than the religious views of some of its citizens. It is clear that fundamentalist sectarian conviction was and is the law's reason for existence.[30]

Although not essential to the holding, the opinion of the Court, written by Justice Fortas, contained some references to state powers in relation to the curriculum of public schools, to freedom of teachers in general, and to the role of the courts. The opinion recognized the "State's undoubted right to prescribe the curriculum for its public schools. . . ."[31] It quoted from some cases involving constitutional rights of teachers, which it said the Court would carefully guard.

Also included was the following, which has become the portion of the opinion most widely quoted by lower courts:

> Judicial interposition in the operation of the public school system of the Nation raises problems requiring care and restraint. Our courts, however, have not failed to apply the First Amendment's mandate in our educational system where essential to safeguard the fundamental values of freedom of speech and inquiry and of belief. By and large, public education in our Nation is committed to the control of state and local authorities. Courts do not and cannot intervene in the resolution of conflicts which arise in the daily operation of school systems and which do not directly and sharply implicate basic constitutional values.[32]

Posting the Ten Commandments

It was not until 1980 that the Court again issued an opinion in the area of religious influences within public schools. The case, involving the posting in classrooms of "The Ten Commandments," was decided on the merits by a vote of five-to-two without oral argument.[33] (The other two Justices simply indicated that they believed the case should have been given plenary consideration with additional briefs and oral argument).

The five-Justice per curiam opinion reversed the Supreme Court of Kentucky, which by an equally divided court had upheld the statute that mandated the posting. The Supreme Court of the United States held that the arrangement violated the first prong of the establishment clause test in that its purpose was not a secular one. Attempts to meet this test had included the requirements that the displays be funded through private contributions (although the state treasurer was to serve as collector) and that the copies were to include "in small print" the notation: "The secular application of the Ten Commandments is clearly seen in its adoption as the fundamental legal code of Western Civilization and the Common Law of the United States."[34]

The Court observed that the Ten Commandments "undeniably" constitute "a sacred text in the Jewish and Christian faiths, and no legislative recitation of a supposed secular purpose can blind us to that fact."[35] It noted that the Commandments are not confined to arguably secular matters, such as murder, adultery, stealing, bearing false witness, and covetousness. Rather, they also concern religious duties such as worshipping the Lord God alone, avoiding idolatry, not using the Lord's name in vain, and observing the sabbath day.

Citing its opinion in *School District of Abington Township*, the Court said that this was not a case in which the Ten Commandments "are integrated into the school curriculum, where the Bible may constitutionally be used in an appropriate study of history, civilization, ethics, comparative religion, or the like."[36] The posting serves no secular educational function. Furthermore, reasoned the Court, the fact that the message is posted, rather than read aloud as in the Bible and prayer cases, is of no constitutional consequence.

The Free Exercise Clause

Flag Salute

In 1940, the Supreme Court decided its first case interpreting the free exercise of religion clause in a public school setting.[37] The case involved the exclusion from school of children of the Jehovah's Witnesses sect because they refused on religious grounds to participate in a flag-salute-and-pledge-of-allegiance ceremony required of students at the start of each school day. The Court said its task was to consider when the constitutional guarantee of religious freedom "compel[s] exemption from doing what society thinks necessary for the promotion of some great common end, or from a penalty for conduct which appears dangerous to the general good."[38] The Court decided that national "cohesion" or "unity" was an "interest inferior to none in the hierarchy of legal values"[39] and that state legislative bodies should be permitted to select appropriate means for its attainment. It was not, said the Court, a function of judges to evaluate the efficacy of the method adopted, nor to require that "dissidents" be exempted when there was a basis for a legislative judgment that exemptions might weaken the effect of the exercise.

This decision, issued at a time when World War II had begun in Europe and nationalism ran high in the United States, was used as a rationale for various types of persecutions of Jehovah's Witnesses. That situation, plus much scholarly criticism of the decision, apparently prompted three of the eight Justices in the majority in the case to state in dissent in a 1942 case (involving the conviction of a member of Jehovah's Witnesses for violating an anti-peddling ordinance)[40] that they had come to believe that the flag salute case had been wrongly decided.

In a 1943 case, these three Justices, plus two Justices appointed during the interim, and the lone dissenter in 1940 (Justice Stone, who in 1943 was Chief Justice) constituted a six-member majority that overruled the 1940 decision.[41] The vehicle for this act by the Court was a case in which all of the key operative facts were similar to those in *Minersville School District v. Gobitis:* a condition precedent to attendance at public school was participation in the patriotic ceremony; nonattendance could lead to delinquency proceedings against the children and prosecution of their parents; and the reason offered for refusal was a tenet of faith of Jehovah's Witnesses precluding bowing down to a graven image, which the flag was considered by them to be.

The Court observed that recitation of the pledge requires affirmation of a belief and an attitude of mind. As "censorship" (prevention of expression) had long been held to be permissible only when the expression presented a clear and present danger of action of a kind that government could prevent and punish, the Court said "involuntary affirmation could be commanded only on even more immediate and urgent grounds than silence."[42] Here there was no allegation that remaining passive during the ceremony created any danger. Thus, the state had no power to require such a ritual.

The Court said that it had assumed in *Minersville* (as did the arguments in that case and the present case) that the power to impose the flag salute discipline upon students, in general, did belong to the state, with the question being one of immunity on religious grounds from an unquestioned general rule. In *West Virginia State Board of Education v. Barnette,* however, it addressed the question which properly should underlie the flag salute controversy: "whether such a ceremony so touching matters of opinion and political attitude may be imposed upon the individual by official authority under powers committed to any political organization under our Constitution."[43]

It should be observed that the question was *not* cast in terms of *religious* rights. Indeed, the Court said, "Nor does the issue as we see it turn on one's possession of particular religious views or the sincerity with which they are held."[44] At other points, the opinion encompassed a broader spectrum than the religion-based objections to participation that precipitated this case. One such point is the following widely quoted passage with which the opinion ended:

> If there is any fixed star in our constitutional constellation, it is that no official, high or petty, can prescribe what shall be orthodox in politics, nationalism, religion, or other matters of opinion or force citizens to confess by word or act their faith therein. If there are any circumstances which permit an exception, they do not now occur to us.
>
> We think the action of the local authorities in compelling the flag salute and pledge transcends constitutional limitations on their power and invades the sphere of intellect and spirit which it is the purpose of the First Amendment to our Constitution to reserve from all official control.[45]

The Court had observed earlier in the opinion that the freedom asserted by the students did not interfere with rights of others to participate in the ceremony. Also, the behavior of those not wishing to participate was peaceable and orderly.

The Court modified the point made in the 1940 opinion that the courts should not get involved in matters better left to legislatures and to educational experts as follows:

> The very purpose of a Bill of Rights was to withdraw certain subjects from the vicissitudes of political controversy, to place them beyond the reach of majorities and officials and to establish them as legal principles to be applied by the courts. One's right to life, liberty, and property, to free speech, a free press, freedom of worship and assembly, and other fundamental rights may not be submitted to vote; they depend on the outcome of no elections.
>
> . . . .
>
> Nor does our duty to apply the Bill of Rights to assertions of official authority depend upon our possession of marked competence in the field where the invasion of rights occurs. . . . [W]e act in these matters not by authority of our competence but by force of our commissions. We cannot, because of modest estimates of our competence in such specialties as public education, withhold the judgment that history authenticates as the function of this Court when liberty is infringed.[46]

The Amish and One Aspect of Compulsory Education

The question of the free exercise of religion in an educational setting arose again in 1972 in the "Amish case" involving compulsory school attendance to age sixteen.[47] The tenet of the Amish faith violated by school attendance beyond eighth grade and age fourteen was described by the Court as follows:

> Formal high school education beyond the eighth grade is contrary to Amish beliefs not only because it places Amish children in an environment hostile to Amish beliefs with increasing emphasis on competition in class work and sports and with pressures to conform to the styles, manners, and ways of the peer group, but because it takes them away from their community, physically and emotionally, during the crucial and formative adolescent period of life. During this period, the children must acquire Amish attitudes favoring manual work and self-reliance and the specific skills needed to perform the adult role of an Amish farmer or housewife. They must learn to enjoy physical labor. Once a child has learned basic reading, writing, and elementary mathematics, these traits, skills, and attitudes admittedly fall within the category of those best learned through example and "doing" rather than in a classroom. And, at this time in life, the Amish child must also grow in his faith and his relationship to the Amish community if he is to be prepared to accept the heavy obligations imposed by adult baptism. In short, high school attendance with teachers who are not of the Amish faith—and may even be hostile to it—interposes a serious barrier to the integration of the Amish child into the Amish religious community.[48]

The Court observed that the Amish views had been conscientiously adhered to for almost 300 years (over 200 years in this country—even before the Constitution was adopted); that scholars testified that the requirement of an additional one or two years not only could result in substantial psychological harm to Amish children because of the conflicts it would produce, but would ultimately result in the destruction of the Old Order Amish church community; that the Amish in the county affected had never been known to commit crimes, receive public assistance, or be unemployed; and that the amount of education at issue was minimal, especially since the young Amish pursued a type of vocational learning-by-doing that the state was not precluded from regulating to a degree.

These factors led the Court to reject Wisconsin's claim that the statute was valid because it was motivated by legitimate secular concerns related to preparation of effective citizens. "A regulation neutral on its face may, in its application, nonetheless offend the constitutional requirement for governmental neutrality if it unduly burdens the free exercise of religion."[49] Further, "[t]he essence of all that has been said and written on the subject is that only those interests of the highest order and those not otherwise served can overbalance legitimate claims to the free exercise of religion."[50]

An Exception for Colleges

The Court, in 1981, with one dissent, answered in the negative the question of "whether a state university, which makes its facilities generally available for the activities of registered student groups, may close its facilities to a registered student group desiring to use the facilities for religious worship and religious discussion."[51] The University of Missouri at Kansas City had refused to allow a religious group to conduct meetings in facilities used by over 100 recognized student groups. The Court ruled that the state's interest in neither supporting, nor appearing to confer approval on, religious sects or practices was not "sufficiently 'compelling' to justify content-based discrimination against respondents' religious speech."[52] The religious group's use of the forum, which had been created by the university, would not be a violation of the establishment clause.

The Court in two footnotes distinguished the case from ones involving religious activities in public graded schools by observing that facilities in those schools are not generally open to other groups and that university students are less impressionable than younger students.[53] Six days after this opinion was issued, the Court unanimously denied certiorari on a decision that had upheld a ban on the holding of prayer meetings by students in a public graded school classroom prior to the start of the school day.[54]

---

1. People of State of Ill. *ex rel.* McCollum v. Board of Educ. of School Dist. No. 71, Champaign Cty., 333 U.S. 203, 68 S. Ct. 461 (1948) [hereinafter cited as McCollum].
2. *Id.* at 210, 68 S. Ct. at 464.
3. Everson v. Board of Educ., 330 U.S. 1, 15-16, 67 S. Ct. 504, 511-512 (1947).
4. McCollum, 333 U.S. at 209-210, 68 S. Ct. at 464.
5. *Id.* at 212, 68 S. Ct. at 465-466.
6. Zorach v. Clauson, 343 U.S. 306, 72 S. Ct. 679 (1952).
7. *Id.* at 311-312, 72 S. Ct. at 682-683.
8. *Id.* at 312, 72 S. Ct. at 683.
9. *Id.* at 313-314, 72 S. Ct. at 683-684.
10. *Id.* at 314, 72 S. Ct. at 684.
11. *Id.*
12. *Id.* at 315, 72 S. Ct. at 685.
13. Engel v. Vitale, 370 U.S. 421, 82 S. Ct. 1261 (1962).
14. *Id.* at 425, 82 S. Ct. at 1264.
15. *Id.* at 429-430, 82 S. Ct. at 1266.

16. *Id.* at 430-431, 82 S. Ct. at 1266-1267.
17. *Id.* at 435, 82 S. Ct. at 1269.
18. *Id.* n.21.
19. School Dist. of Abington Township, Pa. v. Schempp, 374 U.S. 203, 83 S. Ct. 1560 (1963) [hereinafter cited as Abington].
20. The Baltimore case was captioned *Murray v. Curlett.*
21. Abington, 374 U.S. at 217, 83 S. Ct. at 1569.
22. *Id.* at 222, 83 S. Ct. at 1571.
23. *Id.*
24. *Id.* at 223, 83 S. Ct. at 1572.
25. *Id.*
26. *Id.* at 225, 83 S. Ct. at 1573.
27. Epperson v. Arkansas, 393 U.S. 97, 89 S. Ct. 266 (1968).
28. Scopes v. State of Tenn., 154 Tenn. 105, 289 S.W. 363 (1927).
29. Epperson v. Arkansas, 393 U.S. 97, 103, 89 S. Ct. 266, 270.
30. *Id.* at 106-108, 89 S. Ct. at 271-272.
31. *Id.* at 107, 89 S. Ct. at 272.
32. *Id.* at 104, 89 S. Ct. at 270.
33. Stone v. Graham, 449 U.S. 39, 101 S. Ct. 192 (1980).
34. *Id.* at 39-40 n.1, 101 S. Ct. at 193 n.1.
35. *Id.* at 41, 101 S. Ct. at 194.
36. *Id.*
37. Minersville School Dist. v. Gobitis, 310 U.S. 586, 60 S. Ct. 1010 (1940).
38. *Id.* at 593, 60 S. Ct. at 1012.
39. *Id.* at 595, 60 S. Ct. at 1013.
40. Jones v. Opelika, 316 U.S. 584, 62 S. Ct. 1231 (1942). The holding to which the dissent was attached was overruled in Murdock v. Pennsylvania, 319 U.S. 105, 63 S. Ct. 870 (1943).
41. West Virginia State Bd. of Educ. v. Barnette, 319 U.S. 624, 63 S. Ct. 1178 (1943).
42. *Id.* at 633, 63 S. Ct. at 1183.
43. *Id.* at 636, 63 S. Ct. at 1184.
44. *Id.* at 634, 63 S. Ct. at 1183.
45. *Id.* at 642, 63 S. Ct. at 1187.
46. *Id.* at 638-640, 63 S. Ct. at 1185-1186.
47. Wisconsin v. Yoder, 406 U.S. 205, 92 S. Ct. 1526 (1972). Observations of the Court regarding parent rights in general are discussed in chapter 2.
48. *Id.* at 211, 92 S. Ct. at 1531.
49. *Id.* at 220, 92 S. Ct. at 1536.
50. *Id.* at 215, 92 S. Ct. at 1533.
51. Widmar v. Vincent, ____ U.S. ____, 102 S. Ct. 269, 271-272 (1981).
52. *Id.* at ____, 102 S. Ct. at 277.
53. *Id.* nn.13-14.
54. Brandon v. Board of Educ. of Guilderland School Dist., 635 F.2d 971 (2d Cir. 1980), *cert. denied,* ____ U.S. ____, 102 S. Ct. 970 (1981).

CHAPTER 7

Race and Education: 1955 and Before

May 17, 1954: The Constitutional Mandate

"Does segregation of children in public schools solely on the basis of race, even though the physical facilities and other 'tangible' factors may be equal, deprive the children of the minority group of equal educational opportunities? We believe that it does."[1]

Therefore, said the Supreme Court on May 17, 1954, in *Brown v. Board of Education*, the laws of twenty-one states requiring or permitting racial segregation in public schools are in violation of the equal protection clause of the fourteenth amendment. In a companion case, the Court held that the due process clause of the fifth amendment commanded the same result in the federal jurisdiction of the District of Columbia.[2] In *Brown I* the Court spoke with one voice. Not only were there no dissents, but there were no concurring opinions.

Lower courts until this point in time had adhered to the doctrine of "separate but equal," announced by the Supreme Court in 1896 as satisfying the equal protection clause in the matter of separate railroad cars for whites and nonwhites who were travelling within one state.[3] With only the dissent of Justice Harlan (who expressed the memorable words: "Our Constitution is color-blind, and neither knows nor tolerates classes among citizens"[4]), the Court had upheld the state's power to require the intrastate separate-car arrangement. In the opinion other walks of life in which racial separation was practiced were mentioned. These were areas, the Court observed, that did not involve political equality of the races or place any badge of slavery or inferiority on blacks. The distinctions were social and therefore not affected by the thirteenth and fourteenth amendments. The Court commented that "the most common instance of this is connected with the establishment of separate schools for white and colored children, which has been held to be a valid exercise of the legislative power even by courts of States where the political rights of the colored race have been longest and most earnestly enforced"[5] and which has been mandated by Congress for the District of Columbia. The Court said it had struck down in the past and would continue to invalidate discrimination implying inferiority in civil society and pointed to its having required that blacks be allowed to sit upon juries. The Court said, "We consider the underlying fallacy of the plaintiff's argument to consist in the assumption that the enforced separation of the two races stamps the colored race with a badge of inferiority."[6]

In 1954, however, the Court based its opinion in *Brown I* on the conclusion that the "fallacy" was in reality "fact." It stated:

> In approaching this problem, we cannot turn the clock back to 1868 when the [Fourteenth] Amendment was adopted, or even to 1896 when *Plessy v. Ferguson* was written. We must consider public education in the light of its full development and its present place in American life throughout the Nation. Only in this way can it be determined if segregation in public schools deprives these plaintiffs of the equal protection of the laws.
>
> . . . .
>
> . . . To separate [black students] from others of similar age and qualifications solely because of their race generates a feeling of inferiority as to their status in the community that may affect their hearts and minds in a way unlikely ever to be undone. The effect of this separation on their educational opportunities was well stated by a finding in the Kansas case by a court which nevertheless felt compelled to rule against the Negro plaintiffs:

> > "Segregation of white and colored children in public schools has a detrimental effect upon the colored children. The impact is greater when it has the sanction of the law; for the policy of separating the races is usually interpreted as denoting the inferiority of the Negro group. A sense of inferiority affects the motivation of a child to learn. Segregation with the sanction of law, therefore, has a tendency to retard the educational and mental development of Negro children and to deprive them of some of the benefits they would receive in a racially integrated school system."

> Whatever may have been the extent of psychological knowledge at the time of *Plessy v. Ferguson*, this finding is amply supported by modern authority. Any language in *Plessy v. Ferguson* contrary to this finding is rejected.
>
> We conclude that in the field of public education the doctrine of "separate but equal" has no place. Separate educational facilities are inherently unequal. Therefore, we hold that the plaintiffs and others similarly situated for whom the actions have been brought are, by reason of the segregation complained of, deprived of the equal protection of the laws guaranteed by the Fourteenth Amendment.[7]

Earlier in the opinion, the Court presented the following analysis of the role of public education:

> Today, education is perhaps the most important function of state and local governments. Compulsory school attendance laws and the great expenditures for education both demonstrate our recognition of the importance of education to our democratic society. It is required in the performance of our most basic public responsibilities, even service in the armed forces. It is the very foundation of good citizenship. Today it is a principal instrument in awakening the child to cultural values, in preparing him for later professional training, and in helping him to adjust normally to his environment. In these days, it is doubtful that any child may reasonably be expected to succeed in life if he is denied the opportunity of an education. Such an opportunity, where the state has undertaken to provide it, is a right which must be made available to all on equal terms.[8]

Before reaching this conclusion, the Court reviewed the history of the fourteenth amendment and its prior decisions related to segregated education. It found the circumstances surrounding the adoption of the fourteenth amendment to be inconclusive with respect to segregated schools, to a considerable extent because public education was not very mature at the time, particularly in the South. It noted that only two cases involving segregated public graded schools previously had been before the Court, and in neither had the "separate but equal" doctrine been questioned. There had been four cases dealing with segregation in public higher education, all of which were decided in favor of the black plaintiffs without reexamination of the doctrine.

Earlier Public School Cases

The first education case was decided only three years after *Plessy*. Black taxpayers sought an injunction to require a school board in Georgia to discontinue the operation of a high school for white children until one for blacks that had been discontinued was reopened.[9] The reason for the closing was financial. In the record there was no evidence of hostility toward blacks, and an elementary school was being maintained for them. In the posture of the case—granting an injunction to close the white school would not help the blacks—the Supreme Court, in a unanimous opinion written by Justice Harlan, stated that it could interfere with the management of state-operated schools only if there were "a clear and unmistakable disregard of rights secured by the supreme law of the land."[10] The

Court found that this was not the situation in the case as presented. The opinion contained a hint that perhaps the wrong relief had been sought in the lower courts.

The other public school case, decided in 1927, presented, in the words of the Court, "[t]he question . . . whether a Chinese citizen of the United States is denied equal protection of the laws when he is classed among the colored races and furnished facilities for education equal to that offered to all, whether white, brown, yellow, or black."[11] The constitution of Mississippi provided that separate schools must be maintained for children of "the white and colored races," and the Supreme Court of Mississippi interpreted the provision to mean that there were two categories: white and nonwhite. The assignment of the child of Chinese ancestry to the nonwhite school was upheld by the Supreme Court of the United States as being "within the discretion of the state in regulating its public schools and does not conflict with the Fourteenth Amendment."[12] The Court unanimously observed that a claim that no nonwhite school was within convenient reach of the child's residence would have presented a different question.

Earlier College Cases

In each of the four race-state-education cases encompassing professional or graduate school education, the Court ruled in favor of the black plaintiff without being required to question the "separate but equal" doctrine. In 1938, the Court answered in the negative "the question whether the provision for the legal education in other states of Negroes resident in Missouri is sufficient to satisfy the constitutional requirement of equal protection."[13] The state provided for the tuition of blacks to be paid if they attended schools in other states for studies not provided in the university that the state operated for blacks. The Supreme Court, by a vote of seven-to-two, said the state could comply with the fourteenth amendment in affording equal protection of the law only within its own jurisdiction. Further, the right of the plaintiff was a personal one, unaffected by the fact that there was only a limited demand in Missouri for legal education of blacks.

A decade later, when a black student sought admission to the state university's law school, Oklahoma tried to avoid the preceding holding on the ground that the black woman had not given sufficient notice of her intent to apply so that the state could establish separate facilities.[14] In a short opinion, the Court rejected the contention and said that the state must provide a legal education for the plaintiff "as soon as it does for applicants of any other group."[15] Thus, although the Court did not expressly say so, the state could not admit any new white students to the state-operated law school unless it admitted the plaintiff black student or established at once a separate school for blacks.

Oklahoma higher education authorities were back before the Supreme Court two years later, and again, the Court unanimously ruled against them.[16] Acting under the *Sipuel* decision, a lower court had ordered a black man, who had a master's degree and substantial teaching experience, admitted to the graduate program in education. The university authorities responded by requiring that instruction within the university be on a segregated basis. In operation, this meant that the student was required to sit at a special desk set up in an anteroom adjoining the classroom, to sit at a designated desk on the mezzanine of the library, and to sit at a designated table and eat at a different time from other students in the university cafeteria. Before the case reached the Supreme Court, some adjustments in his treatment were made: he could sit in the classroom in a special row for blacks, he was assigned to a table on the main floor of the library, and he could eat at the same time as the white students (but at a different table).

The Court, in this case, as in a case from Texas decided the same day,[17] referred to "intangible" factors related to equality. It said that by the aforementioned practices, the black student was "handicapped in his pursuit of effective graduate instruction. Such restrictions impair and inhibit his ability to study, to engage in discussion and exchange views with other students, and, in general, to learn his profession."[18] It held that the black student "must receive the same treatment at the hands of the State as students of other races."[19]

It was in the Texas case, where a black sought admission to the all-white University of Texas Law School, that a unanimous Court discussed with more specificity "intangibles" intrinsically interwoven with the meaning of "equal" in the field of education.[20] During pendency of the suit, state authorities had established a law school for blacks. The Court, still not required directly to confront the "separate but equal" doctrine (although urged to do so), ruled for the plaintiff by finding the new school not to be equal, not only on objective criteria like size of faculty and library, but also because the University of Texas Law School possessed

> to a far greater degree those qualities which are incapable of objective measurement but which make for greatness in a law school. Such qualities, to name but a few, include reputation of the faculty, experience of the administration, position and influence of the alumni, standing in the community, traditions and prestige. It is difficult to believe that one who had a free choice between these law schools would consider the question close.[21]

The application of "separate but equal" was directly presented four years later in *Brown I*, where the Court said:

> Here, unlike *Sweatt v. Painter*, there are findings below that the Negro and white schools involved have been equalized, or are being equalized, with respect to buildings, curricula, qualifications and salaries of teachers, and other "tangible" factors. Our decision, therefore, cannot turn on merely a comparison of these tangible factors in the Negro and white schools involved in each of the cases. We must look instead to the effect of segregation itself on public education.[22]

May 31, 1955: "With All Deliberate Speed"

Aware of the significance and impact of its 1954 holding in *Brown I* that state-required segregation was unconstitutional, the Court declined to issue a decree at that time as to remedy, but rather posed certain questions regarding relief for the litigants to address in further arguments the following Term. (The Court at the end of the 1952-53 Term had followed the same procedure in approaching the *Brown I* series of cases and had posed questions to be reargued in the 1953-54 Term during which the *Brown I* opinion was issued.)

The implementation decree, announced May 31, 1955 in *Brown II*,[23] established the structure for moving to dismantle dual school systems:

> Full implementation of these constitutional principles may require solution of varied local school problems. School authorities have the primary responsibility for elucidating, assessing, and solving these problems; courts will have to consider whether the action of school authorities constitutes good faith implementation of the governing constitutional principles. Because of their proximity to local conditions and the possible need for further hearings, the courts which originally heard these cases can best perform this judicial appraisal.[24]

The Court said that the lower courts were to apply traditional equitable principles, which permitted practical flexibility in adjusting and reconciling competing interests. The courts were instructed to have blacks admitted to schools "as soon as practicable on a non-discriminatory basis."[25] Although this might involve eliminating a variety of obstacles, "it should go without saying that the vitality of [the *Brown I*] constitutional principles cannot be allowed to yield simply because of disagreement with them."[26]

The following more concrete instructions were given to the lower courts:

While giving weight to these public and private considerations, the courts will require that the defendants make a
prompt and reasonable start toward full compliance with our
May 17, 1954 ruling. Once such a start has been made, the
courts may find that additional time is necessary to carry out
the ruling in an effective manner. The burden rests upon the
defendants to establish that such time is necessary in the public
interest and is consistent with good faith compliance at the
earliest practicable date. To that end, the courts may consider
problems related to administration, arising from the physical
condition of the school plant, the school transportation system,
personnel, revision of school districts and attendance areas into
compact units to achieve a system of determining admission to
the public schools on a nonracial basis, and revision of local
laws and regulations which may be necessary in solving the
foregoing problems. They will also consider the adequacy of
any plans the defendants may propose to meet these problems
and to effectuate a transition to a racially nondiscriminatory
school system. During this period of transition, the courts will
retain jurisdiction of these cases.[27]

The district courts were instructed to "take such proceedings and
enter such orders and decrees consistent with this opinion as are
necessary and proper to admit to public schools on a racially non-
discriminatory basis with all deliberate speed the parties to these
cases."[28]

---

1. Brown v. Board of Educ., 347 U.S. 483, 493, 74 S. Ct. 686, 691 (1954) [hereinafter
cited as Brown I]. For this opinion, the Court consolidated cases from Delaware, Kansas,
South Carolina, and Virginia.

2. Bolling v. Sharpe, 347 U.S. 497, 74 S. Ct. 693 (1954).

3. Plessy v. Ferguson, 163 U.S. 537, 16 S. Ct. 1138 (1896).

4. *Id.* at 559, 16 S. Ct. at 1146.

5. *Id.* at 544, 16 S. Ct. at 1140.

6. *Id.*

7. Brown I, 347 U.S. at 492-495, 74 S. Ct. at 691-692.

8. *Id.* at 493, 74 S. Ct. at 691.

9. Cumming v. Richmond Cty. Bd. of Educ., 175 U.S. 528, 20 S. Ct. 197 (1899).

10. *Id.* at 545, 20 S. Ct. at 201.

11. Gong Lum v. Rice, 275 U.S. 78, 85, 48 S. Ct. 91, 93 (1927).

12. *Id.* at 87, 48 S. Ct. at 94.

13. State of Missouri *ex rel.* Gaines v. Canada, 305 U.S. 337, 59 S. Ct. 232 (1938).

14. Sipuel v. Board of Regents of Univ. of Okla., 332 U.S. 631, 68 S. Ct. 299 (1948).

15. *Id.* at 633, 68 S. Ct. at 299.

16. McLaurin v. Oklahoma State Regents for Higher Educ., 339 U.S. 637, 70 S. Ct. 851
(1950).

17. Sweatt v. Painter, 339 U.S. 629, 70 S. Ct. 848 (1950).

18. McLaurin, 339 U.S. at 641, 70 S. Ct. at 853.

19. *Id.* at 642, 70 S. Ct. at 854.

20. Sweatt, 339 U.S. 629, 70 S. Ct. 848 (1950).

21. *Id.* at 634, 70 S. Ct. at 850.
22. Brown I, 347 U.S. at 492, 74 S. Ct. at 690-691.
23. Brown v. Board of Educ., 349 U.S. 294, 75 S. Ct. 753 (1955) [hereinafter cited as Brown II].
24. *Id.* at 299, 75 S. Ct. at 756.
25. *Id.*
26. *Id.*
27. *Id.*
28. *Id.* at 301, 75 S. Ct. at 757.

CHAPTER 8

Race and Education: Refinement of the Constitutional Mandate

State-level Interference

Following its opinions in *Brown I* and *Brown II*, the Supreme Court rendered no opinions in the substantive area of school desegregation for eight years. It did, however, decide one case growing out of a desegregation situation which attracted wide attention both legally and politically.[1] The school board of Little Rock, Arkansas, was proceeding to move toward desegregation, and its plan had been accepted by the district court and the court of appeals and ordered into effect. Concurrently, the state legislature had taken some actions to impede desegregation in the state, and on the day before the proposed enrollment of nine black students at Central High School, Governor Orval Faubus dispatched units of the Arkansas National Guard to place the school "off limits" to the blacks. The action was without request by, or consultation with, either school or municipal authorities. The result of various statements by political figures and the action by the governor was the hardening of a core of emotional and physical resistance to compliance with the district court's order. That court requested the Attorney General of the United States to enter the proceedings to seek an injunction against the governor's attempts to prevent obedience with the court order. The court, after a hearing, enjoined the governor from so using the Arkansas National Guard and from acts of interference. After the Court of Appeals for the Eighth Circuit affirmed the injunction, the Guard was withdrawn.

On the next school day, local and state police were on hand to protect the nine black children, but the children were removed from the school later that day because of the difficulties of controlling a large crowd of demonstrators. Two days later, President Eisenhower dispatched federal troops to the scene to effect the admission of the blacks. The regular army troops remained for over two months, with federalized National Guardsmen replacing them for the rest of the school year. Eight of the nine black students remained in the school throughout the year.

The situation prompted the school board eventually to request the district court to allow the blacks to be withdrawn from the school and to have the whole desegregation plan postponed for two and one-half years. The request was granted by the district court in June because the situation was termed "intolerable." It involved "chaos, bedlam and turmoil" at the school; "repeated incidents of more or less serious violence directed against the Negro students and their property;" "tension and unrest" among staff, students, and parents; a "serious financial burden" on the school district; and the need for a continuation of "military assistance or its equivalent." The court of appeals held a special session in August and reversed the district court.

The Supreme Court convened in Special Term in late August and unanimously held that the desegregation plan must be implemented. It emphasized that it accepted the good faith of the board in requesting the delay and the findings of the district court that the educational progress of all students had suffered and would continue to do so unless conditions changed from the preceding year. However, the Court said that the conditions are "directly traceable to the actions of legislators and executive officials of the State of Arkansas, taken in their official capacities, which reflect their own determination to resist this Court's decision in the *Brown* case and which have brought about violent resistance to that decision in Arkansas."[2] It added that "the constitutional rights of [black children] are not to be sacrificed or yielded to the violence and disorder which have followed upon the actions of the Governor and Legislature. . . . Thus law and order are not here to be preserved by depriving the Negro children of their constitutional rights."[3]

The Court reviewed its decisions beginning in 1803 establishing the position that it was the Court's role to say what the Constitution means and that all state officials are bound thereby. In the present circumstances, it observed that the *Brown* decisions had enunciated the application of the fourteenth amendment to segregation in public schools. The Court continued:

> It is, of course, quite true that the responsibility for public education is primarily the concern of the States, but it is equally true that such responsibilities, like all other state activity, must be exercised consistently with federal constitutional requirements as they apply to state action. The Constitution created a government dedicated to equal justice under law. The Fourteenth Amendment embodied and emphasized that ideal. State support of segregated schools through any arrangement, management, funds, or property cannot be squared with the Amendment's command that no State shall deny to any person within its jurisdiction the equal protection of the laws. . . . The basic decision in *Brown* was unanimously reached by this Court only after the case had been briefed and twice

argued and the issues had been given the most serious consideration. Since the first *Brown* opinion three new Justices have come to the Court. They are at one with the Justices still on the Court who participated in that basic decision as to its correctness, and that decision is now unanimously reaffirmed. The principles announced in that decision and the obedience of the States to them, according to the command of the Constitution, are indispensable for the protection of the freedoms guaranteed by our fundamental charter for all of us. Our constitutional ideal of equal justice under law is thus made a living truth.[4]

Invalid Student Transfer Plan

The first Supreme Court opinion specifically treating the adequacy of a desegregation plan came eight years, almost to the day, after *Brown II.*[5] The case involved desegregation plans that had been approved by lower federal courts for two Tennessee school districts (Knoxville and Davidson County). Each school district was to be rezoned without reference to race, but there was to be a transfer plan whereby a student who was assigned to a school where the majority of students were "of a different race" could be transferred to a school where his race was in the majority.

The Supreme Court reversed the lower courts and invalidated the transfer provision. It declared:

It is readily apparent that the transfer system proposed lends itself to perpetuation of segregation. Indeed, the provisions can work only toward that end. While transfers are available to those who choose to attend school where their race is in the majority, there is no provision whereby a student might transfer upon request to a school in which his race is in a minority, unless he qualifies for a "good cause" transfer. . . . Here the right of transfer, which operates solely on the basis of a racial classification, is a one-way ticket leading to but one destination, i.e., the majority race of the transferee and continued segregation.

. . . Classifications based on race for purposes of transfers between public schools, as [operating] here, violate the Equal Protection Clause of the Fourteenth Amendment. . . . The recognition of race as an absolute criterion for granting transfers which operate only in the direction of schools in which the transferee's race is in the majority is no less unconstitutional than its use for original admission or subsequent assignment to public schools.[6]

The Court emphasized that it was the particular transfer plan presented here that was unconstitutional. It said the issue would be different if the transfers were unrestricted as to race of transferee and as to racial composition of schools. It added that due to the passage of time, "the context in which we must interpret and apply [the criterion from *Brown II* of 'all deliberate speed'] to plans for desegregation has been significantly altered. . . . The transfer provisions here cannot be deemed to be reasonably designed to meet legitimate local problems, and therefore do not meet the requirements of *Brown*."[7]

Invalid School Closing

A year later, the Court said, "the time for mere 'deliberate speed' has run out."[8] The case was the result of the only complete shutdown of a public school system in the wake of desegregation. Although compulsory education laws had been repealed in a few states and legislation authorizing closings was included in the wave of statutes aimed at stopping or slowing desegregation, only Prince Edward County, Virginia, (one of the five districts in the *Brown* litigation) actually closed its public schools. For the five school years beginning in 1959, a private group, aided by public funds, operated private schools for white children in that county. Having rejected an offer to set up segregated private schools for their children, blacks in the county continued to work through the courts for desegregation in public education. For four years, there was no formal education for the black children, who comprised about fifty-five percent of school-age residents of the county. In 1963, federal, state, and local authorities cooperated with a private organization to start classes for blacks.

The Supreme Court held not only that the closing of the schools was unconstitutional but that the district court was empowered to order their reopening. Basic to the decision was the fact that public schools were being maintained throughout Virginia except in the one county. The Court said:

> Virginia law, as here applied, unquestionably treats the school children of Prince Edward differently from the way it treats the school children of all other Virginia counties. Prince Edward children must go to a private school or none at all; all other Virginia children can go to public schools. Closing Prince Edward's schools bears more heavily on Negro children in Prince Edward County since white children there have accredited private schools which they can attend, while colored children until very recently have had no available private schools, and even the school they now attend is a temporary

expedient. Apart from this expedient, the result is that Prince Edward County school children, if they go to school in their own county, must go to racially segregated schools which, although designated as private, are beneficiaries of county and state support.

. . . [T]he record in the present case could not be clearer that Prince Edward's public schools were closed and private schools operated in their place with state and county assistance, for one reason, and one reason only: to ensure, through measures taken by the county and the State, that white and colored children in Prince Edward County would not, under any circumstances, go to the same school. Whatever nonracial grounds might support a State's allowing a county to abandon public schools, the object must be a constitutional one, and grounds of race and opposition to desegregation do not qualify as constitutional.[9]

The Court took notice that the case began in 1951 and had been delayed "by resistance at the state and county levels, by legislation, and by lawsuits. The original plaintiffs have doubtless all passed high school age. There has been entirely too much deliberation and not enough speed in enforcing the constitutional rights which we held in *Brown I* had been denied Prince Edward County Negro children."[10]

Relief for Some Black Students

The Court's concern with the pace of desegregation was further expressed in December, 1965.[11] The Ft. Smith, Arkansas school system had adopted a grade-a-year desegregation plan that began with first grade in 1957-58, and thus, for 1965-66, had left 10th, 11th, and 12th grades segregated. In a short per curiam opinion, the Court said that the black students in those still-segregated grades were entitled to immediate relief. Their "assignments are constitutionally forbidden not only for the reasons stated in [*Brown I*], but also because [they] are thereby prevented from taking certain courses offered only at another high school limited to white students. . . ."[12] Instead of a remand for further proceedings on relief, the Court ordered that black students desiring courses not offered in their segregated high school be allowed immediate transfer.

Three Inadequate Freedom-of-Choice Plans

In 1968, the Court decided three cases from three circuits in each of which the basic issue was the adequacy of a desegregation plan. Each plan involved the "freedom-of-choice" concept that had been widely instituted in the South in the 1960's. In essence, this arrangement involved no reassignments by order of school authorities. Children whose parents expressed a preference for them to attend a school other than the one to which they normally would be assigned would be reassigned if feasible. The concept was grounded in the erroneous notion that the dropping of prior compulsory segregation was all that was required constitutionally. Furthermore, because the starting point was a school assignment based entirely on race, in effect only those who wished to leave a school where their race was predominant in order to attend a school where their race was in the minority would ask for transfers. "Black" and "white" school designations in the minds of community members would be changed only if large numbers of students transferred. It is not surprising that only small numbers of blacks moved to "white" schools, and an insignificant number of whites moved to "black" schools.

The setting for the principal case[13] was New Kent County, Virginia, in which there were only two schools being operated. Until 1965, no mixing of the races in school had occurred. At that time, in order to remain eligible for federal funds, a freedom-of-choice plan was adopted. In the next three years no white child had chosen to attend the "black" school, and eighty-five percent of the black children remained in that school. The Court, in holding that the plan was insufficient, said:

> In other words, the school system remains a dual system. Rather than further the dismantling of the dual system, the plan has operated simply to burden children and their parents with a responsibility which *Brown II* placed squarely on the School Board. The Board must be required to formulate a new plan and, in light of other courses which appear open to the Board, such as zoning, fashion steps which promise realistically to convert promptly to a system without a "white" school and a "Negro" school, but just schools.[14]

The Court declined to rule that freedom-of-choice could have no place in a desegregation plan. "We do not hold that a 'freedom-of-choice' plan might of itself be unconstitutional, although that argument has been urged upon us."[15] The Court observed that "general experience under 'freedom-of-choice' to date has been such as to indicate its ineffectiveness as a tool of desegregation,"[16] but it recognized the possibility that it might work under some unspecified circumstance. However, "if there are reasonably available other ways, such for illustration as zoning, promising speedier and more effective conversion to a unitary, nonracial school system, 'freedom-of-choice' must be held unacceptable."[17]

The Court took the opportunity to redefine the legal duty of boards of education in formerly de jure segregated districts. It said that *Brown II* had established that such a board was "clearly charged with the affirmative duty to take whatever steps might be necessary to convert [the dual system] to a unitary system in which racial discrimination would be eliminated root and branch."[18] It decreed that henceforth boards and reviewing courts should apply an "effects" test in assessing adequacy of desegregation measures. The concept, which was to replace the *Brown II* standard of "all deliberate speed," was expressed in these words: "The burden on a school board today is to come forward with a plan that promises realistically to work, and promises realistically to work *now*."[19]

In the second case,[20] from Arkansas, the fact situation was very similar to that in *Green*. In *Raney* the Court, relying on the *Green* reasoning to find the freedom-of-choice plan inadequate, added the direction to lower courts that it was their responsibility not to dismiss a segregation case until it was clear that disestablishment of the dual system actually had been achieved. The Court said that the lower courts should retain jurisdiction to insure both that a constitutionally acceptable plan is adopted and that it is operated so that the "'goal of a desegregated, non-racially operated school system is rapidly and finally achieved.'"[21] In the third case, arising in Tennessee, the Court struck down a "free transfer" provision that in effect negated an assignment plan that otherwise was capable of producing meaningful desegregation.[22] The Court, referring to its decision five years before in *Goss*, said:

> While we there indicated that "free-transfer" plans under some circumstances might be valid, we explicitly stated that "no official transfer plan or provision of which racial segregation is the inevitable consequence may stand under the Fourteenth Amendment." [*Goss*] So it is here; no attempt has been made to justify the transfer provision as a device designed to meet "legitimate local problems;" rather it patently operates as a device to allow *resegregation* of the races to the extent desegregation would be achieved by geographically drawn zones. Respondent's argument in this Court reveals its purpose. We are frankly told in the Brief that without the transfer option it is apprehended that white students will flee the school system altogether. "But it should go without saying that the vitality of these constitutional principles cannot be allowed to yield simply because of disagreement with them." [*Brown II*]
>
> We do not hold that "free transfer" can have no place in a desegregation plan. But like "freedom of choice," if it cannot be shown that such a plan will further rather than delay conversion to a unitary, nonracial, nondiscriminatory school system, it must be held unacceptable.[23]

Teacher Desegregation Required

The topic of faculty desegregation was treated by the Supreme Court for the first time in November, 1965, over a decade after the *Brown II* desegregation-implementation opinion. The case was a suit against the Board of Education of Richmond, Virginia, contesting a plan that was being put into effect to desegregate the schools.[24] The Court of Appeals for the Fourth Circuit had affirmed a district court's holding that omission from the plan of any provision requiring the assignment of faculty personnel on a nonracial basis was not sufficient cause to require rejection of the plan. The appellate court had ruled that it was proper to defer inquiry into the appropriateness of teacher assignments and other "supplemental measures" until the effects of the "direct measures" regarding pupil reassignments could be determined.

The Supreme Court disagreed. It ordered immediate hearings on the question of faculty assignments, saying:

> There is no merit to the suggestion that the relation between faculty allocation on an alleged racial basis and the adequacy of the desegregation plans is entirely speculative. Nor can we perceive any reason for postponing these hearings: Each plan had been in operation for at least one academic year; these suits had been pending for several years; and more than a decade has passed since we directed desegregation of public school facilities "with all deliberate speed." ... Delays in desegregation of school systems are no longer tolerable.[25]

Less than a month later, the Court answered a key question of standing to sue for the desegregation of teaching staffs by stating that students not yet in desegregated classes could challenge the racial allocation of faculty on two theories: that it denies them equality of educational opportunity without regard to segregation of students, and that it renders inadequate an otherwise constitutional student desegregation plan soon to be applied to their grades.[26]

The first Supreme Court opinion dealing expressly with the implementation of a faculty desegregation plan came in 1969 in a case that arose in Montgomery County, Alabama.[27] The district judge had ordered the school board to move toward a goal under which the ratio of white to black faculty members in each school was substantially the same as it was within the system as a whole. Also, for the 1968-69 school year, each school was to have at least one full-time teacher of the minority race of teachers in that school. In schools with twelve or more teachers, the race of at least one out of every six faculty and staff members was required to be different from the race of the majority of faculty and staff members in that school. The Court of Appeals for the

Fifth Circuit had modified the ratio pattern for 1968-69 to require only "approximately" the ratio and had held that the ratio concept should be eliminated in the future with compliance not tested solely by the achievement of ratios. The two-to-one decision of the appellate panel was left in effect by the rejection, in a six-to-six vote, of a rehearing by all judges on the circuit court.

The Supreme Court reversed, ordering the ratio arrangement to be put into immediate effect. The key reasoning was as follows:

> Judge Johnson's order now before us was adopted in the spirit of this Court's opinion in [*Green*] in that his plan "promises realistically to work, and promises realistically to work *now*." The modifications ordered by the panel of the Court of Appeals, while of course not intended to do so, would, we think, take from the order some of its capacity to expedite, by means of specific commands, the day when a completely unified, unitary, nondiscriminatory school system becomes a reality instead of a hope. We believe it best to leave Judge Johnson's order as written rather than as modified by the 2-1 panel, particularly in view of the fact that the Court of Appeals as a whole was evenly divided on this subject. We also believe that under all the circumstances of this case we follow the original plan outlined in *Brown II*, as brought up to date by this Court's opinions in [*Green*] and [*Griffin*], by accepting the more specific and expeditious order of Judge Johnson, whose patience and wisdom are written for all to see and read on the pages of the five-year record before us.[28]

"With All Deliberate Speed" Replaced by "Terminate at Once"

In the fall of 1969 the Supreme Court issued a brief order that fundamentally changed the pace of desegregation.[29] The vehicle was an appeal from the granting to certain Mississippi school districts by lower courts of additional time before desegregation plans were to be put into effect. The Court said:

> The question presented is one of paramount importance, involving as it does the denial of fundamental rights to many thousands of school children, who are presently attending Mississippi schools under segregated conditions contrary to the applicable decisions of this Court. Against this background the Court of Appeals should have denied all motions for additional time because continued operation of segregated schools under a standard of allowing "all deliberate speed" for desegregation is no longer constitutionally permissible. Under explicit

holdings of this Court the obligation of every school district is to terminate dual school systems at once and to operate now and hereafter only unitary schools.[30]

This decision required that lower courts no longer allow the status quo of complete or substantial segregation to continue while arguments and appeals dragged on in the courts. It was now a matter of "integrate now and litigate later." Objections to plans ordered would be considered by the courts after they were in operation, not before, as had been the typical situation.

The 1971 Cases: Specifics for Desegregating Dual School Systems

As expected, many types of arrangements were ordered by lower federal courts. The parameters of the constitutional mandate and the techniques that federal judges could order were discussed at length by the Court in 1971 in a series of cases. The case utilized by the Court for its primary exposition was from Charlotte, North Carolina, where lower courts had ordered a plan involving the most politically volatile of the techniques—busing.[31] The Court unanimously held that the technique could be utilized and that under the circumstances, the order was reasonably within the trial judge's discretionary power. It observed that nationwide approximately thirty-nine percent of all public school children were bused, that busing had been used extensively in Charlotte over the years, and that the new busing plan, which included the consideration of desegregation, compared favorably with the existing one as to time spent by students on buses. It said:

> In these circumstances, we find no basis for holding that the local school authorities may not be required to employ bus transportation as one tool of school desegregation. Desegregation plans cannot be limited to the walk-in school.
>
> An objection to transportation of students may have validity when the time or distance of travel is so great as to either risk the health of the children or significantly impinge on the educational process. . . . The reconciliation of competing values in a desegregation case is, of course, a difficult task with many sensitive facets but fundamentally no more so than remedial measures courts of equity have traditionally employed.[32]

The Court also addressed what it called "racial balances or racial quotas." The district court had ordered that efforts be made to reach a seventy-one percent to twenty-nine percent ratio of white to black students in the various schools so that there would be no basis for contending that one school was racially different from the others. The Court found the guideline to be within the equity power of the federal court that was charged with fashioning a remedy for the constitutional violation. The Court said:

> If we were to read the holding of the District Court to require, as a matter of substantive constitutional right, any particular degree of racial balance or mixing, that approach would be disapproved and we would be obliged to reverse. The constitutional command to desegregate schools does not mean that every school in every community must always reflect the racial composition of the school system as a whole.[33]

On the point of altering attendance zones to "break up the dual school system," the Court stated:

> Absent a constitutional violation there would be no basis for judicially ordering assignment of students on a racial basis. All things being equal, with no history of discrimination, it might well be desirable to assign pupils to schools nearest their homes. But all things are not equal in a system that has been deliberately constructed and maintained to enforce racial segregation. The remedy for such segregation may be administratively awkward, inconvenient, and even bizarre in some situations and may impose burdens on some; but all awkwardness and inconvenience cannot be avoided in the interim period when remedial adjustments are being made to eliminate the dual school systems.[34]

The Court addressed the question of the continued existence in a former dual school system of schools attended almost entirely by students of one race. It commented that there might be circumstances where a small number of schools served essentially one race. No clear-cut rule could govern all circumstances. However, the Court said:

> [I]n a system with a history of segregation the need for remedial criteria of sufficient specificity to assure a school authority's compliance with its constitutional duty warrants a presumption against schools that are substantially disproportionate in their racial composition. Where the school authority's proposed plan for conversion from a dual to. a unitary system contemplates the continued existence of some schools that are all or predominately of one race, they have the burden of showing that such school assignments are genuinely nondiscriminatory. The court should scrutinize such schools, and the burden upon the school authorities will be to satisfy the court that their racial composition is not the result of present or past discriminatory action on their part.[35]

In this opinion, the Court reiterated that district courts must correct faculty segregation and that ratios may be used as starting points. It also expressed the following view on school construction in systems being transformed from a dual to a unitary operation:

> The construction of new schools and the closing of old ones are two of the most important functions of local school authorities and also two of the most complex. They must decide questions of location and capacity. . . .
>
> In the past, choices in this respect have been used as a potent weapon for creating or maintaining a state-segregated school system. In addition to the classic pattern of building schools specifically intended for Negro or white students, school authorities have sometimes, since *Brown,* closed schools which appeared likely to become racially mixed through changes in neighborhood residential patterns. This was sometimes accompanied by building new schools in the areas of white suburban expansion farthest from Negro population centers in order to maintain the separation of the races with a minimum departure from the formal principles of "neighborhood zoning." . . .
>
> In ascertaining the existence of legally imposed school segregation, the existence of a pattern of school construction and abandonment is thus a factor of great weight. In devising remedies where legally imposed segregation has been established, it is the responsibility of local authorities and district courts to see to it that future school construction and abandonment are not used and do not serve to perpetuate or re-establish the dual system.[36]

Decided at the same time as *Swann* were three other cases. In one, the Court declared unconstitutional a North Carolina statute forbidding assignment of students on the basis of race and the use of involuntary busing "for the purpose of creating a balance or ratio of race."[37] The basis of the decision was that the statute would deprive school authorities of the ability to execute their constitutional duty to disestablish dual school systems.

In a case from Alabama, the Court affirmed the use of ratios as starting points for faculty and staff desegregation and disapproved of a desegregation plan because "inadequate consideration was given to the possible use of bus transportation and split zoning."[38]

In the third case, the Court reversed a judgment of the Supreme Court of Georgia that had enjoined a school desegregation plan on the ground that it "treat[ed] students differently because of their race."[39] The Court tersely remarked that the school board had properly taken race of students into account because "any other approach would freeze the status quo that is the very target of all desegregation processes.[40]

1. Cooper v. Aaron, 358 U.S. 1, 78 S. Ct. 1401 (1958).
2. *Id.* at 15, 78 S. Ct. at 1408.
3. *Id.* at 16, 78 S. Ct. at 1409.
4. *Id.* at 19-20, 78 S. Ct. at 1410.
5. Goss v. Board of Educ., 373 U.S. 683, 83 S. Ct. 1405 (1963).
6. *Id.* at 686-688, 83 S. Ct. at 1408-1409.
7. *Id.* at 689, 83 S. Ct. at 1409.
8. Griffin v. County School Bd. of Prince Edward Cty., 377 U.S. 218, 234, 84 S. Ct. 1226, 1235 (1964).
9. *Id.* at 230-231, 84 S. Ct. at 1233.
10. *Id.* at 229, 84 S. Ct. at 1232.
11. Rogers v. Paul, 382 U.S. 198, 86 S. Ct. 358 (1965).
12. *Id.* at 199, 86 S. Ct. at 359-360.
13. Green v. County School Bd. of New Kent Cty., 391 U.S. 430, 88 S. Ct. 1689 (1968).
14. *Id.* at 441-442, 88 S. Ct. at 1696.
15. *Id.* at 439, 88 S. Ct. at 1695.
16. *Id.*
17. *Id.* at 441, 88 S. Ct. at 1696.
18. *Id.* at 437-438, 88 S. Ct. at 1694.
19. *Id.*
20. Raney v. Board of Educ. of Gould School Dist., 391 U.S. 443, 88 S. Ct. 1697 (1968).
21. *Id.* at 449, 88 S. Ct. at 1700.
22. Monroe v. Board of Comm'rs of City of Jackson, Tenn., 391 U.S. 450, 88 S. Ct. 1700 (1968).
23. *Id.* at 459, 88 S. Ct. at 1705.
24. Bradley v. School Bd., City of Richmond, 382 U.S. 103, 86 S. Ct. 224 (1965).
25. *Id.* at 105, 86 S. Ct. at 225-226.
26. Rogers v. Paul, 382 U.S. 198, 86 S. Ct. 358 (1965).
27. United States v. Montgomery Cty. Bd. of Educ., 395 U.S. 225, 89 S. Ct. 1670 (1969).
28. *Id.* at 235-236, 89 S. Ct. at 1675-1676.
29. Alexander v. Holmes Cty. Bd. of Educ., 396 U.S. 19, 90 S. Ct. 29 (1969).
30. *Id.*
31. Swann v. Charlotte-Mecklenburg Bd. of Educ., 402 U.S. 1, 91 S. Ct. 1267 (1971).
32. *Id.* at 30-31, 91 S. Ct. at 1283.
33. *Id.* at 24, 91 S. Ct. at 1280.
34. *Id.* at 28, 91 S. Ct. at 1282.
35. *Id.* at 26, 91 S. Ct. at 1281.
36. *Id.* at 20-22, 91 S. Ct. at 1278-1279.
37. North Carolina State Bd. of Educ. v. Swann, 402 U.S. 43, 91 S. Ct. 1284 (1971).
38. Davis v. Board of School Comm'rs of Mobile Cty., 402 U.S. 33, 38, 91 S. Ct. 1289, 1292 (1971).
39. McDaniel v. Barresi, 402 U.S. 39, 41, 91 S. Ct. 1287, 1288 (1971).
40. *Id.*, 91 S. Ct. at 1289.

CHAPTER 9

Race and Education: Continuing Application of the Constitutional Mandate

Altering School District Boundaries while Desegregating

The remarkable unanimity of the Justices of the Supreme Court in school desegregation cases came to an end in 1972 in a case involving changes in boundaries of school districts in states dismantling dual school systems.[1] In another boundary case decided at the same time, however, the opinion was unanimous.[2] The disagreement in the first case, from Virginia, was not on the legal principles to be applied but on their application to the facts. In each case, the district court had enjoined the creation of a new school district, and in each, the court of appeals had reversed. The Supreme Court held that the court of appeals was incorrect in both cases.

In the first case, the Court majority of five said that a proposal

> to erect new boundary lines for the purpose of school attendance . . . where a dual school system had long flourished . . . must be judged according to whether it hinders or furthers the process of school desegregation. If the proposal would impede the dismantling of the dual system, then a district court, in the exercise of its remedial discretion, may enjoin it from being carried out.[3]

The conclusion of the majority was that the totality of circumstances surrounding the establishment by a municipality of a school district separate from the county in which the municipality was located would impede the process of desegregation in the county that had operated as one segregated system. The individual factors leading to that conclusion were that the differences in racial percentages in the two districts would begin somewhat out of balance and would, according to lower court findings, soon become wider; the two formerly all-white schools were located in the city, while all the schools in the surrounding county were formerly all-black; the buildings in the city were on better sites and were better equipped; and the intention to change to a separate district was announced by the city council two weeks after the entry of the first desegregation decree that would have caused more than a little change in the attendance pattern of the formerly segregated single system.

The majority said that it was proper in such a case to examine the effects on desegregating school systems, with no necessity for proof of a discriminatory motive on the part of officials. The minority said that because the city had a right to establish a separate system under state law that was not related to segregation, the findings of the district court as to discriminatory effects, especially in future projections, were not sufficient to support a federal injunction against the action. The four Justices emphasized, however, that "[i]f it appeared that the city of Emporia's operation of a separate school system would either perpetuate racial segregation in the schools of the Greensville County area or otherwise frustrate the dismantling of the dual system in that area, [we] would unhesitatingly join in [the majority judgment]."[4]

In the second case, all nine Justices voted to invalidate a North Carolina statute that authorized the creation of a new school district for the city of Scotland Neck, a part of the Halifax County school district then in the process of dismantling a dual school system. The Court found that the disparity in the racial composition of the two school districts to be formed by the separation would be "substantial" (fifty-seven percent white in one and eleven percent white in the other). The four Justices who had dissented in the Emporia case joined in a concurring opinion explaining that in the Scotland Neck case not only would the disparity in racial composition of the schools be great, but also that there was no reason for the legislation except to avoid impending desegregation in the area.

The Denver Case: De Jure Segregation outside the South

Until 1973 Supreme Court opinions had dealt only with school desegregation in states that had required (or expressly permitted local districts to require) separation of the races in public schools. That the segregation to be corrected in those cases had been governmentally imposed (*i.e.*, de jure segregation) rather than adventitiously growing out of the uniform application of racially neutral student assignment policies (*i.e.*, de facto segregation) was uncontestable. Several times in the *Swann* opinion, the Court emphasized that it was discussing only de jure segregation. Such segregation, however, was not confined to those states that once required it by state constitution or statute. Some of the school segregation in the North and West erroneously was considered by many to be de facto segregation. The existence of de jure segregation outside of the South was essentially a question of proof. Lower federal (and state) courts had decided several cases bearing on the point, and remedial court orders to correct what was judicially found to be de jure segregation in the North and West were unsuccessfully appealed to the Supreme Court beginning in 1961.[5] However, the Court's first opinion involving segregation outside the South came nineteen years after *Brown I.*

At that time, the Supreme Court decided the widely publicized "Denver case."[6] The Denver school board never had taken overt action to separate the races by gerrymandering attendance zones or manipulating student assignments, as had the other districts outside the South that had been ordered by lower courts to correct de jure situations. What the Denver board initially had done was to open an elementary school in 1960 with an enrollment which was virtually one hundred percent minority students, ninety-three percent "Negro" and seven percent "Hispano." The trial court found that a series of acts by the school board, beginning with the establishment of that school and its attendance zone, had the effect of creating a segregated condition in one section of the city at the time of the trial in 1969. Thus, the segregation was deemed de jure and a remedial order was issued.

The order to effectuate desegregation of these schools was affirmed by the Court of Appeals for the Tenth Circuit. The trial court, however, also examined segregated core city schools. It found these to be de facto segregated, but "educationally inferior" to the predominantly "Anglo" schools in other parts of the district. It ordered the board to provide "equal educational opportunity" to the predominantly "Negro" and "Hispano" students assigned there by providing "compensatory education in an integrated environment." The court of appeals reversed the order affecting the core city schools.

By a vote of seven-to-one, the Supreme Court affirmed the order to desegregate the schools that were found to be de jure segregated. It vacated the part of the decree of the Tenth Circuit that had reversed the trial court's judgment regarding the core city schools. The Court vacated, rather than reversed, so that further proceedings could take place in the trial court in accordance with principles announced by the Supreme Court.

The first "new" principle was that in defining a "segregated" school, "Negroes" and "Hispanos" must be considered in one category because "in Denver [they] suffer identical discrimination in treatment when compared with the treatment afforded Anglo students."[7] On the key question of whether the Denver school board could be ordered to eliminate the segregation in the core city schools, the Supreme Court held that the lower courts had applied an incorrect legal standard. It noted that some thirty-eight percent of Denver's total "Negro" school students (including over two-thirds of the "Negro" junior high students) were segregated in schools in the section of the district that the lower courts had found to be the object of an unconstitutional policy of deliberate racial segregation. Furthermore, there was uncontroverted evidence that for many years teachers and staff had been assigned on a basis of minority-teacher-to-minority-school. The Court said that it had never suggested that plaintiffs in school desegregation cases must bear the burden of proving the elements of de jure segregation in connection with each and every school within the system. It stated that, to the contrary, it had held that when plaintiffs could prove that a current condition of segregated schooling existed within a district where a dual system was statutorily compelled or authorized at the time of the *Brown I* decision, the state automatically must assume an affirmative duty to effectuate a transition to a racially nondiscriminatory school system.

Recognizing that a statutory dual school system had never existed in Denver, the Court stated that "where plaintiffs prove that the school authorities have carried out a systematic program of segregation affecting a substantial portion of the students, schools, teachers, and facilities within the school system, it is only common sense to conclude that there exists a predicate for a finding of the existence of a dual school system."[8] The impact of racially inspired school board actions goes beyond the particular schools that are the subjects of those actions. "[A] finding of intentionally segregative school board actions in a meaningful portion of a school system, as in this case, creates a presumption that other segregated schooling within the system is not adventitious."[9]

The Court acknowledged the "rare" possibility that there might be a situation where the geographical structure of, or the natural boundaries within, a school district could have the effect of dividing the district into "separate, identifiable and unrelated"[10] units. Since determining whether an exception exists is essentially a question of fact, which in the first instance must be resolved by a trial court, the Court remanded the case to the trial court to determine if the de jure segregated area was a "separate, identifiable and unrelated" section that should be treated as isolated from the rest of the district. If the school board failed to prove that contention, the lower court was directed to ascertain whether the board's policy of deliberate racial segregation in the Park Hill schools constituted the entire school system a dual school system. If so, the school board must be ordered to desegregate the whole system completely. If not, the board must affirmatively show that the segregation in the core city schools was not the result of intentional action. The reason for this shift of burden of proof was that intentional illegal actions had been proved for one section of the city. If the board failed to rebut the prima facie case in regard to

the core city schools, the trial court was instructed to order desegregation of this cluster of schools. (On remand, it was held that the
evidence established Denver to be a dual school system and thus subject
to a system-wide desegregation order.[11])

In the *Denver* case, the Supreme Court took the opportunity to stress
that it was dealing with de jure segregation. It clearly stated the legal
test for such a determination: "We emphasize that the differentiating
factor between *de jure* segregation and so-called *de facto* segregation
. . . is *purpose* or *intent* to segregate."[12]

Excessive Court-ordered Remedies

In 1974 the Court examined the extent of the power of federal courts
to order remedies for segregation which would directly affect school
districts other than the one at bar in a given case. Specifically, if a
formerly de jure segregated district contains at the time of adjudication
such a high percent of blacks that meaningful racial mixing cannot take
place because of the small percent of whites attending the district's
schools, does the federal Constitution require that adjacent districts
that are heavily populated by whites participate in remediating the
situation?

By a five-to-four vote, the Court answered, in effect, "not if those
surrounding districts were not themselves involved in discriminatory
acts."[13] The Court said:

> We granted certiorari . . . to determine whether a federal
> court may impose a multidistrict, areawide remedy to a single
> district de jure segregation problem absent any finding that the
> other included school districts have failed to operate unitary
> school systems within their districts, absent any claim or find-
> ing that the boundary lines of any affected school district were
> established with the purpose of fostering racial segregation in
> public schools, absent any finding that the included districts
> committed acts which effected segregation within the other
> districts, and absent a meaningful opportunity for the included
> neighboring school districts to present evidence or be heard on
> the propriety of a multidistrict remedy or on the question of
> constitutional violations by those neighboring districts.[14]

In so framing the issue, the Court set out the flaws in the lower
courts' disposition of the case, which had been to conclude that the
only feasible desegregation plan involved the crossing of the boundary
lines between the Detroit school district and adjacent or nearby school
districts for the limited purpose of providing an effective desegregation
plan. The Sixth Circuit Court of Appeals had said that such a plan

would be appropriate because of certain acts of the state and that it could be implemented because of the state's authority to control local school districts. (The board of education of Detroit was an instrumentality of the state, and the state legislature and state board of education contributed to the Detroit situation by certain actions and inactions in regard to funding, construction, and transportation.) The district court had been ordered, however, to give those suburban school districts that might be affected by an interdistrict order an opportunity to be heard with respect to the scope and implementation of such a remedy.

That there was de jure segregation in Detroit was affirmed by the Supreme Court, and the lower courts were instructed to formulate promptly a decree to eliminate it within the district. But the Court rejected the lower courts' approach to school district boundaries. It said:

> Boundary lines may be bridged where there has been a constitutional violation calling for interdistrict relief, but, the notion that school district lines may be casually ignored or treated as a mere administrative convenience is contrary to the history of public education in our country. No single tradition in public education is more deeply rooted than local control over the operation of schools; local autonomy has long been thought essential both to the maintenance of community concern and support for public schools and to quality of the educational process.[15]

The Court expressed concern about problems that would develop if the fifty-four independent school districts included in the possible metropolitan plan were, in effect, consolidated. Included would be 276,000 students in Detroit and some 503,000 students in the other fifty-three districts in the "desegregation area." The Court stated:

> Entirely apart from the logistical and other serious problems attending large-scale transportation of students, the consolidation would give rise to an array of other problems in financing and operating this new school system. Some of the more obvious questions would be: What would be the status and authority of the present popularly elected school boards? Would the children of Detroit be within the jurisdiction and operating control of a school board elected by the parents and residents of other districts? What board or boards would levy taxes for school operations in these 54 districts constituting the consolidated metropolitan area? What provisions could be made for assuring substantial equality in tax levies among the 54 districts, if this were deemed requisite? What provisions would be made for financing? Would the validity of long-term bonds be jeopardized unless approved by all of the component

districts as well as the State? What body would determine that portion of the curricula now left to the discretion of local school boards? Who would establish attendance zones, purchase school equipment, locate and construct new schools, and indeed attend to all the myriad day-to-day decisions that are necessary to school operations affecting potentially more than three-quarters of a million pupils.[16]

The Court further observed that in resolving the problems, the district court would first have to take on a legislative function and then an administrative one. "This is a task which few, if any, judges are qualified to perform and one which would deprive the people of control of schools through their elected representatives."[17]

Also stressed was the fact that evidence of de jure segregation was confined to Detroit schools (with only one relatively minor instance involving another district). The Court further stated that "[t]he constitutional right of the Negro respondents residing in Detroit is to attend a unitary school system in that district,"[18] and that unless the district lines were discriminatorily drawn or only white students were allowed to attend schools in adjoining districts, there was no constitutional duty to make provisions for black students to do so.

It must be emphasized that the Court did not rule out interdistrict remedies per se. It set the standards to be met before a federal court could order them as follows:

> [I]t must first be shown that there has been a constitutional violation within one district that produces a significant segregative effect in another district. Specifically, it must be shown that racially discriminatory acts of the state or local school districts, or of a single school district have been a substantial cause of interdistrict segregation. Thus an interdistrict remedy might be in order where the racially discriminatory acts of one or more school districts caused racial segregation in an adjacent district, or where district lines have been deliberately drawn on the basis of race. In such circumstances an interdistrict remedy would be appropriate to eliminate the interdistrict segregation directly caused by the constitutional violation.[19]

In 1976, the Court considered a case in which a district judge had required periodic readjustments in student assignment patterns to reflect demographic changes in population subsequent to the implementation of an initial student assignment plan.[20] After de jure segregation had been found to exist in Pasadena, California, the school board was ordered in 1970 to institute a plan that would result in no school having "a majority of any minority students." In 1974, when the board sought to modify this requirement, the judge said that the order "meant to me that at least during my lifetime there would be no majority of any minority in any school in Pasadena."[21] The Supreme Court, in holding that the judge had exceeded his authority, pointed to the facts that the initial order, which had encompassed a plan to correct existing de jure segregation, had accomplished that objective and that changes between 1970 and 1974 in enrollments in five of thirty-two schools were not due to any acts of the school authorities but were the result of changes in residential patterns. The Court declared:

> That being the case, the District Court was not entitled to require the [school district] to rearrange its attendance zones each year so as to ensure that the racial mix desired by the court was maintained in perpetuity. For having once implemented a racially neutral attendance pattern in order to remedy the perceived constitutional violations on the part of the [school district], the District Court had fully performed its function of providing the appropriate remedy for previous racially discriminatory attendance patterns.[22]

Appropriate Court-ordered Remedies

A year later, the Court considered further the extent of the remedial powers of federal courts in school desegregation cases.[23] Following the decision in 1974 of *Milliken I* that upheld the finding of de jure segregation in the Detroit public schools and ordered it corrected within that system, certain prescriptions were made by the district court and upheld by the Court of Appeals for the Sixth Circuit. Four components of the court-ordered desegregation plan were challenged in *Milliken II*. They were: (1) a remedial reading and communications skills program, (2) an inservice education program to assist teachers in coping with problems in the desegregation process, (3) a new testing program free from racial, ethnic or cultural bias, and (4) an expanded counseling and career guidance program.

The rationale of the challenge was described by the Court as follows:

> In challenging the order before us, petitioners do not specifically question that the District Court's mandated programs are designed, as nearly as practicable, to restore the schoolchildren of Detroit to a position they would have enjoyed absent constitutional violations by state and local officials. And, petitioners do not contend, nor could they, that the prerogatives of the Detroit School Board have been abrogated by the decree, since of course the Detroit School Board itself proposed incorporation of these programs in the

first place. Petitioners' sole contention is that, under *Swann*, the District Court's order exceeds the scope of the constitutional violation. Invoking our holding in *Milliken I*, petitioners claim that, since the constitutional violation found by the District Court was the unlawful segregation of students on the basis of race, the court's decree must be limited to remedying unlawful pupil assignments.[24]

A unanimous Court, stating that "[t]his contention misconceives the principle petitioners seek to invoke,"[25] rejected the argument and explained the principle in these words:

> The well-settled principle that the nature and scope of the remedy are to be determined by the violation means simply that federal court decrees must directly address and relate to the constitutional violation itself. Because of this inherent limitation upon federal judicial authority, federal court decrees exceed appropriate limits if they are aimed at eliminating a condition that does not violate the Constitution or does not flow from such a violation, or if they are imposed upon governmental units that were neither involved in nor affected by the constitutional violation, as in *Milliken I*. But where, as here, a constitutional violation has been found, the remedy does not "exceed" the violation if the remedy is tailored to cure the "'*condition* that offends the Constitution'."
>
> The "condition" offending the Constitution is Detroit's *de jure* segregated school system, which was so pervasively and persistently segregated that the District Court found that the need for the educational components flowed directly from constitutional violations by both state and local officials. These specific educational remedies, although normally left to the discretion of the elected school board and professional educators, were deemed necessary to restore the victims of discriminatory conduct to the position they would have enjoyed in terms of education had these four components been provided in a nondiscriminatory manner in a school system free from pervasive *de jure* racial segregation.
>
> . . . .
>
> . . . In a word, discriminatory student assignment policies can themselves manifest and breed other inequalities built into a dual system founded on racial discrimination. Federal courts need not, and cannot, close their eyes to inequalities, shown by the record, which flow from a longstanding segregated system.[26]

Also of significance in this case was the affirmance of an order that the cost of these programs was to be borne equally by the state and the local board. The Court observed that state officials, as well as local ones, had been found responsible for unconstitutional conduct in connection with the Detroit school system's de jure segregation. It held that federal courts do not violate the eleventh amendment when they prospectively "enjoin state officials to conform their conduct to requirements of federal law, notwithstanding a direct and substantial impact on the state treasury."[27]

Findings Required to Support a Remedy

On the same day the Court issued the decision in *Milliken II*, it delivered another unanimous decision concerning remedies for correcting de jure segregation.[28] The *Dayton I* case essentially involved questions of proof and of functions of federal district courts and courts of appeals. The district court (after two reversals by the Sixth Circuit Court of Appeals) had ordered an extensive system-wide busing plan for Dayton, Ohio. This third plan was affirmed by the court of appeals. While expressly reaffirming the principles of *Keyes*, the Supreme Court found the remedy to be "entirely out of proportion to the constitutional violations found by the district court,"[29] as revealed in the record of the case. It emphasized, however, that this conclusion "is not to say that the last word has been spoken as to the correctness of the District Court's findings as to unconstitutionally segregative actions"[30] on the part of the school board. The Court stated that a remand was necessary so that the district court could make more specific findings, taking additional evidence if necessary. The court of appeals, after accepting or rejecting the specific findings of fact and reviewing the district court's interpretation of the applicable law, would affirm, reverse or modify the district court's order, giving its reasons so that its opinion could be ultimately reviewed by the Supreme Court. The two reversals in the present litigation by the court of appeals had, in effect, required an extensive remedy based on recorded facts that did not suffice to support it.

The Court outlined the procedural steps as follows:

> The duty of both the District Court and the Court of Appeals, in a case such as this, where mandatory segregation by law of the races in the schools has long since ceased, is to first determine whether there was any action in the conduct of the business of the School Board which was intended to, and did in fact, discriminate against minority pupils, teachers, or staff. . . . If such violations are found, the District Court in the first instance, subject to review by the Court of Appeals, must determine how much incremental segregative effect these

violations had on the racial distribution of the Dayton school population as presently constituted, when that distribution is compared to what it would have been in the absence of such constitutional violations. The remedy must be designed to redress that difference, and only if there has been a systemwide impact may there be a systemwide remedy.

We realize that this is a difficult task, and that it is much easier for a reviewing court to fault ambiguous phrases such as "cumulative violation" than it is for the finder of fact to make the complex factual determinations in the first instance. Nonetheless, that is what the Constitution and our cases call for, and that is what must be done in this case.[31]

In commenting on a "three-part cumulative violation" that had been found and was apparently the central predicate for the system-wide order, the Court observed that (1) the fact of pupil population disparities among schools *alone* does not violate the fourteenth amendment, (2) the rescission of a previously adopted school board resolution (recognizing its fault in not taking affirmative action sooner) was "of questionable validity" in establishing a constitutional violation, and (3) prior zoning regulations for the high schools that might warrant corrective action did not appear to affect lower grades. Nevertheless, the Supreme Court left the plan in effect for the upcoming school year.

Systemwide Plans Justified in Ohio

Almost precisely two years after *Dayton I*, the Court upheld on the merits a system-wide desegregation plan for Dayton that had been imposed by the court of appeals.[32] Following the remand in 1977, the district court ruled that there was no constitutional violation at all, and it dismissed the suit. For the third time, the court of appeals reversed. It set out sufficient facts and conclusions of law to satisfy a Supreme Court majority that a system-wide remedy was warranted.

The Supreme Court summarized the judgment it affirmed in the following language:

The basic ingredients of the Court of Appeals' judgment was that at the time of *Brown I*, the Dayton Board was operating a dual school system, that it was constitutionally required to disestablish that system and its effects, that it had failed to discharge this duty, and that the consequences of the dual system, together with the intentionally segregative impact of various practices since 1954, were of systemwide import and an appropriate basis for a systemwide remedy. In arriving at these conclusions, the Court of Appeals found that in some instances the findings of the District Court were clearly erroneous and that in other respects the District Court had made errors of law.[33]

The racial composition of students and staff at various schools in 1954, coupled with some clearly racially motivated acts prior to 1954, meant that the board was placed under an affirmative duty to correct its purposeful operation of segregated schools. As the segregation encompassed a substantial portion of the district, under the holding in *Keyes*, there arose an inference that segregation elsewhere in the system was intentional. The inference was not rebutted. Further, not only had the board, subsequent to 1954, changed its arrangements only slightly, but it "had engaged in many post-*Brown I* actions that had the effect of increasing or perpetuating segregation."[34] The Court said that the court of appeals was "quite justified in utilizing the Board's total failure to fulfill its affirmative duty—and indeed its conduct resulting in increased segregation—to trace the current, systemwide segregation back to the purposefully dual system of the 1950's and to the subsequent acts of intentional discrimination."[35]

On the same day that it issued the preceding five-to-four decision, the Court released a seven-to-two decision affirming a court-ordered system-wide desegregation plan for Columbus, Ohio.[36] Two of the dissenters in the preceding case joined the majority essentially because they believed the findings of trial judges should be given more weight than those of judges of courts of appeals in such cases. Here, the district court and the court of appeals agreed that in Columbus in 1954 there existed as the direct result of cognitive acts or omissions of the school board an enclave of separate schools for black students; that the board did not assume its affirmative duty to correct the situation; and that the extent of the segregation had been increased by subsequent acts of the board so that it had become sufficient to support an order for a system-wide desegregation plan to bring each school in the system roughly within proportionate racial balance. In the years since 1954 the intentional segregative acts included assigning black teachers only to schools with predominantly black student bodies, manipulation of attendance zones, and site selections for new schools that had the "foreseeable and anticipated effect of maintaining the racial separation of the schools."[37] The Court observed that there was more evidence of intent of certain actions than merely foreseeable disparate impact, but that in any event such foreseeability was a relevant element of evidence supporting a conclusion of forbidden purpose.

Referenda Related to Desegregation

In 1982, the Supreme Court rendered two decisions related to the constitutionality of referenda having the effect of limiting busing of students for purposes of better racial balance within the schools of a district. In one, an eight-Justice majority agreed that implementation of the referendum did not violate the equal protection clause of the fourteenth amendment.[38] In the other, the vote was five-to-four to declare the result of the referendum unconstitutional.[39]

In the Los Angeles case, the referendum had amended the state constitution to prohibit state courts from ordering "mandatory pupil assignment or transportation unless a federal court would do so to remedy a [federal constitutional] violation."[40] Some years before, the Supreme Court of California had interpreted the state constitution to require correction of de facto segregation as well as de jure segregation, and the Los Angeles school board had been ordered by a state trial court to implement a plan that included substantial busing. The state constitutional amendment was attacked as a violation of the equal protection clause. However, the Supreme Court said that it "reject[s] the contention that once a State chooses to do 'more' than the Fourteenth Amendment requires, it may never recede. We reject an interpretation of the Fourteenth Amendment so destructive of a State's democratic processes and of its ability to experiment."[41]

The Court said that the amendment

> does not embody a racial classification. It neither says nor implies that persons are to be treated differently on account of their race. It simply forbids state courts from ordering pupil school assignment or transportation in the absence of a Fourteenth Amendment violation. The benefit it seeks to confer—neighborhood schooling—is made available regardless of race in the discretion of school boards.[42]

Furthermore, added the Court, discriminatory motive could not be imputed to the almost sixty-nine percent of the electorate that voted for the amendment.

In the Seattle case, the challenged referendum was an initiative measure providing that, in general, no school board could require a student to attend a school other than one of the two nearest his residence that offered a given course of study, or employ any of seven methods of "indirect" student assignment, including redefining attendance zones and pairing of schools. The Seattle school district was one of three in Washington that for several years had been attempting for educational reasons to achieve a better racial balance in the schools of the district. The Court found "little doubt that the initiative was effectively drawn for racial purposes."[43] It said:

> The initiative removes the authority to address a racial problem—and only a racial problem—from the existing decision-making body, in such a way as to burden minority interests.

Those favoring the elimination of *de facto* school segregation now must seek relief from the state legislature, or from the statewide electorate. Yet authority over all other student assignment decisions, as well as over most other areas of educational policy, remains vested in the local school board.... [T]he community's political mechanisms are modified to place effective decisionmaking authority over a racial issue at a different level of government.[44]

The Court, however, expressly recognized that the power of a state over its educational system is broad. "Washington could have reserved to state officials the right to make all decisions in the areas of education and student assignment. It has chosen, however, to use a more elaborate system; having done so, the State is obligated to operate that system within the confines of the Fourteenth Amendment."[45]

---

1. Wright v. Council of City of Emporia, 407 U.S. 451, 92 S. Ct. 2196 (1972).

2. United States v. Scotland Neck City Bd. of Educ., 407 U.S. 484, 92 S. Ct. 2214 (1972).

3. Wright v. Council of City of Emporia, 407 U.S. at 460, 92 S. Ct. at 2202.

4. *Id.* at 471, 92 S. Ct. at 2207.

5. Taylor v. Board of Educ. of City School Dist. of New Rochelle, 294 F.2d 36 (2d Cir. 1961), *cert. denied*, 368 U.S. 940, 82 S. Ct. 382 (1961).

6. Keyes v. School Dist. No. 1, Denver, Colo., 413 U.S. 189, 93 S. Ct. 2686 (1973).

7. *Id.* at 198, 93 S. Ct. at 2692.

8. *Id.* at 201, 93 S. Ct. at 2694.

9. *Id.* at 208, 93 S. Ct. at 2697.

10. *Id.* at 203, 93 S. Ct. at 2695.

11. Keyes v. School Dist. No. 1, Denver, Colo., 368 F. Supp. 207 (D. Colo. 1973), *aff'd on this point*, 521 F.2d 465 (10th Cir. 1975).

12. Keyes v. School Dist. No. 1, Denver, Colo., 413 U.S. 189, 208, 93 S. Ct. 2686, 2697 (1973).

13. Milliken v. Bradley, 418 U.S. 717, 94 S. Ct. 3112 (1974) [hereinafter cited as Milliken I].

14. *Id.* at 721-722, 94 S. Ct. at 3116.

15. *Id.* at 741-742, 94 S. Ct. at 3125-3126.

16. *Id.* at 743, 94 S. Ct. at 3126.

17. *Id.* at 744, 94 S. Ct. at 3127.

18. *Id.* at 746, 94 S. Ct. at 3128.

19. *Id.* at 745, 94 S. Ct. at 3127.

20. Pasadena City Bd. of Educ. v. Spangler, 427 U.S.424, 96 S. Ct. 2697 (1976).

21. *Id.* at 433, 96 S. Ct. at 2703.

22. *Id.* at 436-437, 96 S. Ct. at 2705.

23. Milliken v. Bradley, 433 U.S. 267, 97 S. Ct. 2749 (1977) [hereinafter cited as Milliken II].

24. *Id.* at 281, 97 S. Ct. at 2757-2758.

25. *Id.*, 97 S. Ct. at 2758.

26. *Id.* at 281-283, 97 S. Ct. at 2758-2759.

27. *Id.* at 289, 97 S. Ct. at 2762.

28. Dayton Bd. of Educ. v. Brinkman, 433 U.S. 406, 97 S. Ct. 2766 (1977) [hereinafter cited as Dayton I].

29. *Id.* at 418, 97 S. Ct. at 2774.

30. *Id.*

31. *Id.* at 420, 97 S. Ct. at 2775-2776.
32. Dayton Bd. of Educ. v. Brinkman, 443 U.S. 526, 99 S. Ct. 2971 (1979) [hereinafter cited as Dayton II].
33. *Id.* at 534, 99 S. Ct. at 2977.
34. *Id.* at 538, 99 S. Ct. at 2979.
35. *Id.* at 541, 99 S. Ct. at 2981.
36. Columbus Bd. of Educ. v. Penick, 443 U.S. 449, 99 S. Ct. 2941 (1979).
37. *Id.* at 462, 99 S. Ct. at 2949.
38. Crawford v. Board of Educ. of City of Los Angeles, 50 U.S.L.W. 5016 (U.S. June 30, 1982).
39. Washington v. Seattle School Dist. No. 1, 50 U.S.L.W. 4998 (U.S. June 30, 1982).
40. Crawford, 50 U.S.L.W. at 5017.
41. *Id.* at 5018.
42. *Id.* at 5019.
43. Washington, 50 U.S.L.W. at 5002.
44. *Id.* at 5002-5003.
45. *Id.* at 5006.

CHAPTER 10

Teacher Rights: The Loyalty Turmoil

Loyalty Oaths: A Tedious Evolution

Loyalty oaths for educational personnel existed in thirty states in 1953.[1] They differed widely in specific provisions. Beginning in 1949 there had been a wave of enactments of a type of oath that might be termed "non-disloyalty" because it prescribed that one not do certain things relating to unlawful overthrow of the government. In 1952, the Supreme Court issued its first opinion on such an oath required of educators.[2] A year before, the Court upheld a requirement (implementing a 1941 city charter provision) that public employees of the city of Los Angeles swear that they would not advocate the overthrow of the government by unlawful means, or belong to an organization so advocating, and that they had done neither for the preceding five years.[3] The Court then had viewed the matter as an employment qualification that was permissible if the proscription applied only to activities knowingly engaged in and if those who had not taken the oath as so interpreted were given an opportunity to do so. (It seems certain that today the oath would not be enforceable for reasons developed in subsequent cases discussed later in this section.)

In *Wieman*, the Court unanimously invalidated a similar oath after the Supreme Court of Oklahoma refused to require that membership be with knowledge of the nature of a proscribed organization. Membership alone was the basis of disqualification for all current and prospective public officers and employees, with employees of school districts specifically covered. The case was brought by members of the faculty and staff of Oklahoma Agricultural and Mechanical College. The Court pointed out:

> [M]embership may be innocent. A state servant may have joined a proscribed organization unaware of its activities and purposes. In recent years, many completely loyal persons have severed organizational ties after learning for the first time of the character of groups to which they had belonged. "They had joined, [but] did not know what it was; they were good, fine young men and women, loyal Americans, but they had been trapped into it—because one of the great weaknesses of all Americans, whether adult or youth, is to join something."

[Testimony of J. Edgar Hoover, head of Federal Bureau of Investigation.] At the time of affiliation, a group itself may be innocent, only later coming under the influence of those who would turn it toward illegitimate ends. Conversely, an organization formerly subversive and therefore designated as such may have subsequently freed itself from the influences which originally led to its listing.

. . . Yet under the Oklahoma Act, the fact of association alone determines disloyalty and disqualification; it matters not whether association existed innocently or knowingly. To thus inhibit individual freedom of movement is to stifle the flow of democratic expression and controversy at one of its chief sources. . . . Indiscriminate classification of innocent with knowing activity must fall as an assertion of arbitrary power. The oath offends due process.[4]

In 1961, the Supreme Court again unanimously struck down a loyalty oath.[5] The reasoning was that the vagueness of the provisions of the oath rendered it unconstitutional. This was the first of many oaths to be invalidated by the Court because of their content. The challenge by a public school teacher to the Florida oath, in the words of the Court, presented the following question:

The issue to be decided, then, is whether a State can constitutionally compel those in its service to swear that they have never "knowingly lent their aid, support, advice, counsel, or influence to the Communist Party." More precisely, can Florida consistently with the Due Process Clause of the Fourteenth Amendment force an employee either to take such an oath, at the risk of subsequent prosecution for perjury, or face immediate dismissal from public service.[6]

The Court pointed out that nothing in the oath was susceptible of objective measurement, such as would be advocacy of the violent overthrow of the government or affiliation with the Communist Party. The Court posed possibilities, the "very absurdity" of which brought into focus the extraordinary ambiguity of the language used. Observing that in the past, Communist Party candidates legally had run in elections and that the Party had on occasion endorsed candidates nominated by others, the Court rhetorically asked:

Could one who had ever cast his vote for such a candidate safely subscribe to this legislative oath? Could a lawyer who had ever represented the Communist Party or its members swear with either confidence or honesty that he had never knowingly lent his "counsel" to the Party? Could a journalist who had ever defended the constitutional rights of the Communist Party conscientiously take an oath that he had never lent the Party his "support"? Indeed, could anyone honestly subscribe to this oath who had ever supported any cause with contemporaneous knowledge that the Communist Party also supported it?[7]

Quoting from cases with other subject matter, the Court emphasized that "a statute which either forbids or requires the doing of an act in terms so vague that men of common intelligence must necessarily guess at its meaning and differ as to its application, violates the first essential of due process of law."[8] It added that "[t]he vice of unconstitutional vagueness is further aggravated where, as here, the statute in question operates to inhibit the exercise of individual freedoms affirmatively protected by the Constitution."[9]

The Court added that it was not questioning the basic power of a state to safeguard the public service from disloyalty, but was requiring that such be done without infringing upon the constitutional rights of individuals.

In 1964, in a case brought by University of Washington personnel, the Court struck down two oaths on the same grounds as in the preceding case.[10] One oath, enacted in 1955, was of the non-disloyalty type. The other, which had been in effect since 1931, exacted a promise that the teacher would "by precept and example promote respect for the flag and the institutions of the United States of America and the State of Washington, reverence for law and order and undivided allegiance to the government of the United States."[11]

The Court's holding that this was unconstitutionally vague was partially buttressed as follows:

> The range of activities which are or might be deemed inconsistent with the required promise is very wide indeed. The teacher who refused to salute the flag or advocated refusal because of religious beliefs might well be accused of breaching his promise. . . . And what are "institutions" for the purposes of this oath? . . . The oath may prevent a professor from criticizing his state judicial system or the Supreme Court or the institution of judicial review. Or it might be deemed to proscribe advocating the abolition, for example, of the Civil Rights Commission, the House Committee on Un-American Activities, or foreign aid.
>
> It is likewise difficult to ascertain what might be done without transgressing the promise to "promote undivided allegiance to the government of the United States." It would not be unreasonable for the serious-minded oathtaker to conclude that he should dispense with lectures voicing far-reaching criticism of any old or new policy followed by the Government of the United States. He could find it questionable under this language to ally himself with any interest

group dedicated to opposing any current public policy or law of the Federal Government, for if he did, he might well be accused of placing loyalty to the group above allegiance to the United States.[12]

The opinion of the Court repeated the *Cramp* dictum that it did not question the power of a state to take proper measures to safeguard the public service from disloyal conduct. In this case, two Justices dissented.

In the next loyalty oath case, in 1966, there were four dissenters from a decision invalidating an Arizona oath and accompanying statute that provided for criminal penalties, as well as discharge, for anyone taking the oath who knowingly became or remained a member of the Communist Party or of an organization having for one of its purposes the overthrow of the government by force or violence.[13] The majority opinion tied together the question of the oath itself and criminal penalties attached to the violation thereof. The minority dwelt on the oath and did not specifically say whether or not it thought such membership could be made a crime.

The heart of the majority opinion was that "[a] law which applies to membership without the 'specific intent' to further the illegal aims of the organization infringes unnecessarily on protected freedoms. It rests on the doctrine of 'guilt by association' which has no place here."[14]

The Supreme Court further commented:

> One who subscribes to this Arizona oath and who is, or thereafter becomes, a knowing member of an organization which has as "one of its purposes" the violent overthrow of the government, is subject to immediate discharge and criminal penalties. . . . Would it be legal to join a seminar group predominantly Communist and therefore subject to control by those who are said to believe in the overthrow of the government by force and violence? Juries might convict though the teacher did not subscribe to the wrongful aims of the organization. And there is apparently no machinery provided for getting clearance in advance.
>
> Those who join an organization but do not share its unlawful purposes and who do not participate in its unlawful activities surely pose no threat, either as citizens or as public employees. Laws such as this which are not restricted in scope to those who join with the "specific intent" to further illegal action impose, in effect, a conclusive presumption that the member shares the unlawful aims of the organization. . . .
>
> This Act threatens the cherished freedom of association protected by the First Amendment, made applicable to the States through the Fourteenth Amendment.[15]

Similar reasoning led to a six-to-three invalidation of a series of Maryland statutes, including an oath objected to by one who was offered a teaching position at the University of Maryland.[16] The oath specified that the affiant was "not engaged in one way or another in the attempt to overthrow" federal, state, or local government. Another section of Maryland law included a broad definition of "subversive." The attorney general of the state and the board of regents of the university had construed the oath narrowly, excluding "alteration" of the government by peaceful "revolution" and excluding reference to membership in "subversive" groups. This, however, did not meet constitutional requirements in the eyes of the Court. "We are in the First Amendment field. The continuing surveillance which this type of law places on teachers is hostile to academic freedom."[17] The Court said that there was the possibility that there could be "oppressive or capricious application as regimes change. That very threat . . . may deter the flowering of academic freedom as much as successive suits for perjury [penalties for which were prescribed in the oath provision]."[18]

In 1971 the Court issued its first opinion on affirmative-type oaths (those to support federal and state constitutions and to faithfully discharge duties).[19] It stated unanimously that an oath "requiring all applicants to pledge to support the Constitution of the United States and of the State of Florida demands no more of Florida public employees than is required [by the Constitution] of all state and federal officers . . . [and thus the] validity . . . of the oath would appear settled."[20] In the same short per curiam opinion, the Court invalidated a provision requiring a sworn statement that one did "not believe in the overthrow of the Government of the United States or of the State of Florida by force or violence" because "it falls within the ambit of decisions of this Court proscribing summary dismissal from public employment without hearing or inquiry required by due process."[21] Three Justices added that belief in overthrow could never be a basis for government action adverse to a person.

The latter position was expressly enunciated in the Court's 1972 opinion in a loyalty oath case.[22] By a four-to-three vote, the Court upheld, as a requirement for public employment, an oath phraseology that, in addition to "uphold and defend" the constitutions of state and nation (which all Justices agreed was constitutional), required that one "oppose the overthrow of" state or federal government "by force, violence or by any illegal or unconstitutional method." The majority rejected claims of vagueness, saying:

> The second clause does not expand the obligation of the first; it simply makes clear the application of the first clause to a particular issue. Such repetition, whether for emphasis or cadence,

seems to be the wont of authors of oaths. That the second clause may be redundant is no ground to strike it down; we are not charged with correcting grammar but with enforcing a constitution.[23]

Other Loyalty Statutes

In 1953 half of the states had legislation providing specifically for the exclusion of disloyal teachers without requiring oaths.[24] Bans against "subversive" activities were generally focused on advocacy of alleged subversive doctrines and membership in alleged subversive organizations. The most extensive legislation covering only educators was enacted in New York. Originally, in 1949, it applied only to public schools, but it was extended in 1953 to publicly-controlled higher education. This legislation, known as the Feinberg Law,[25] set up elaborate arrangements essentially to implement two existing laws. One was a 1917 statute providing for the removal of school personnel for "the utterance of any treasonable or seditious word or words or the doing of any treasonable or seditious act or acts;"[26] the other was a 1939 ban on advocating or teaching the violent overthrow of the government or on joining any group so advocating.[27]

The Feinberg Law directed the Board of Regents (the state body in charge of education on all levels) to take affirmative action to meet a legislatively-found menace derived from infiltration into the education system of Communists and other subversives. The board was instructed to adopt rules of enforcement for the two existing provisions and to report annually to the legislature. The board, after inquiry, notice, and hearing, was to compile a list of subversive organizations, membership in which would constitute prima facie evidence of disqualification for appointment or retention in a position in public education.

The statute and the rules established by the regents were each challenged on their face (that is, without anyone having been adversely affected by operation of the law). The Supreme Court upheld the statute in 1952 by a vote of six-to-three (six-to-two on the merits).[28] It said that persons who advocated subversive doctrines or were members of subversive organizations were not deprived of the right to assemble, speak, or believe as they wished. However, such persons

> have no right to work for the State in the school system on their own terms. . . . They may work for the school system upon the reasonable terms laid down by the proper authorities of New York. If they do not choose to work on such terms, they are at liberty to retain their beliefs and associations and go elsewhere.[29]

This formulation (implying that public employment could be conditioned upon the surrender of constitutional rights that could not be directly abridged by government action) was circumscribed a few months later in *Wieman v. Updegraff*[30] and expressly rejected fifteen years later in *Keyishian v. Board of Regents of the University of the State of New York*[31] based on the reasoning developed in the cases in the preceding section. However, several points from the *Adler* decision have survived. Perhaps most are in the following paragraph:

> A teacher works in a sensitive area in a schoolroom. There he shapes the attitude of young minds towards the society in which they live. In this, the state has a vital concern. It must preserve the integrity of the schools. That the school authorities have the right and the duty to screen the officials, teachers, and employees as to their fitness to maintain the integrity of the schools as a part of ordered society, cannot be doubted. One's associates, past and present, as well as one's conduct, may properly be considered in determining fitness and loyalty.[32]

In 1967 in *Keyishian,* when aspects of implementation of the Feinberg Law were brought before the Court, by a five-to-four vote, the entire New York structure for eliminating alleged subversives from public schools and colleges was declared unconstitutional.[33] The occasion was a suit brought by some members of the faculty of the formerly privately-operated University of Buffalo who had become state employees when that university was merged into the state university system. At that time, they were required to execute a certificate that they then were not Communists and that if they once were, the fact had been communicated to the president of the state university system. (The Communist Party of the United States and the Communist Party of New York had been listed in 1958 as subversive organizations by the regents under the Feinberg mandates.)

Preliminarily, the Court noted that in its 1952 *Adler* decision, it had not considered the argument of unconstitutional vagueness because the challenge had not been made in the lower courts. Considering that argument this time, the Court found the array of cumulative statutory and administrative provisions existing in 1967 to be fatally vague. and threatening to teachers' first amendment rights. It stated:

> We do not have the benefit of a judicial gloss by the New York courts enlightening us as to the scope of this complicated plan. In light of the intricate administrative machinery for its enforcement this is not surprising. The very intricacy of the plan and the uncertainty as to the scope of its proscriptions make it a highly efficient *in terrorem* mechanism. It would be a bold

teacher who would not stay as far as possible from utterances or acts which might jeopardize his living by enmeshing him in this intricate machinery. The uncertainty as to the utterances and acts proscribed increases that caution in "those who believe the written law means what it says."[34]

Citing the same types of uncertainties it had found in the loyalty oath legislation discussed in the preceding section, the Court concluded:

The regulatory maze created by New York is wholly lacking in "terms susceptible of object measurement." . . . Vagueness of wording is aggravated by prolixity and profusion of statutes, regulations, and administrative machinery, and by manifold cross-references to interrelated enactments and rules.[35]

The Court emphasized that "[t]here can be no doubt of the legitimacy of New York's interest in protecting its education system from subversion. But 'even though the governmental purpose be legitimate and substantial, that purpose cannot be pursued by means that broadly stifle fundamental personal liberties when the end can be more narrowly achieved.'"[36] It continued:

Our Nation is deeply committed to safeguarding academic freedom, which is of transcendent value to all of us and not merely to the teachers concerned. That freedom is therefore a special concern of the First Amendment, which does not tolerate laws that cast a pall of orthodoxy over the classroom. "The vigilant protection of constitutional freedoms is nowhere more vital than in the community of American schools." The classroom is peculiarly the "marketplace of ideas." The Nation's future depends upon leaders trained through wide exposure to that robust exchange of ideas which discovers truth "out of a multitude of tongues, [rather] than through any kind of authoritative selection."[37]

The Court also specifically struck down the discrete provision that made the fact of Communist Party membership prima facie evidence of disqualification for a position in the educational system. "[T]o the extent that *Adler* sustained the provision of the Feinberg Law constituting membership in an organization advocating forceful overthrow of government a ground for disqualification, pertinent constitutional doctrines have since rejected the premises upon which that conclusion rested."[38] The Court said that "constitutional doctrine which has emerged since [*Adler*] has rejected its major premise . . . [which] was that public employment, including academic employment, may be conditioned upon the surrender of constitutional rights which could not be abridged by direct government action."[39] Citing its holding the year before in *Elfbrandt v. Russell*,[40] the Court restated the standard set out there: "legislation which sanctions membership unaccompanied by specific intent to further the unlawful goals of the organization or which is not active membership violates constitutional limitations."[41]

Loyalty Investigations

In the context of loyalty, the Supreme Court has considered two aspects of the question of whether a publicly-employed teacher may be disciplined for refusing to answer questions related to out-of-school activities. The cases were decided two years apart, each by a five-to-four vote.

The first involved an associate professor on tenure at a New York City public college who was questioned by a United States Senate subcommittee investigating "subversive influences in the American educational system."[42] Recognizing that education was primarily a state function, the subcommittee said it was limiting itself to considerations affecting national security. The professor, when called to testify, stated that he was not presently a member of the Communist Party and that he would answer all questions about his associations since 1941; but he refused to answer questions about membership during 1940 and 1941 on the fifth amendment ground that his answers might tend to incriminate him. This claim was accepted by the subcommittee as a valid assertion of a constitutional right.

Shortly after his refusal to testify, Professor Slochower was summarily dismissed under a provision of the New York City Charter that prescribed termination of employment for any employee utilizing the privilege against self-incrimination to avoid answering a question relating to his official conduct. The Supreme Court held that the automatic dismissal violated the due process clause.

Reviewing previous decisions in the area of loyalty of public employees, the Court said that when it had upheld state requirements or regulations, the government had offered a reason related to a legitimate objective. Here, the justification offered was that invoking the fifth amendment led to only two possible inferences, either of which would justify termination. The possible inferences were that the answering of the question would tend to prove the professor guilty of a crime in some way connected to his official conduct, or that perjury was committed if the privilege were falsely invoked. The Court found this reasoning unacceptable. It said:

> [W]e must condemn the practice of imputing a sinister meaning to the exercise of a person's constitutional right under the Fifth Amendment. The right of an accused person to refuse to testify, which had been in England merely a rule of evidence,

was so important to our forefathers that they raised it to the dignity of a constitutional enactment. . . .[43]

The Court observed that in the present situation, no consideration was given to "such factors as the subject matter of the questions, remoteness of the period to which they are directed, or justification for exercise of the privilege. It matters not whether the plea resulted from mistake, inadvertence or legal advice conscientiously given, whether wisely or unwisely."[44]

The Court noted that the Board of Higher Education made no criticism of the professor's qualifications to hold his position. (He had taught on the college level for twenty-seven years.) It further observed that information presented to the Senate subcommittee about Slochower's alleged Communist involvement had been known to the board for some twelve years, but it had done nothing about it over that period. Then it "seized upon his claim of privilege before the federal committee and converted it through the use of [the provision in the charter] into a conclusive presumption of guilt. Since no inference of guilt was possible from the claim before the federal committee, the discharge falls of its own weight as wholly without support."[45]

The Court concluded its opinion as follows:

> This is not to say that Slochower has a constitutional right to be an associate professor of German at Brooklyn College. The State has broad powers in the selection and discharge of its employees, and it may be that proper inquiry would show Slochower's continued employment to be inconsistent with a real interest of the State. But there has been no such inquiry here. We hold that the summary dismissal of appellant violates due process of law.[46]

Two years later, the Court upheld the discharge of a public school teacher who refused to answer questions about his loyalty posed by the superintendent in the superintendent's office.[47] The Court synopsized the case as follows:

> The question before us is whether the Board of Public Education for the School District of Philadelphia, Pennsylvania, violated the Due Process Clause of the Fourteenth Amendment to the Constitution of the United States when the Board, purporting to act under the Pennsylvania Public School Code, discharged a public school teacher on the ground of "incompetency," evidenced by the teacher's refusal of his Superintendent's request to confirm or refute information as to the teacher's loyalty and his activities in certain allegedly subversive organizations. . . . [W]e hold that it did not.[48]

The teacher was told by the superintendent of schools that the superintendent had information reflecting adversely on the teacher's loyalty and that he wanted to determine its truth or falsity. The first question was whether the teacher had been an officer of a particular Communist organization in 1944. The teacher requested and was granted permission to consult counsel before answering. This was shortly before a summer recess, and the question was not reposed until the fall semester. At that time, the teacher said that he had consulted counsel and that he declined to answer the question. He said further that he would not answer any questions similar to it. He was told that the superintendent in these sessions (attended only by the superintendent, the teacher, and a board attorney) was investigating the teacher's fitness for continued employment and that failure to answer might lead to dismissal.

Subsequently, after a hearing at which the teacher had counsel and did not testify, he was dismissed on a statutory charge of "incompetency." It had been agreed that any evidence of disloyalty would not be relevant. Thus, "[t]he only question before [the Court was] whether the Federal Constitution prohibits petitioner's discharge for statutory 'incompetency' based on his refusal to answer the Superintendent's questions."[49]

The Court commented that a teacher was implicitly bound by "obligations of frankness, candor and cooperation in answering inquiries made of him by his employing Board examining into his fitness to serve it as a public school teacher."[50] The question asked was held to be relevant to the inquiry, and, furthermore, the teacher had made it clear that he would not answer any other questions of the same type as the one asked. Thus he "blocked from the beginning any inquiry into his Communist activities, however relevant to his present loyalty."[51] The Court emphasized that the dismissal was not based on the alleged activities of the teacher, but on his insubordination and lack of frankness and candor.

The Court stated that "incompetency," as a disqualifying factor, encompassed a broad area. It said, "We find no requirement in the Federal Constitution that a teacher's classroom conduct be the sole basis for determining his fitness. Fitness for teaching depends on a broad range of factors."[52]

The Court decided two other cases directly involving loyalty inquiries in the field of education. In 1957, by a vote of six-to-two, it held that a guest lecturer at a public college could not be compelled to disclose the content of his lecture to the state attorney general, who was authorized by the legislature to investigate subversive activities in the state.[53] Other refusals by the person also were at issue in the case, as was the extent of the legislature's charge to the attorney general. There was no opinion subscribed to by a majority of the Court, but on the point presented here, there was agreement among six Justices that first amendment rights of the teacher in the setting of the university would be infringed by requiring him to respond to questions of the attorney general about the lecture.

Two years later, a majority of five Justices described the preceding case as follows:

> The vice existing there was that the questioning of Sweezy, who had not been shown ever to have been connected with the Communist Party, as to the contents of a lecture he had given at the University of New Hampshire, and as to his connections with the Progressive Party, then on the ballot as a normal political party in some 26 States, was too far removed from the premises on which the constitutionality of the State's investigation had to depend to withstand attack under the Fourteenth Amendment. . . . This is a very different thing from inquiring into the extent to which the Communist Party has succeeded in infiltrating into our universities, or elsewhere, persons and groups committed to furthering the objective of overthrow.[54]

The *Barenblatt* case was one in which the power of Congress to require testimony was contested primarily on the basis of the first amendment's guarantees of speech and association. Use of the fifth amendment's self-incrimination clause was expressly not relied upon by a college instructor who had been convicted of contempt of Congress for refusal to answer questions about associations with alleged Communist Party activities at educational institutions in the United States. The power of Congress to inquire under the circumstances into the matters in the field of education was upheld. The competing considerations were discussed as follows:

> In the present case congressional efforts to learn the extent of a nationwide, indeed worldwide, problem have brought one of its investigating committees into the field of education. Of course, broadly viewed, inquiries cannot be made into the teaching that is pursued in any of our educational institutions. When academic teaching-freedom and its corollary learning-freedom, so essential to the well-being of the Nation, are claimed, this Court will always be on the alert against intrusion by Congress into this constitutionally protected domain. But this does not mean that the Congress is precluded from interrogating a witness merely because he is a teacher. An educational institution is not a constitutional sanctuary from inquiry into matters that may otherwise be within the constitutional legislative domain merely for the reason that inquiry is made of someone within its walls.[55]

The first amendment defense of the instructor against disclosure was held insufficient in light of the evidence before Congress of "Communist infiltration furthering the alleged ultimate purpose of overthrow" and the fact that *all* questioning was rejected by the instructor. The Court noted some factors absent here that could have led to a different conclusion. It said:

> There is no indication in this record that the Subcommittee was attempting to pillory witnesses. Nor did petitioner's appearance as a witness follow from indiscriminate dragnet procedures lacking in probable cause for belief that he possessed information which might be helpful to the Subcommittee. And the relevancy of the questions put to him by the Subcommittee is not open to doubt.[56]

1. W.S. ELSBREE & E.E. REUTTER, JR., STAFF PERSONNEL IN THE PUBLIC SCHOOLS 311-315 (Englewood Cliffs, N.J.: Prentice-Hall, Inc., 1954).
2. Wieman v. Updegraff, 344 U.S. 183, 73 S. Ct. 215 (1952).
3. Garner v. Board of Pub. Works of City of Los Angeles, 341 U.S. 716, 71 S. Ct. 909 (1951).
4. Wieman v. Updegraff, 344 U.S. at 190-191, 73 S. Ct. at 218-219.
5. Cramp v. Board of Pub. Instruction of Orange Cty., Fla., 368 U.S. 278, 82 S. Ct. 275 (1961).
6. *Id.* at 285, 82 S. Ct. at 280.
7. *Id.*
8. *Id.*
9. *Id.* at 287, 82 S. Ct. at 281.
10. Baggett v. Bullitt, 377 U.S. 360, 84 S. Ct. 1316 (1964).
11. *Id.* at 362, 84 S. Ct. at 1317.
12. *Id.* at 371-372, 84 S. Ct. at 1322.
13. Elfbrandt v. Russell, 384 U.S. 11, 86 S. Ct. 1238 (1966).
14. *Id.* at 19, 86 S. Ct. at 1242.
15. *Id.* at 16-18, 86 S. Ct. at 1241.
16. Whitehill v. Elkins, 389 U.S. 54, 88 S. Ct. 184 (1967).
17. *Id.* at 59-60, 88 S. Ct. at 187.
18. *Id.* at 62, 88 S. Ct. at 188.
19. Connell v. Higginbotham, 403 U.S. 207, 91 S. Ct. 1772 (1971).
20. *Id.* at 208, 91 S. Ct. at 1773.
21. *Id.*
22. Cole v. Richardson, 405 U.S. 676, 92 S. Ct. 1332 (1972).
23. *Id.* at 684, 92 S. Ct. at 1337.
24. ELSBREE & REUTTER, *supra* note 1, at 315-319.
25. N.Y. EDUC. LAW § 3022 (McKinney 1949).
26. N.Y. EDUC. LAW § 3021 (McKinney 1917).
27. N.Y. CIV. SERV. LAW § 12-a (McKinney 1939).
28. Adler v. Board of Educ., 342 U.S. 485, 72 S. Ct. 380 (1952).
29. *Id.* at 492, 72 S. Ct. at 384-385.
30. 344 U.S. 183, 73 S. Ct. 215 (1952).
31. 385 U.S. 589, 87 S. Ct. 675 (1967).
32. Adler v. Board of Educ., 342 U.S. at 493, 72 S. Ct. at 385.
33. Keyishian v. Board of Regents of Univ. of State of N.Y., 385 U.S. 589, 87 S. Ct. 675 (1967).

34. *Id.* at 601, 87 S. Ct. at 682-683.
35. *Id.* at 604, 87 S. Ct. at 684.
36. *Id.* at 602, 87 S. Ct. at 683.
37. *Id.*
38. *Id.* at 595, 87 S. Ct. at 679.
39. *Id.* at 605, 87 S. Ct. at 685.
40. 384 U.S. 11, 86 S. Ct. 1238 (1966).
41. Keyishian, 385 U.S. at 608, 87 S. Ct. at 686.
42. Slochower v. Board of Higher Educ. of N.Y.C., 350 U.S. 551, 76 S. Ct. 637 (1956).
43. *Id.* at 557, 76 S. Ct. at 640.
44. *Id.* at 558, 76 S. Ct. at 641.
45. *Id.*
46. *Id.*
47. Beilan v. Board of Pub. Educ., 357 U.S. 399, 78 S. Ct. 1317 (1958).
48. *Id.* at 400, 78 S. Ct. at 1319.
49. *Id.* at 404, 78 S. Ct. at 1321.
50. *Id.*
51. *Id.* at 405, 78 S. Ct. at 1322.
52. *Id.*
53. Sweezy v. New Hampshire, 354 U.S. 234, 77 S. Ct. 1203 (1957).
54. Barenblatt v. United States, 360 U.S. 109, 129, 79 S. Ct. 1081, 1094 (1959).
55. *Id.* at 112, 79 S. Ct. at 1085.
56. *Id.* at 134, 79 S. Ct. at 1097.

CHAPTER 11

Teacher Rights: Expression and Due Process

Expression

Public

In 1968, for the first time, the Supreme Court issued a full opinion dealing with teachers' first amendment rights to freedom of expression in a case not involving some aspect of loyalty or alleged subversive activities.[1] The decision, with only one Justice in partial dissent, was grounded on the view, refined in the series of loyalty cases discussed in Chapter 10, that although one has no constitutional right to public employment, he may not be excluded therefrom for an unconstitutional reason. Reiterating the very special place in the order of American law occupied by the constitutional guarantee of freedom of expression, the Court forbade the dismissal of Marvin Pickering because he had written a letter to a newspaper criticizing the way in which the board and superintendent of schools had informed, or prevented the informing of, the voters relative to proposals to raise new revenue for the schools. The letter also expressed the view that the board was undesirably emphasizing athletics to the detriment of academics and charged the superintendent with attempting to prevent teachers from opposing or criticizing financial proposals of the board.

The Court established the framework for analysis as follows:

> To the extent that the Illinois Supreme Court's opinion may be read to suggest that teachers may constitutionally be compelled to relinquish the First Amendment rights they would otherwise enjoy as citizens to comment on matters of public interest in connection with the operation of the public schools in which they work, it proceeds on a premise that has been unequivocally rejected in numerous prior decisions of this Court. "[T]he theory that public employment which may be denied altogether may be subjected to any conditions, regardless of how unreasonable, has been uniformly rejected." At the same time it cannot be gainsaid that the State has interests as an employer in regulating the speech of its employees that differ significantly from those it possesses in connection with regulation of the speech of the citizenry in general. The problem in any case

is to arrive at a balance between the interests of the teacher, as a citizen, in commenting upon matters of public concern and the interest of the State, as an employer, in promoting the efficiency of the public services it performs through its employees.[2]

Although stating that it did not deem it either appropriate or feasible to attempt to lay down a general standard against which all such statements may be judged, the Court proceeded to discuss some factors of importance. As to the contents of the letter, the Court noted that the statements were not directed toward a person with whom the teacher would be in daily contact. "Thus no question of maintaining either discipline by immediate superiors or harmony among coworkers is presented here."[3] As to statements in the letter that were false, the Court said that there was no evidence that they were made knowingly or recklessly, and the board easily could have corrected them by writing a letter or otherwise. Essentially, the errors were in figures that were a matter of public record and regarding which his position as teacher did not qualify Pickering to speak with any greater authority than any other taxpayer. The case was not one in which a breach of confidentiality was involved, nor one in which a teacher made false statements about matters that would be difficult to counter because of the teacher's presumed greater access to the real facts.

Regarding the effects of the letter, the Court observed that it was not written until after the defeat at the polls of the proposed tax increase, so it could not have affected that. Further, as far as the record revealed, the letter had no effects on the operation of the schools—it "was greeted by everyone but its main target, the Board, with massive apathy and total disbelief."[4]

The Court emphasized that the general subject which the letter addressed was a matter of public concern and that the input of teachers was an ingredient essential to informed debate. This point was expressed in these words:

> More importantly, the question whether a school system requires additional funds is a matter of legitimate public concern on which the judgment of the school administration, including the School Board, cannot, in a society that leaves such questions to popular vote, be taken as conclusive. On such a question free and open debate is vital to informed decision-making by the electorate. Teachers are, as a class, the members of a community most likely to have informed and definite opinions as to how funds allotted to the operation of the schools should be spent. Accordingly, it is essential that they be able to speak out freely on such questions without fear of retaliatory dismissal.[5]

Pickering quickly became a much cited case in education law because so many teacher termination cases contain at least a sliver of a first amendment consideration. Four years later, the Court re-emphasized the broad protections of the first amendment by expressly answering in the negative the question of "whether [a teacher's] lack of a contractual or tenure right to re-employment, taken alone, defeats his claim that the nonrenewal of his contract [by a public college] violated the First and Fourteenth Amendments."[6] The Court said that the teacher loyalty cases, as well as cases in other areas, had "made clear" that although government can deny a person a benefit for many reasons, it may not do so

> on a basis that infringes his constitutionally protected interests —especially, his interest in freedom of speech. For if the government could deny a benefit to a person because of his constitutionally protected speech or associations, his exercise of those freedoms would in effect be penalized and inhibited. This would allow the government to "produce a result which [it] could not command directly."[7]

Intertwined with Conduct

Practically speaking, however, most adverse teacher personnel decisions are based on more than one factor. Thus, it is essential to determine the extent to which a protected activity of a teacher figured in the adverse personnel action. For to bar any action against a teacher who was inadequate on other grounds simply because he also displeased school authorities by engaging in a constitutionally protected act would place that teacher in a favored position over teachers similarly situated except for the constitutionally protected act. This dilemma was resolved in a unanimous decision by the Supreme Court in 1977.[8]

The case involved the nonrenewal of a nontenured teacher partially on the ground that he had called a radio station and told a disc jockey of a proposed dress code for teachers with the result that the disc jockey announced the adoption of the code as a news item. There was no question but that this incident was a factor in the board's decision not to renew the teacher's contract. There also was no question but that there were other acts of the teacher unrelated to freedom of expression that figured in the decision. The way such a situation should be resolved by the trial court was outlined by the Supreme Court as follows:

> Initially ... the burden [is] properly placed upon [the teacher] to show that his conduct was constitutionally protected, and that this conduct was a "substantial factor"—or to put it in other words, that it was a "motivating factor" in the

Board's decision not to rehire him. . . . [If this burden is carried, the court must] determine whether the Board [has] shown by a preponderance of the evidence that it would have reached the same decision as to [the teacher's] reemployment even in the absence of the protected conduct.[9]

Private

In a unanimous 1979 decision, the Supreme Court, for the first time, expressly held that the first amendment's protection of a public employee's speech includes private as well as public communication.[10] The case involved a teacher who had been terminated for, among other reasons, allegedly making petty and unreasonable demands on the principal in a manner variously described by the principal as "insulting," "hostile," "loud," and "arrogant." The subject of the black teacher's comments to the white principal was racial discrimination in employment policies and practices in the school system, which was under a court-ordered desegregation plan. The trial court had decided the case before the Supreme Court's decision in *Mt. Healthy* and had not followed the steps established there. In *Givhan*, there was some evidence of conduct on the part of the teacher that, if proved, might have precipitated her dismissal were the first amendment issue not involved. Therefore, the Supreme Court remanded the case after reviewing its holdings in *Pickering*, *Perry*, and *Mt. Healthy* and after articulating the point of constitutional law that private expression (here, to the principal) was entitled to constitutional protection. Freedom of speech, said the Court, is not "lost to the public employee who arranges to communicate privately with his employer rather than to spread his views before the public."[11]

The Court added, however:

> When a teacher speaks publicly, it is generally the *content* of his statements that must be assessed to determine whether they "in any way either impeded the proper performance of his daily duties in the classroom or . . . interfered with the regular operation of the schools generally." Private expression, however, may in some situations bring additional factors to the *Pickering* calculus. When a government employee personally confronts his immediate superior, the employing agency's institutional efficiency may be threatened not only by the content of the employee's message, but also by the manner, time, and place in which it is delivered.[12]

Addressing the contention that the principal was a captive audience for the remarks of the teacher, the Court said, "Having opened his office door to petitioner, the principal was hardly in a position to argue that he was the *'unwilling recipient'* of her views."[13]

To School Board

In 1976, the Supreme Court unanimously answered the following question in the negative: "[W]hether a State may constitutionally require that an elected Board of Education prohibit teachers, other than union representatives, to speak at open meetings, at which public participation is permitted, if such speech is addressed to the subject of pending collective-bargaining negotiations?"[14]

One of the bargaining issues was whether the contract should include an agency shop provision (called a "fair share" clause in Wisconsin). Due to a stalemate in the negotiations, the teachers' union arranged to have pickets present at a public board meeting and to have some 350 teachers in attendance to support the union's position. During the portion of the meeting provided for comments by the public, the president of the union spoke on the teachers' position and presented a petition signed by some 1,350 teachers. Then the floor was obtained by a teacher who, although part of the bargaining unit, was not a member of the union. The teacher said that he desired to inform the board, as he had already informed the union, that an informal survey he had conducted concerning the fair share clause revealed much confusion about the meaning of the proposal. He stated that a large number of teachers had already signed a petition taking no stand on the proposal but arguing that all alternatives be presented clearly to the teachers and the general public before action was taken. The statement was two-and-one-half minutes in length, and the only board response was a question by the president asking if the petition would be presented to the board (the teacher answering affirmatively). Later that evening, the board met in executive session and voted to accept all of the union's demands except the fair share proposal. The next day, the union negotiators accepted the board's proposal and a contract was subsequently signed.

A few weeks later, the union filed a prohibited labor practices complaint with the Wisconsin Employment Relations Commission against the board for permitting the teacher to speak. The claim was that what had transpired constituted negotiations with a member of the bargaining unit other than the exclusive representative. The commission (and the Wisconsin courts) agreed and ordered the school board not to permit employees other than representatives of the union to appear and speak at board meetings on matters subject to collective bargaining.

In reversing, the Supreme Court emphasized that first amendment rights were violated. The Court said:

> [T]he participation in public discussion of public business cannot be confined to one category of interested individuals. To

permit one side of a debatable public question to have a monopoly in expressing its views to the government is the antithesis of constitutional guarantees. Whatever its duties as an employer, when the board sits in public meetings to conduct public business and hear the views of citizens, it may not be required to discriminate between speakers on the basis of their employment, or the content of their speech.[15]

Procedural Due Process

Liberty and Property Concepts

IN GENERAL. In 1972, the Court considered the question of whether a public employee whose fixed-term contract was not renewed had a constitutional right to a statement of reasons and a hearing on the decision not to rehire.[16] By a vote of five-to-three, the answer was that he did not. The Court's opinion, dealing also with special conditions under which the answer could be different, became the touchstone for the constitutional resolution of hundreds of cases in the years following.

The plaintiff in *Roth* had been hired as an assistant professor for a fixed term of one academic year at Wisconsin State University-Oshkosh. When his contract was not renewed, Roth raised substantive first amendment objections and also procedural due process claims. Only the fourteenth amendment procedural due process issue was before the Supreme Court.

The Court began its analysis with the following observation:

> The requirements of procedural due process apply only to the deprivation of interests encompassed by the Fourteenth Amendment's protection of liberty and property. When protected interests are implicated, the right to some kind of prior hearing is paramount. But the range of interests protected by procedural due process is not infinite.
>
> ... [T]o determine whether due process requirements apply in the first place, we must look not to the "weight" but to the *nature* of the interest at stake. We must look to see if the interest is within the Fourteenth Amendment's protection of liberty and property.[17]

The Court explained:

> "Liberty" and "property" are broad and majestic terms. They are among the "[g]reat [constitutional] concepts ... purposely left to gather meaning from experience. ... [T]hey relate to the whole domain of social and economic fact, and

the statesmen who founded this Nation knew too well that only a stagnant society remains unchanged." . . . The Court has . . . made clear that the property interests protected by procedural due process extend well beyond actual ownership of real estate, chattels, or money. By the same token, the Court has required due process protection for deprivations of liberty beyond the sort of formal constraints imposed by the criminal process.

Yet, while the Court has eschewed rigid or formalistic limitations on the protection of procedural due process, it has at the same time observed certain boundaries. For the words "liberty" and "property" in the Due Process Clause of the Fourteenth Amendment must be given some meaning.[18]

The Court suggested two types of circumstances under which a public employer's refusal to re-employ would implicate liberty interests. It discussed them as follows:

The State, in declining to rehire the respondent, did not make any charge against him that might seriously damage his standing and associations in his community. It did not base the nonrenewal of his contract on a charge, for example, that he had been guilty of dishonesty, or immorality. Had it done so, this would be a different case. For "[w]here a person's good name, reputation, honor, or integrity is at stake because of what the government is doing to him, notice and an opportunity to be heard are essential." In such a case, due process would accord an opportunity to refute the charge before University officials. (The purpose of such notice and hearing is to provide the person an opportunity to clear his name. Once a person has cleared his name at a hearing, his employer, of course, may remain free to deny him future employment for other reasons.)
. . .

Similarly, there is no suggestion that the State, in declining to re-employ the respondent, imposed on him a stigma or other disability that foreclosed his freedom to take advantage of other employment opportunities. The State, for example, did not invoke any regulations to bar the respondent from all other public employment in state universities. Had it done so, this, again, would be a different case. For "[t]o be deprived not only of present government employment but of future opportunity for it certainly is no small injury . . . ."[19]

Regarding procedural protection of property rights, the Court reviewed many prior decisions and summed up in these words:

Certain attributes of "property" interests protected by procedural due process emerge from these decisions. To have a property interest in a benefit, a person clearly must have more than an abstract need or desire for it. He must have more than a unilateral expectation of it. He must, instead, have a legitimate claim of entitlement to it. It is a purpose of the ancient institution of property to protect those claims upon which people rely in their daily lives, reliance that must not be arbitrarily undermined. It is a purpose of the constitutional right to a hearing to provide an opportunity for a person to vindicate those claims.

Property interests, of course, are not created by the Constitution. Rather they are created and their dimensions are defined by existing rules or understandings that stem from an independent source such as state law—rules or understandings that secure certain benefits and that support claims of entitlement to those benefits.[20]

Roth's contract specifically provided that his employment would terminate on June 30th, and there was no state statute, university rule, or university policy that created any claim to renewal. Therefore, although he "surely had an abstract concern in being rehired, . . . he did not have a *property* interest sufficient to require the University authorities to give him a hearing when they declined to renew his contract of employment."[21]

On the same day, another case was decided in which the Court stated that a property right could be derived from other than a formal statute or express contractual provision.[22] In *Perry v. Sindermann*, the plaintiff had been employed in the state college system of Texas for ten years and at Odessa Junior College for four successive years under a series of one-year contracts. On the question of whether he was entitled to a statement of reasons and a hearing when the governing board voted not to offer him a contract for the next year, the Court expressly recognized the possibility that a property right could have been created by an unwritten understanding fostered by the college administration. As an integral part of the allegation of the existence of a de facto tenure system, Sindermann cited the following provision from the College's official Faculty Guide:

"Teacher Tenure: Odessa College has no tenure system. The Administration of the College wishes the faculty member to feel that he has permanent tenure as long as his teaching services are satisfactory and as long as he displays a cooperative attitude toward his co-workers and his superiors, and as long as he is happy in his work."[23]

There was also a claim that the statewide coordinating board for higher education in the state had promulgated guidelines providing that one who had been in the state college and university system for at least seven years had a form of job tenure.

The Court said that property interests subject to procedural due process protection "are not limited by a few rigid, technical forms. .... A person's interest in a benefit is a 'property' interest for due process purposes if there are such rules or mutually explicit understandings that support his claim of entitlement to the benefit and that he may invoke at a hearing."[24] The Court analogized the situation to the law of contracts wherein certain agreements, though not explicitly formalized, may be implied from the promisor's words and conduct in the light of surrounding circumstances and wherein the meaning of the promisor's words and acts may be determined by reference to usage of the past. The Court continued:

> A teacher, like the respondent, who has held his position for a number of years, might be able to show from the circumstances of this service—and from other relevant facts —that he has a legitimate claim of entitlement to job tenure. Just as this Court has found there to be a "common law of a particular industry or of a particular plant" that may supplement a collective-bargaining agreement, so there may be an unwritten "common law" in a particular university that certain employees shall have the equivalent of tenure. This is particularly likely in a college or university, like Odessa Junior College, that has no explicit tenure system even for senior members of its faculty, but that nonetheless may have created such a system in practice.[25]

Thus, although "a mere subjective 'expectancy'" is not protected by procedural due process, Sindermann was entitled to try to prove his claim to due process in light of the policies and practices existing at the institution. "Proof of such a property interest would not, of course, entitle him to reinstatement. But such proof would obligate college officials to grant a hearing at his request, where he could be informed of the grounds for his nonretention and challenge their sufficiency."[26]

IN SPECIFIC SITUATIONS. The Supreme Court, in 1976, decided three cases outside the field of education that further refined the concept of deprivation of liberty as the basis for invoking constitutional procedural due process. The first was a five-to-three decision in which the Court held that the distribution by local police of a flyer depicting "active shoplifters" did not deprive one pictured therein of any liberty triggering the need for due process.[27] The plaintiff at the time of the release of his picture in the flyer had been arrested for shoplifting, but the charge later was dismissed. The Court said that, although the facts could be the basis of a defamation action in a state court, they did not state a constitutional liberty claim. It explicated *Board of Regents of State Colleges v. Roth* as follows:

> While *Roth* recognized that governmental action defaming an individual in the course of declining to rehire him could entitle the person to notice and an opportunity to be heard as to the defamation, its language is quite inconsistent with any notion that a defamation perpetrated by a government official but unconnected with any refusal to rehire would be actionable under the Fourteenth Amendment. . . . Certainly there is no suggestion in *Roth* to indicate that a hearing would be required each time the State in its capacity as employer might be considered responsible for a statement defaming an employee who continues to be an employee.[28]

The Court also reiterated the *Roth* point that any constitutional property claim would have to be grounded in state law. In *Paul v. Davis,* no state law guaranteed an enjoyment of reputation that might have been altered by the police chief's action (although state tort law made recovery of damages possible).

In another 1976 case, the Court in a five-Justice opinion addressed the question of whether "assuming that the explanation for [a police officer's] discharge was false, . . . that false explanation deprived him of an interest in liberty protected by [the Due Process] Clause."[29] Prior to reaching that question, the majority of Justices had accepted the interpretation by lower federal courts of a state statutory situation on which the state courts had not definitively ruled. The issue was whether a local police officer had a property right to continued employment or only to compliance with specified procedures before removal. (Four Justices believed the former to be the correct interpretation of the state law and, thus, that the officer could be removed only for proven cause.) The majority, holding that there was no property right, went on to discuss the liberty issue involved. In the posture of the case, the Court was required to assume that the reasons given for the discharge constituted a stigma and, further, that they were false.

On the point of disclosure of the reasons, the Court observed that they were revealed in only two ways by the city manager, who had dismissed the officer. They were disclosed orally to the officer in private, and they were divulged in writing in answer to interrogatories after the present litigation began. Neither way could afford any basis for culpability of the city manager; otherwise forthright and truthful communication between employer and employee and between litigants would be jeopardized.

On the point of falsity, the Court reasoned as follows:

> [T]he reasons stated to him in private had no different impact on his reputation than if they had been true. And the answers to his interrogatories, whether true or false, did not cause the discharge. The truth or falsity of the City Manager's statement determines whether or not his decision to discharge the petitioner was correct or prudent, but neither enhances nor diminishes petitioner's claim that his constitutionally protected interest in liberty has been impaired. A contrary evaluation of his contention would enable every discharged employee to assert a constitutional claim merely by alleging that his former supervisor made a mistake.[30]

The Court then encapsulated the role of the federal judiciary in cases of adverse personnel actions in the domain of public employment.

> The federal court is not the appropriate forum in which to review the multitude of personnel decisions that are made daily by public agencies. We must accept the harsh fact that numerous individual mistakes are inevitable in the day-to-day administration of our affairs. The United States Constitution cannot feasibly be construed to require federal judicial review for every such error. In the absence of any claim that the public employer was motivated by a desire to curtail or to penalize the exercise of an employee's constitutionally protected rights, we must presume that official action was regular and, if erroneous, can best be corrected in other ways. The Due Process Clause of the Fourteenth Amendment is not a guarantee against incorrect or ill-advised personnel decisions.[31]

The next year a Court majority of five held that a hearing is not required for an alleged liberty deprivation when the truthfulness of a stigmatizing impression is not challenged.[32] A probationary police officer, who had been terminated, claimed that he was entitled to a hearing because of the stigmatizing effect of certain material put in his personnel file. The former officer had authorized the release of information in the file. A subsequent employer dismissed him after that employer "gleaned" that the termination from the police department was based on an apparent suicide attempt.

The Court declined to consider whether the report in question was of a stigmatizing nature or whether the circumstances of its apparent dissemination were such as to fall within the scope of *Roth* because the due process requirement enunciated in *Roth* was an opportunity to refute the charge. "But if the hearing mandated by the Due Process Clause is to serve any useful purpose, there must be some factual dispute between an employer and a discharged employee which has some significant bearing on the employee's reputation."[33] If the employee "does not challenge the substantial truth of the material in question, no hearing would afford a promise of achieving that result for him."[34]

The Court said it was not resting its conclusion on a procedural point, but on the fact that the record as a whole made no mention that the incident did not take place as reported. The former officer "has therefore made out no claim under the Fourteenth Amendment that he was harmed by the denial of a hearing, even were we to accept in its entirety the determination by the Court of Appeals that the creation and disclosure of the file report otherwise amounted to stigmatization within the meaning of [*Roth*]."[35]

Elements of Process

The following 1961 observation by the Supreme Court about constitutional procedural due process has been quoted by the Court frequently in subsequent cases: "The very nature of due process negates any concept of inflexible procedures universally applicable to every imaginable situation."[36] However, absolutely central to the notion of procedural due process is the requirement of a hearing. "The fundamental requisite of due process of law is the opportunity to be heard,"[37] said the Court in 1914. In the 1974 case of *Arnett v. Kennedy*,[38] the Court held that the hearing did not always have to precede the termination of a public employee who statutorily could be discharged only for cause. In *Arnett*, the federal employee was granted the statutory protection along with provisions for determining whether cause existed. The procedures provided for a pre-termination appearance of the employee in which he could answer charges and for a post-termination hearing if he were removed and requested the hearing. Back pay would be awarded if the employee prevailed. Five Justices in two separate opinions agreed on the point that the post-termination hearing arrangement was not unconstitutional.

The impartiality of those conducting a termination hearing was considered by the Court in a school-related case in 1976.[39] It is, of course, self-evident that "a biased decisionmaker [is] constitutionally unacceptable."[40] Further, "our system of law has always endeavored to prevent even the probability of unfairness."[41] In the *Hortonville* case teachers in a Wisconsin school district had been on strike contrary to state law. The reason for the strike was that by March no agreement had been reached for the year that was then two-thirds over. The board, after two weeks of conducting classes with substitute teachers, decided to hold disciplinary hearings for each striking teacher. The teachers, however, appeared before the board with counsel and indicated that they wished to be treated as a group. The board heard the claims that the strike had been provoked by actions of the board and that the board was not sufficiently impartial to exercise discipline over the striking teachers. Subsequently, the board voted to terminate the employment of the striking teachers, but invited them to reapply for teaching positions. Only one teacher accepted the invitation and returned to work. The remaining positions were filled by new teachers. The discharged teachers sought judicial relief for alleged due process violations.

A majority of six Justices agreed that the due process clause did not prohibit "this School Board from making the decision to dismiss teachers admittedly engaged in a strike and persistently refusing to return to their duties."[42] The Court noted that the Supreme Court of Wisconsin had held that state law prohibited the strike and that termination of the strikers' employment was within the board's authority. As the teachers admitted they were engaged in a strike, there was no factual matter to be resolved at the hearing. Thus, the only decision before the board was how to exercise its discretion in carrying out its duties. The Court discussed the situation as follows:

> The Board's decision whether to dismiss striking teachers involves broad considerations, and does not in the main turn on the Board's view of the "seriousness" of the teachers' conduct or the factors they urge mitigated their violation of state law. It was not an adjudicative decision, for the Board had an obligation to make a decision based on its own answer to an important question of policy: what choice among the alternative responses to the teachers' strike will best serve the interests of the school system, the interests of the parents and children who depend on the system, and the interests of the citizens whose taxes support it? The Board's decision was only incidentally a disciplinary decision; it had significant governmental and public policy dimensions as well.[43]

On the point of bias of the board members, the Court said that there was no evidence that the board members "had the kind of personal or financial stake in the decision that might create a conflict of interest, and there is nothing in the record to support charges of personal animosity."[44] In fact, the Wisconsin Supreme Court, which had ruled that the board was disqualified from deciding whether the teachers should be dismissed, said it was not suggesting that the board members were other than dedicated public servants. The United States Supreme Court also observed that the board was required by statute to participate in the negotiations that preceded the strike, and thus the involvement, without more, would not disqualify the board. The Court said:

Mere familiarity with the facts of a case gained by an agency in the performance of its statutory role does not . . . disqualify a decisionmaker. Nor is a decisionmaker disqualified simply because he has taken a position, even in public, on a policy issue related to the dispute, in the absence of a showing that he is not "capable of judging a particular controversy fairly on the basis of its own circumstances."[45]

The Court concluded that there was no federal right to have a body other than the school board make or review the decision to terminate the teachers. It observed:

[T]he state legislature has given to the Board the power to employ and dismiss teachers, as a part of the balance it has struck in the area of municipal labor relations; altering those statutory powers as a matter of federal due process clearly changes that balance. Permitting the Board to make the decision at issue here preserves its control over school district affairs, leaves the balance of power in labor relations where the state legislature struck it, and assures that the decision whether to dismiss the teachers will be made by the body responsible for that decision under state law.[46]

---

1. Pickering v. Board of Educ. of Township H.S. Dist. 205, 391 U.S. 563, 88 S. Ct. 1731 (1968).
2. *Id.* at 568, 88 S. Ct. at 1734-1735.
3. *Id.* at 570, 88 S. Ct. at 1735.
4. *Id.* at 570, 88 S. Ct. at 1736.
5. *Id.*
6. Perry v. Sindermann, 408 U.S. 593, 92 S. Ct. 2694 (1972). The eight participating Justices agreed on this point.
7. *Id.* at 597, 92 S. Ct. at 2697.
8. Mount Healthy City School Dist. v. Doyle, 429 U.S. 274, 97 S. Ct. 568 (1977).
9. *Id.* at 287, 97 S. Ct. at 576.
10. Givhan v. Western Line Consolidated School Dist., 439 U.S. 410, 99 S. Ct. 693 (1979).
11. *Id.* at 415-416, 99 S. Ct. at 696-697.
12. *Id.* at 415 n.4, 99 S. Ct. at 696 n.4.
13. *Id.* at 415, 99 S. Ct. at 696.
14. City of Madison, Joint School Dist. No. 8 v. Wisconsin Employment Relations Comm'n, 429 U.S. 167, 169, 97 S. Ct. 421, 423 (1976).
15. *Id.* at 175-176, 97 S. Ct. at 426.
16. Board of Regents of State Colleges v. Roth, 408 U.S. 564, 92 S. Ct. 2701 (1972) [hereinafter cited as Roth].
17. *Id.* at 569-571, 92 S. Ct. at 2705-2706.
18. *Id.* at 571-572, 92 S. Ct. at 2706.
19. *Id.* at 573-574, 92 S. Ct. at 2707.
20. *Id.* at 577, 92 S. Ct. at 2709.
21. *Id.* at 578, 92 S. Ct. at 2710.

22. Perry v. Sindermann, 408 U.S. 593, 92 S. Ct. 2694 (1972). The three Justices who dissented in *Roth* found it unnecessary to deal with this point in the present case.

23. *Id.* at 600, 92 S. Ct. at 2699.

24. *Id.*

25. *Id.* at 602, 92 S. Ct. at 2700.

26. *Id.*

27. Paul v. Davis, 424 U.S. 693, 96 S. Ct. 1155 (1976).

28. *Id.* at 709-710, 96 S. Ct. at 1164-1165.

29. Bishop v. Wood, 426 U.S. 341, 343, 96 S. Ct. 2074, 2077 (1976).

30. *Id.* at 349, 96 S. Ct. at 2079-2080.

31. *Id.* at 349-350, 96 S. Ct. at 2080.

32. Codd v. Velger, 429 U.S. 624, 97 S. Ct. 882 (1977).

33. *Id.* at 627, 97 S. Ct. at 884.

34. *Id.*

35. *Id.* at 628-629, 97 S. Ct. at 884-885.

36. Cafeteria Workers v. McElroy, 367 U.S. 886, 895, 81 S. Ct. 1743, 1748 (1961).

37. Grannis v. Ordean, 234 U.S. 385, 394, 34 S. Ct. 779, 783 (1914).

38. 416 U.S. 134, 94 S. Ct. 1633 (1974).

39. Hortonville Joint School Dist. No. 1 v. Hortonville Educ. Ass'n, 426 U.S. 482, 96 S. Ct. 2308 (1976) [hereinafter cited as Hortonville].

40. Withrow v. Larkin, 421 U.S. 35, 47, 95 S. Ct. 1456, 1464 (1975).

41. *In re* Murchison, 349 U.S. 133, 136, 75 S. Ct. 623, 625 (1955).

42. Hortonville, 426 U.S. at 488, 96 S. Ct. at 2312.

43. *Id.* at 495, 96 S. Ct. at 2315.

44. *Id.* at 492, 96 S. Ct. at 2314.

45. *Id.* at 493, 96 S. Ct. at 2314.

46. *Id.* at 496, 96 S. Ct. at 2316.

CHAPTER 12

Teacher Rights:
Conditions of Employment

The Impairment of Contracts Clause

The Supreme Court has decided three education cases involving a primary claim that a state had impaired the obligation of a contract contrary to Article I, Section 10, the express federal constitutional provision forbidding it. The cases were decided during two consecutive terms in 1937 and 1938. The first was a challenge to a New Jersey statute enacted during the Depression to permit local boards to reduce the salaries of teachers.[1] The plaintiff, who was a tenured teacher, argued that the statewide tenure law was in the nature of a contract of indefinite duration beyond the power of the state to alter. The state's highest court held that no contract was formed, tenure being a legislative status rather than a contractual one. The Supreme Court said that although it was "not bound by the decision of a state court as to the existence and terms of a contract, the obligation of which is asserted to be impaired, . . . where a statute is claimed to create a contractual right we give weight to the construction of the statute by the courts of the state."[2] The unanimous Court's analysis of the situation included the following:

> Although after the expiration of the first three years of service the employe [sic] continued in his then position and at his then compensation unless and until promoted or given an increase in salary for a succeeding year, we find nothing in the record to indicate that the board was bound by contract with the teacher for more than the current year. The employe assumed no binding obligation to remain in service beyond that term. Although the [tenure law] prohibited the board, a creature of the state, from reducing the teacher's salary or discharging him without cause, we agree with the courts below that this was but a regulation of the conduct of the board and not a term of a continuing contract of indefinite duration with the individual teacher.[3]

The board's method of reduction was to group salaries into six ranges and to reduce salaries in each range by a fixed percent. The result was that in some instances a teacher receiving the lowest salary in a bracket wound up with a figure below the salary of the highest teacher in the next lower bracket. To this, the Court responded:

> We think it was reasonable and proper that the teachers employed by the board should be divided into classes for the application of the percentage reduction. All in a given class were treated alike. Incidental individual inequality resulting in some instances from the operation of the plan does not condemn it as an unreasonable or arbitrary method of dealing with the problem of general salary reductions or deny the equality guaranteed by the Fourteenth Amendment.[4]

In the second case, the issue was whether allowances of a certain type paid to retired teachers could be reduced.[5] The allowances in question were financed solely by the state, with no portion based on teacher contributions. (In Illinois, there was also a system of retirement payments based on joint contributions of teachers and public employers.) Illinois courts had construed statutes of the type at bar as being subject to alteration by the legislature rather than as being contractual. As in the preceding case, the Court said that "[w]hile we are required to reach an independent judgment as to the existence and nature of the alleged contract, we give great weight to the views of the highest court of the state touching these matters."[6]

A point emphasized by the plaintiff teachers was that the present statute referred to the payments as an "annuity" rather than a "pension." ("Annuity" is used technically to denote payments out partially based on payments in—a contractual arrangement—whereas a "pension" is a gift.) The state's highest court attached no significance to the word used to describe the payments. The Supreme Court, without dissent, said:

> We are of the same opinion, particularly as an examination of the Illinois statutes indicates that, in acts dealing with the subject, the Legislature has apparently used the terms "pensions," "benefits," and "annuities" interchangeably as having the same connotation.[7]

In the third case, the Court, by a seven-to-one vote, held that an Indiana tenure law had created a contractual relationship with certain teachers.[8] The legislation was described by the Supreme Court as follows:

> The title of the act is couched in terms of contract. It speaks of the making and canceling of indefinite contracts. In the body the word "contract" appears ten times in section 1, defining the relationship; eleven times in section 2, relating to the

termination of the employment by the employer; and four times in section 4, stating the conditions of termination by the teacher.

The tenor of the act indicates that the word "contract" was not used inadvertently or in other than its usual legal meaning. ... Examination of the entire act convinces us that the teacher was by it assured of the possession of a binding and enforceable contract against school districts [sic].[9]

In a statute amending the act, a certain class of school districts was omitted from coverage by the provisions. When a teacher in such a district sought to block her dismissal, the board responded that the tenure protections had been repealed. The Supreme Court, however, held that a contract existed that, although under some conditions could be altered by the state under the state's police power, could not be altered under present facts without violating the Constitution. The Court stated:

Our decisions recognize that every contract is made subject to the implied condition that its fulfillment may be frustrated by a proper exercise of the police power, but we have repeatedly said that, in order to have this effect, the exercise of the power must be for an end which is in fact public and the means adopted must be reasonably adapted to that end, and the Supreme Court of Indiana has taken the same view in respect of legislation impairing the obligation of the contract of a state instrumentality. The causes of cancellation provided in the act of 1927 and the retention of the system of indefinite contracts in all municipalities except townships by the act of 1933 are persuasive that the repeal of the earlier act by the later was not an exercise of the police power for the attainment of ends to which its exercise may properly be directed.[10]

Pre-employment Inquiries

The first opinion of the Supreme Court pertaining to prerequisites for initial employment of teachers (other than requirements directly tied to loyalty) was issued in 1960.[11] By a vote of five-to-four the Court held unconstitutional an Arkansas statute compelling every teacher in a school or college receiving state funds to file annually an affidavit listing every organization to which he had belonged or to which he had made regular contributions within the preceding five years.

Four Justices, although expressing displeasure with the provision, believed that there was a legitimate basis for the inquiry and that the Court should await possible abuses before striking down the requirement. The majority, however, emphasized that teachers in Arkansas were employed on a year-to-year basis with no civil service or tenure protection, and that there was no stipulation that the information be kept confidential by school authorities. The majority reasoned as follows:

> Even if there were no disclosure to the general public, the pressure upon a teacher to avoid any ties which might displease those who control his professional destiny would be constant and heavy. Public exposure, bringing with it the possibility of public pressures upon school boards to discharge teachers who belong to unpopular or minority organizations, would simply operate to widen and aggravate the impairment of constitutional liberty.
>
> The vigilant protection of constitutional freedoms is nowhere more vital than in the community of American schools. . . . [I]n view of the nature of the teacher's relation to the effective exercise of the rights which are safeguarded by the Bill of Rights and by the Fourteenth Amendment, inhibition of freedom of thought, and of action upon thought, in the case of teachers brings the safeguards of those amendments vividly into operation.[12]

The Court highlighted the constitutional flaw in the statute by pointing out what it was *not* deciding.

> The question to be decided here is not whether the State of Arkansas can ask certain of its teachers about all their organizational relationships. It is not whether the State can ask all of its teachers about certain of their associational ties. It is not whether teachers can be asked how many organizations they belong to, or how much time they spend in organizational activity. The question is whether the State can ask every one of its teachers to disclose every single organization with which he has been associated over a five-year period. The scope of the inquiry required by Act 10 is completely unlimited. . . . It requires him to list, without number, every conceivable kind of associational tie—social, professional, political, avocational, or religious. Many such relationships could have no possible bearing upon the teacher's occupational competence or fitness.[13]

Such "comprehensive interference with associational freedom goes far beyond what might be justified in the exercise of the State's legitimate inquiry into the fitness and competency of its teachers."[14] However, the Court set forth as a "basic postulate" that "[t]here can be no doubt of the right of a state to investigate the competence and fitness of those whom it hires to teach in its schools, as this Court before now has had occasion to recognize."[15]

Citizenship

The next time a question of teachers' initial employment qualifications was decided in a nonloyalty context was almost two decades later. In 1979, the Court, by a one-vote margin, upheld the power of a state to require that public school teachers be United States citizens (or be in the process of applying for citizenship).[16] It emphasized the important governmental role of public education "in the preparation of individuals for participation as citizens and in the preservation of the values on which our society rests."[17]

Public education was analogized to the police function, an area in which a citizenship requirement previously had been sustained. Although the citizen/alien distinction is normally irrelevant to private activity, the Court said it is crucial to government (the Constitution itself using the distinction eleven times). The Court observed that a teacher has substantial responsibility and discretion in fulfilling a significant governmental role. It said:

> No amount of standardization of teaching materials or lesson plans can eliminate the personal qualities a teacher brings to bear .... Further, a teacher serves as a role model for his students, exerting a subtle but important influence over their perceptions and values. Thus, through both the presentation of course materials and the example he sets, a teacher has an opportunity to influence the attitudes of students toward government, the political process, and a citizen's social responsibilities. This influence is crucial to the continued good health of a democracy.
>
> ... [A] State properly may regard all teachers as having an obligation to promote civic virtues and understanding in their classes, regardless of the subject taught. Certainly a State also may take account of a teacher's function as an example for students, which exists independently of particular classroom subjects.[18]

Residency

Whether public employees can be required to take up and maintain residence within the geographic boundaries of the political units by which they are employed was decided affirmatively by the Supreme Court in 1976.[19] The case before the Court involved a firefighter whose employment was terminated when he moved his permanent residence outside the city of Philadelphia in violation of a regulation. The Court's opinion was a terse per curiam one for six Justices, three voting to hear arguments. It said that it previously had "held that this kind of ordinance is not irrational"[20] by virtue of its having dismissed an appeal from a state court decision upholding a similar rule for want of a substantial federal question.[21] It also cited with approval a holding of the Court of Appeals for the Sixth Circuit sustaining a residence requirement for public school teachers in Cincinnati.[22] The court of appeals had accepted reasons offered by the school authorities related to obtaining teachers committed to urban education, such as that they were more likely to support tax levies, less likely to engage in strikes, more likely to be involved in community activities, and more likely to encourage integration in society and in the schools. Finally, the Supreme Court rejected the contention that the constitutionally recognized right to travel interstate was impaired. It emphasized that the *McCarthy* case did not require prior residency of a given duration in order to be eligible for a benefit by the state, but rather required continuing residency during employment.

Two years later, the Court unanimously held that Alaska could not require that preference be given to residents of the state for employment connected with the development of oil and gas resources in the state.[23] The decision was based squarely on Article IV, Section 2 of the Constitution, which provides, "The citizens of each state shall be entitled to all privileges and immunities of citizens in the several states." The Court said that the clause required any distinction between citizens of one state and citizens of other states to be based on a substantial reason related to some evil the discriminatory statute was designed to correct. The reason offered for the Alaska statute was the reduction of unemployment in the state. The evidence, however, indicated that the major cause of unemployment was not the influx of nonresidents seeking employment but the fact that a substantial number of Alaska's jobless residents (especially unemployed Eskimo and Indian residents) were unable to secure employment because of lack of education and job training or because of geographical remoteness from job opportunities. Thus, employment of nonresidents would deny jobs to Alaskans only to the extent that the jobs for which untrained residents were being prepared might be filled by nonresidents before the residents' training was completed. Moreover, said the Court, the across-the-board employment preference offered all Alaskans for all jobs covered by the act did not bear a substantial relationship to the articulated goal of the statute. It added that any policy forcing employers in the state to discriminate against nonresidents "may present serious constitutional questions."[24]

Political Affiliation

The constitutionality of several other terms or conditions of public employment has been decided in contexts other than education, but with applicability to the education sphere. Several concern the involvement of employees in political activities.

In 1973, the Court, by votes of six-to-three and five-to-four, respectively, decided two cases relative to restrictions on political activities of public employees. The first concerned only federal employees and reaffirmed a 1947 holding[25] that the first amendment was not violated by a ban on a federal employee's holding a party office, working at the polls, or acting as party paymaster for other party workers.[26] The Court added that an act of Congress also would

> unquestionably be valid ... if, in plain and understandable language, [it] forbade activities such as organizing a political party or club; actively participating in fund-raising activities for a partisan candidate or political party; becoming a partisan candidate for, or campaigning for, an elective public office; actively managing the campaign of a partisan candidate for public office; initiating or circulating a partisan nominating petition or soliciting votes for a partisan candidate for public office; or serving as a delegate, alternate or proxy to a political party convention.[27]

The second case involved a similar statute in Oklahoma.[28] The basic attack on the statute was on grounds of vagueness and overbreadth, points discussed in the preceding companion case and there rejected as bases for invalidating the act and its implemental rules. The Court in *Broadrick v. Oklahoma* observed that the plaintiffs were charged with clear violations of the act, and it refused to nullify the statute on the ground that the law might conceivably be improperly applied. It found that, in light of the important purposes to be served by a state system of public employment free from untoward partisan influences, some imprecision at the "outermost boundaries" of the restrictions was not relevant in this case of conduct at the "hard core" of the statute's proscriptions—conduct which complainants agreed could constitutionally be forbidden.

In 1980, a six-Justice majority established the criteria under which a public employee could be terminated on the basis of party affiliation.[29] In 1976 the Court had held, by a vote of five-to-three, but with no majority opinion, that certain non-civil-service employees could not be discharged solely on the ground that they were not members of, or supported by, the winning party.[30] In the instant case, two assistant public defenders had been targeted for discharge by a Democrat solely because they were members of the Republican party. The Court based its opinion in *Branti v. Finkel* on an extension of the common threat of the two opinions supporting the holding in the 1976 case—"that the First Amendment prohibits the dismissal of a public employee solely because of his private political beliefs."[31] It formulated the test as being "whether the hiring authority can demonstrate that party affiliation is an appropriate requirement for the effective performance of the public office involved."[32] The Court observed that the work of an assistant public defender did not involve partisan political interests or concerns, and that, therefore, the discharges could not be effectuated.

Agency Shop

Closely related to initial employment is the question of whether a teacher (or other public employee) who does not belong to a union representing all employees can be required to pay a service fee to the union. That actual membership in an organization cannot be made a condition of public employment has become so clear under first amendment associational rights, as delineated over the years, that the explicit issue has never been the precise question before the Supreme Court. Labor union advocates instead have sought imposition by law of the "fair share" or "agency shop" arrangement. In 1977, the Supreme Court unanimously upheld the agency shop with certain provisos.[33]

The Court said that "insofar as the service charge is used to finance expenditures by the Union for the purposes of collective bargaining, contract administration, and grievance adjustment,"[34] there was no first amendment bar to imposing it. The Court recognized the costs of collective bargaining and the rationality of a decision by a government unit to prescribe collective bargaining in the public sector and to arrange for distributing costs among those who benefitted. If the fee is used for political or ideological purposes, however, the assessment would violate the constitutional rights of those opposed to the view espoused. The Court said that, although a union may make expenditures for the expression of political views, such expenditures must be financed by employees "who do not object to advancing those ideas and who are not coerced into doing so against their will by the threat of loss of governmental employment."[35]

The Court added that it was aware that there would be difficulties in drawing lines between collective-bargaining activities and ideological activities unrelated to collective bargaining. It offered no clues, pointing out that the case was devoid of an evidentiary record, being decided on the general pleadings. However, the Court did expressly hold that employees could not be required to register objections to specific expenditures.

> To require greater specificity [than opposition to "ideological expenditures of *any* sort that are unrelated to collective

bargaining"] would confront an individual employee with the dilemma of relinquishing either his right to withhold his support of ideological causes to which he objects or his freedom to maintain his own beliefs without public disclosure.[36]

In-service Requirements

Failure to participate in continuing professional development activities was upheld as a cause for discharge of a teacher on tenure by a unanimous Supreme Court in 1979.[37] Basing salary increases for teachers on the earning of college credits completed after the teachers have been employed is a commonly accepted personnel policy. In Oklahoma, however, a newly enacted statute mandated certain increases in salary for teachers regardless of the continuing education policy. Thus, a local board was confronted with a dilemma: either to retain those teachers holding no degree higher than the bachelor's degree who refused to engage in the earning of five semester hours of college credit every three years, or not to renew the contracts of such teachers. It chose the latter path, and when, after a hearing with counsel present, one teacher refused to comply with the prospective requirement by enrolling in courses, the board voted not to renew her contract for "willful neglect of duty," a specific cause in the Oklahoma tenure law.

The Court found no constitutional flaw in the situation. "The school board's rule is endowed with a presumption of legislative validity, and the burden is on [the teacher] to show that there is no rational connection between the Board's action and the school district's conceded interest in providing its students with competent, well-trained teachers."[38] The Court observed that the board's change of sanction was a response to the legislature's removal of the milder one and that the board made its change prospectively. That the plaintiff was not offered three years after the change of sanction to complete the five credits was of no legal consequence.

The opinion concluded with the following paragraph:

> At bottom, respondent's position is that she is willing to forego routine pay raises, but she is not willing to comply with the continuing education requirement or to give up her job. The constitutional permissibility of a sanction imposed to enforce a valid governmental rule, however, is not tested by the willingness of those governed by the rule to accept the consequences of noncompliance. The sanction of contract nonrenewal is quite rationally related to the Board's objective of enforcing the continuing education obligation of its teachers. Respondent was not, therefore, deprived of equal protection of the laws.[39]

1. Phelps v. Board of Educ., 300 U.S. 319, 57 S. Ct. 483 (1937).
2. *Id.* at 322, 57 S. Ct. at 484-485.
3. *Id.* at 323, 57 S. Ct. at 485.
4. *Id.*
5. Dodge v. Board of Educ., 302 U.S. 74, 58 S. Ct. 98 (1937).
6. *Id.* at 79, 58 S. Ct. at 100.
7. *Id.* at 81, 58 S. Ct. at 101.
8. State *ex rel.* Anderson v. Brand, 303 U.S. 95, 58 S. Ct. 443 (1938).
9. *Id.* at 105, 58 S. Ct. at 448.
10. *Id.* at 108-109, 58 S. Ct. at 450.
11. Shelton v. Tucker, 364 U.S. 479, 81 S. Ct. 247 (1960).
12. *Id.* at 486-487, 81 S. Ct. at 251.
13. *Id.* at 487-488, 81 S. Ct. at 251-252.
14. *Id.* at 490, 81 S. Ct. at 253.
15. *Id.* at 485, 81 S. Ct. at 250.
16. Ambach v. Norwick, 441 U.S. 68, 99 S. Ct. 1589 (1979).
17. *Id.* at 76, 99 S. Ct. at 1594.
18. *Id.* at 78-80, 99 S. Ct. at 1595-1596.
19. McCarthy v. Philadelphia Civil Service Comm'n, 424 U.S. 645, 96 S. Ct. 1154 (1976).
20. *Id.* at 646, 96 S. Ct. at 1155.
21. Detroit Police Officers Ass'n v. City of Detroit, 405 U.S. 950, 92 S. Ct. 1173 (1972).
22. Wardwell v. Board of Educ. of Cincinnati, 529 F.2d 625 (6th Cir. 1976).
23. Hicklin v. Orbeck, 437 U.S. 518, 98 S. Ct. 2482 (1978).
24. *Id.* at 528, 98 S. Ct. at 2488.
25. United Public Workers v. Mitchell, 330 U.S. 75, 67 S. Ct. 556 (1947).
26. United States Civil Service Comm'n v. National Ass'n of Letter Carriers, 413 U.S. 548, 93 S. Ct. 2880 (1973).
27. *Id.* at 556, 93 S. Ct. at 2886.
28. Broadrick v. Oklahoma, 413 U.S. 601, 93 S. Ct. 2908 (1973).
29. Branti v. Finkel, 445 U.S. 507, 100 S. Ct. 1287 (1980).
30. Elrod v. Burns, 427 U.S. 347, 96 S. Ct. 2673 (1976).
31. Branti v. Finkel, 445 U.S. at 516-517, 100 S. Ct. at 1294.
32. *Id.* at 518, 100 S. Ct. at 1295.
33. Abood v. Detroit Bd. of Educ., 431 U.S. 209, 97 S. Ct. 1782 (1977).
34. *Id.* at 225-226, 97 S. Ct. at 1794.
35. *Id.* at 236, 97 S. Ct. at 1800.
36. *Id.* at 241, 97 S. Ct. at 1802.
37. Harrah Independent School Dist. v. Martin, 440 U.S. 194, 99 S. Ct. 1062 (1979).
38. *Id.* at 198, 99 S. Ct. at 1064.
39. *Id.* at 201, 99 S. Ct. at 1065.

CHAPTER 13

Teacher Rights: Discriminatory Employment Practices

Title VII of Civil Rights Act of 1964

The Cornerstone Case

A 1971 Supreme Court opinion construing Title VII of the Civil Rights Act of 1964[1] turned out to be as significant in the area of employment discrimination as was the 1954 decision outlawing racial discrimination in the public schools.[2] The unanimous opinion of the eight participating Justices received little immediate attention in public employment circles, probably because at that time Title VII did not cover public employment. Slightly more than a year later, however, Congress made the statute (and of course its construction by the Supreme Court) applicable to employees of state and local governments.

The key conclusion of the Supreme Court was that "[i]f an employment practice which operates to exclude Negroes cannot be shown to be related to job performance, the practice is prohibited."[3] Although the case concerned discrimination on the basis of race, the holding would be applicable to cases involving discrimination on any of the bases prohibited by Title VII. (See Appendix C.)

The case had been brought as a class action by black employees of a North Carolina plant of the privately owned Duke Power Company. Prior to July of 1965 (the effective date of the Civil Rights Act of 1964), the company openly discriminated on the basis of race in the hiring and assigning of employees at the plant. In 1965 when the company abolished its policy of employing blacks only in one department (the Labor Department), it made the completion of high school a condition for transfer from that department. For a decade there had been the requirement of high school graduation for initial employment in the other departments, which were staffed with whites. However, whites hired before the requirement was instituted continued to advance.

A further requirement added by the company when the federal statute became effective was that new employees in any but the Labor Department must pass two "professionally prepared aptitude tests," as well as have a high school education. Two months later, incumbent employees in the Labor Department who lacked a high school education were permitted to qualify for transfer by passing the Wonderlic Personnel Test (for general intelligence) and the Bennett Mechanical Aptitude Test. The cut-offs approximated the national median scores for high school graduates, and thus were more stringent than the requisite of high school completion.

The Court began its analysis by looking to the intent of Congress:

> The objective of Congress in the enactment of Title VII is plain from the language of the statute. It was to achieve equality of employment opportunities and remove barriers that have operated in the past to favor an identifiable group of white employees over other employees. Under the Act, practices, procedures, or tests neutral on their face, and even neutral in terms of intent, cannot be maintained if they operate to "freeze" the status quo of prior discriminatory employment practices.
>
> ... What is required by Congress is the removal of artificial, arbitrary, and unnecessary barriers to employment when the barriers operate invidiously to discriminate on the basis of racial or other impermissible classification.[4]

It was undisputed that the record in the case showed that whites fared far better than blacks on the company's criteria. For example, in 1960 almost three times as great a percent of North Carolina white males had completed high school as had black males. As for the alternative tests, in one sample using the Wonderlic and Bennett tests as part of a battery, fifty-eight percent of whites passed as compared to only six percent of blacks, a consequence the Court said would appear to be "directly traceable to race. Black intelligence must have the means of articulation to manifest itself fairly in a testing process. Because they are Negroes, petitioners have long received inferior education in segregated schools."[5]

The Court held that Title VII goes beyond prohibiting direct discrimination. It said:

> The Act proscribes not only overt discrimination but also practices that are fair in form, but discriminatory in operation. The touchstone is business necessity. If an employment practice which operates to exclude Negroes cannot be shown to be related to job performance, the practice is prohibited.[6]

The Court's acceptance of a "results" criterion without a need to show segregative intent by the employer was of great significance. It put employers who might have been insensitive "innocents" in the same legally indefensible position as contrivers of plans for discrimination in employment. It placed on all employers a responsibility to eliminate unintentional as well as intentional results of any employment practice that had an actual effect of disadvantaging a protected class of persons unless there was a "business necessity" to support the practice.

Examining the record of the case, the Court concluded:

> On the record before us, neither the high school completion requirement nor the general intelligence test is shown to bear a demonstrable relationship to successful performance of the jobs for which it was used. Both were adopted . . . without meaningful study of their relationship to job-performance ability. . . .
>
> The evidence . . . shows that [white] employees who have not completed high school or taken the tests have continued to perform satisfactorily and make progress in departments for which the high school and test criteria are now used.[7]

The company contended that its general intelligence tests were permitted because the Civil Rights Act specifically authorized the use of "any professionally developed ability test . . . [not] designed, intended, or used to discriminate" against a protected class. The Court disagreed. It examined the records of Congress, which showed that the intent was to permit the use only of "job-related" tests.

However, the Court said, "Nothing in the Act precludes the use of testing or measuring procedures; obviously they are useful. What Congress has forbidden is giving these devices and mechanisms controlling force unless they are demonstrably a reasonable measure of job performance."[8] Furthermore, permissible tests must "measure the person for the job and not the person in the abstract."[9]

In 1975, the Court expanded its reasoning.[10] It said unanimously:

> If an employer does then [after plaintiff has made a prima facie case] meet the burden of proving that its tests are "job related," it remains open to the complaining party to show that other tests or selection devices, without a similarly undesirable racial effect, would also serve the employer's legitimate interest in "efficient and trustworthy workmanship." Such a showing would be evidence that the employer was using its tests merely as a "pretext" for discrimination.[11]

Steps and Burdens of Proof

Two years later, in a unanimous opinion the Court established the order and allocation of proof that was to be observed in a Title VII employment discrimination suit filed by an individual.[12] The initial burden is placed on the complainant to establish a prima facie case of discrimination.

This may be done by showing (i) that he belongs to a racial minority; (ii) that he applied and was qualified for a job for which the employer was seeking applicants; (iii) that, despite his qualifications, he was rejected; and (iv) that, after his rejection, the position remained open and the employer continued to seek applicants from persons of complainant's qualifications.[13]

The burden then shifts to the employer "to articualte some legitimate, nondiscriminatory reason for the employee's rejection."[14] Finally, the complainant must be afforded "a fair opportunity to show that [the employer's] stated reason for [complainant's] rejection was in fact pretext."[15]

In 1978, the Court expressly rejected the contention that the employer, after a prima facie case of discrimination is presented against him, must adopt a method of employment that allows consideration of the qualifications of the largest number of minority applicants.[16] The Court said that such a view would equate the prima facie showing with an ultimate finding of fact as to discriminatory refusal to hire under Title VII. It stated that the prima facie case "raises an inference of discrimination only because we presume these acts, if otherwise unexplained, are more likely than not based on the consideration of impermissible factors."[17] The Court continued:

> [T]he burden which shifts to the employer is merely that of proving that he based his employment decision on a legitimate consideration, and not an illegitimate one such as race. To prove that, he need not prove that he pursued the course which would both enable him to achieve his own business goal *and* allow him to consider the *most* employment applications. Title VII forbids him from having as a goal a work force selected by any proscribed discriminatory practice, but it does not impose a duty to adopt a hiring procedure that maximizes hiring of minority employees. To dispel the adverse inference from a prima facie showing under *McDonnell Douglas*, the employer need only "articulate some legitimate nondiscriminatory reason for the employee's rejection." [*McDonnell Douglas*, 93 S. Ct. at 1824.]
>
> . . . .
>
> This is not to say of course that proof of a justification which is reasonably related to the achievement of some legitimate goal necessarily ends the inquiry. The plaintiff must be given the opportunity to introduce evidence that the proffered justification is merely a pretext for discrimination.[18]

In 1981, the Court was obliged to repeat much of what it had said in the above cases.[19] In unanimously reversing a decision of the Court of

Appeals for the Fifth Circuit, the Court re-emphasized the nature of the burden on the defendant as follows:

> We have stated consistently that the employee's prima facie case of discrimination will be rebutted if the employer articulates lawful reasons for the action; that is, to satisfy this intermediate burden, the employer need only produce admissible evidence which would allow the trier of fact rationally to conclude that the employment decision had not been motivated by discriminatory animus. The Court of Appeals would require the defendant to introduce evidence which, in the absence of any evidence of pretext, would *persuade* the trier of fact that the employment action was lawful. This exceeds what properly can be demanded to satisfy a burden of production.
>
> . . . .
>
> The Court of Appeals also erred in requiring the defendant to prove by objective evidence that the person hired or promoted was better qualified than the plaintiff. *McDonnell Douglas* teaches that it is the plaintiff's task to demonstrate that similarly situated employees were not treated equally. . . . The Court of Appeals' rule would require the employer to show that the plaintiff's objective qualifications were inferior to those of the person selected. If it cannot, a court would, in effect, conclude that it has discriminated.
>
> The court's procedural rule harbors a substantive error. Title VII prohibits all discrimination in employment based upon race, sex and national origin. . . . Title VII, however, does not demand that an employer give preferential treatment to minorities or women. . . . It does not require the employer to restructure his employment practices to maximize the number of minorities and women hired. . . .
>
> The views of the Court of Appeals can be read, we think, as requiring the employer to hire the minority or female applicant whenever that person's objective qualifications were equal to those of a white male applicant. But Title VII does not obligate an employer to accord this preference. Rather, the employer has discretion to choose among equally qualified candidates, provided the decision is not based upon unlawful criteria. The fact that a court may think that the employer misjudged the qualifications of the applicants does not in itself expose him to Title VII liability, although this may be probative of whether the employer's reasons are pretexts for discrimination. . . .
>
> In summary, the Court of Appeals erred by requiring the defendant to prove by a preponderance of the evidence the existence of nondiscriminatory reasons for terminating the respondent and that the person retained in her stead had superior objective qualifications for the position.[20]

Pattern-or-Practice Cases

In 1977 the Court twice dealt with the related question of general discriminatory treatment through the "pattern or practice" of an employer. The major case involved the trucking industry;[21] the other case involved public school teachers.[22] A significant point treated in both cases was the present consequences of discriminatory practices occurring prior to the effective date of Title VII (for private employers, 1965; for state and local governments, 1972). The private company had been found to have discriminated before and after the Act. In the public school case, the lower courts had incorrectly not made the distinction. There were no dissents from the substantive points presented below.

In a pattern-or-practice action the plaintiff is the government, which the Court said initially must "demonstrate that unlawful discrimination has been a regular procedure or policy followed by an employer or group of employers."[23] The burden then shifts to the employer to defeat the prima facie showing of a pattern or practice by "demonstrating that the Government's proof is either inaccurate or insignificant."[24] The Court said that the employer "might show, for example, that the claimed discriminatory pattern is a product of pre-Act hiring rather than unlawful post-Act discrimination, or that during the period it is alleged to have pursued a discriminatory policy it made too few employment decisions to justify the inference that it had engaged in a regular practice of discrimination."[25] If the employer fails to rebut the inference arising from the government's prima facie case, the trial court can order appropriate prospective changes in the employer's employment procedures. Also, of course, it can fashion individual relief for those who suffered from the discriminatory practices. This may take many forms, including employment, particular assignments, retroactive seniority, and awards for lost pay.

On the point of seniority rights, the Court examined the history of Title VII in the Congress and concluded that the section relating to seniority made it "clear that the routine application of a bona fide seniority system would not be unlawful under Title VII."[26] The Court said, "[W]e hold that an otherwise neutral, legitimate seniority system does not become unlawful under Title VII simply because it may perpetuate pre-Act discrimination. Congress did not intend to make it illegal for employees with vested seniority rights to continue to exercise those rights, even at the expense of pre-Act discriminatees."[27]

In the pattern-or-practice case involving public school employment practices in Hazelwood, Missouri, the Court made some additional observations about the use of statistics in establishing a prima facie case. It stated that the "proper comparison was between the racial composition of Hazelwood's teaching staff and the racial composition of the qualified public school teacher population in the relevant labor market."[28] It reiterated that it was only post-Act hiring data that were to be analyzed under Title VII. "A public employer who from that date forward made all its employment decisions in a wholly non-discriminatory way would not violate Title VII even if it had formerly maintained an all-white work force by purposefully excluding Negroes."[29] Recognizing that the significance of the racial statistics would depend on the area elected as the relevant labor market, the Court instructed the trial court to make such a determination. (Whether the city of St. Louis should be included was a major issue.)

Not Restricted to Minorities

That Title VII is not limited to discrimination against minorities was decided by the Court in 1976.[30] All Justices agreed on the point. The context was the discharge of two white employees and the retention of a black employee in a situation in which all were charged with misappropriating some merchandise being transported by the company. The lower courts had dismissed the claim of the white employees as not being cognizable under Title VII. The Court said that the Act "prohibits *all* racial discrimination in employment, without exception for any group of particular employees, and while crime or other misconduct may be a legitimate basis for discharge, it is hardly one for racial discrimination."[31]

Religious Accommodation

The following year, the Court, by a seven-to-two vote, delineated the employer's obligation under Title VII to accommodate an employee whose religious beliefs prohibited him from working on Saturdays in an employment setting that required constant staffing.[32] A 1972 amendment to Title VII requires that the employer must demonstrate that he is "unable to reasonably accommodate to an employee's or prospective employee's religious observance or practice without undue hardship on the conduct of the employer's business." In this case, a collectively bargained seniority system governed work shifts in the twenty-four-hour, seven-day-a-week operation. No volunteers would change shifts so that the airline would have had to deprive another employee of his shift preference at least in part because he did not adhere to a religion that observed the Saturday Sabbath. Citing the preceding case the Court said that Title VII "does not contemplate such unequal treatment . . . [and forbids discrimination] directed against majorities as well as minorities."[33] The Court further stated that there was no requirement that the employer bear more than a nominal cost in order to provide Saturdays off for the complaining worker. Thus, the hiring of a substitute worker definitely would not be required.

Time Limitations

In 1980, the Supreme Court construed the Title VII requirement that an aggrieved person must file a complaint with the Equal Employment Opportunity Commission "within one hundred and eighty days after the alleged unlawful employment practice occurred."[34] The context was a black Liberian's claim of discrimination on the basis of national origin because he was not granted tenure at a state college attended predominantly by blacks. The Court's vote was six-to-three.

In February 1973, the appropriate faculty committee recommended that Professor Ricks not receive an appointment with tenure. The committee agreed to reconsider its decision, and in February 1974, it adhered to its previous decision. In March 1974, the Faculty Senate voted to support the negative recommendation, and later that month, the Board of Trustees formally voted not to grant tenure. Ricks then filed a grievance. On June 26, 1974, the trustees, according to policy, offered Ricks a one-year "terminal" contract that would expire June 30, 1975. He signed the contract. On September 12, 1974, the Board of Trustees notified Ricks that his grievance had been denied.

The Court held that the proper date to begin the 180-day count was June 26, 1974. The key reasoning was that the alleged unlawful practice actually occurred when the trustees "made and communicated to Ricks"[35] their decision to terminate his employment on June 30, 1975. The Court said that the critical point was the time of the alleged discriminatory act, not the time when its consequences took complete effect. Also rejected by the Court was the date the grievance was decided against Ricks. The Court said:

> [W]e think that the Board of Trustees had made clear well before September 12 that it had formally rejected Ricks' tenure bid. The June 26 letter itself characterized that as the Board's "official position." It is apparent, of course, that the Board in the June 26 letter indicated a willingness to change its prior decision if Ricks' grievance were found to be meritorious. But entertaining a grievance complaining of the tenure decision does not suggest that the earlier decision was in any respect tentative. The grievance procedure, by its nature, is a *remedy* for a prior decision, not an opportunity to *influence* that decision before it is made.[36]

In 1981, by a six-to-three vote, the Court held in a brief per curiam opinion that the limitation period for nontenured administrators in the

Puerto Rico Department of Education to file complaints began when they received notification that their appointments would terminate at a specified date.[37] The majority found the case to be controlled by *Delaware State College v. Ricks.*

Constitutional Criteria

In 1976 the Supreme Court sharply distinguished constitutional claims from Title VII claims in the area of employment discrimination. It held by a seven-to-two vote that the disparate impact of a test was not sufficient to establish a prima facie case of discrimination for a claim based on the Constitution.[38] The Court of Appeals for the District of Columbia Circuit had erroneously applied the legal standards applicable to Title VII cases to a case involving a test for police officers in Washington, D.C., that had been begun before Title VII became applicable to public employees. The percentage of blacks who had failed the test was about four times that of whites, and the court of appeals held that this fact alone triggered the need for the employer to establish the validity of the test in terms of job performance. The court held as irrelevant the efforts of the District of Columbia to recruit blacks and the fact that recent hirings were roughly equivalent to the racial composition of the surrounding community. It also found that validation of the test in terms of success in the police training program was not sufficient, but that validation in terms of actual job performance was required.

The Supreme Court, after reviewing cases in several contexts involving the equal protection clause of the fourteenth amendment and the equivalent component in the due process clause of the fifth amendment (applicable in this District of Columbia case), emphasized that intent to discriminate must be shown. It added, however, the observation that the necessary "invidious discriminatory purpose may often be inferred from the totality of the relevant facts, including the fact, if it is true, that the law bears more heavily on one race than another."[39] Further, said the Court, disparate impact may for all practical purposes demonstrate unconstitutionality because in various circumstances the discrimination is very difficult to explain on nonracial grounds. The Court summarized as follows:

> Disproportionate impact is not irrelevant, but it is not the sole touchstone of an invidious racial discrimination forbidden by the Constitution. Standing alone, it does not trigger the rule that racial classifications are to be subjected to the strictest scrutiny and are justifiable only by the weightiest of considerations.[40]

The Court also discussed the test validation question that had been addressed by the lower courts. The test had been validated as to relationship with performance in the recruit training program, but not directly with performance as a police officer. The Court stated that the view that such validation was sufficient was supported by regulations of the Civil Service Commission, by the opinion evidence placed before the trial judge, and by the current views of the Civil Service Commissioners. Further, it was not inconsistent with *Griggs* or *Albemarle Paper Co.*, and "seems to us the much more sensible construction of the job-relatedness requirement."[41]

The impact of the *Washington v. Davis* decision on public employment rights of the classes covered by Title VII was negligible because Congress had made Title VII applicable to public employers almost four years earlier, and post-1972 cases were based on Title VI, not on constitutional equal protection grounds. Where lower federal courts previously had ordered changes based on the Constitution without having required proof of discriminatory intent, the doctrine of res judicata generally prevented reopening the cases if they had been terminated before this decision.

The consequences of the second prong of the holding—that test validation with a training program was sufficient—were of obvious significance. In the field of education, a validation of scores on the National Teacher Examination as measures of knowledge obtainable in teacher preparation programs offered in the state of South Carolina was the basis of a holding, affirmed by a five-to-two vote without opinion by the Supreme Court, that specified scores on the examination were not barred by Title VII as bases for certification or salary despite evidence that blacks performed much more poorly on the test than did whites.[42]

In 1979, the Supreme Court held that states may enforce statutes giving an absolute lifetime preference in public employment to qualified veterans even though the result is to keep a grossly disproportionate number of qualified women from civil service positions.[43] In this seven-to-two holding the Court said that the result was compelled by its holding in *Washington v. Davis* to the effect that a neutral law does not violate the fourteenth amendment solely because its results have a disproportionate impact on a particular class. Title VII, which expressly cannot be construed to modify veterans' rights, was not involved.

In *Personnel Administrator of Massachusetts v. Feeney*, the Court found no trace of deliberate discriminatory intent against women in the installation in 1896 or in later modifications of the principle of veterans' preference in Massachusetts. Although female veterans always had been treated similarly to male veterans, when the present suit was commenced, ninety-eight percent of the veterans in Massachusetts were male. It was argued that this fact demonstrated an impact too inevitable to have been unintended, particularly when coupled with the fact that under federal military policy, the status of "veteran" is reserved primarily for men. However, the argument for such inferred intentional discrimination was internally flawed because the female plaintiff agreed that a more limited hiring preference for veterans could be sustained. The Court observed that "invidious discrimination does not become less so because the discrimination accomplished is of a lesser magnitude."[44] As to foreseeable consequences in relation to discriminatory purpose, the Court said that it "implies that the decisionmaker . . . selected or reaffirmed a particular course of action at least in part 'because of,' not merely 'in spite of,' its adverse effects upon an identifiable group."[45]

Gender-based Policies

Pregnancy and Child-bearing

CONSTITUTIONAL REQUIREMENTS. The common practice of employers to establish personnel policies uniquely applicable to childbearing was successfully challenged before the Supreme Court in 1974.[46] Specifically at bar were the maternity leave policies of the school districts of Cleveland, Ohio, and Chesterfield County, Virginia. By consolidating the cases, the Court was able to discuss the constitutionality of several subpoints. The major question was whether a teacher could be required to take a leave of absence at a fixed point during her pregnancy that is substantially before the expected date of childbirth. One school system specified four months, the other prescribed five months. By a seven-to-two vote, the Court answered in the negative.

The Supreme Court approached the problem as follows:

> By acting to penalize the pregnant teacher for deciding to bear a child, overly restrictive maternity leave regulations can constitute a heavy burden on the exercise of . . . protected freedoms. Because public school maternity leave rules directly affect "one of the basic civil rights of man," the Due Process Clause of the Fourteenth Amendment requires that such rules must not needlessly, arbitrarily, or capriciously impinge upon this vital area of a teacher's constitutional liberty. The question before us in these cases is whether the interests advanced in support of the rules of the Cleveland and Chesterfield County School Boards can justify the particular procedures they have adopted.[47]

The school boards offered two explanations for mandating a firm cut-off date. One was the necessity of maintaining continuity of instruction by obtaining a qualified substitute teacher. The other justification was that, because at least some teachers become physically incapable of adequately performing certain duties during the latter part of pregnancy, the rules would protect the health of the teacher and the unborn child while assuring the presence of a physically capable instructor in the classroom at all times.

The Court recognized continuity of instruction as a significant and legitimate educational goal. It stated that, although a requirement of notice to school authorities of pregnancy and a definite date for the commencement of leave would be constitutionally acceptable, the absolute requirement of termination at the end of the fourth or fifth month of pregnancy was not rational in that the dates would occur at different times in the school year for different teachers. "As long as the teachers are required to give substantial advance notice of their condition, the choice of firm dates later in pregnancy would serve the boards' objectives just as well, while imposing a far lesser burden on the women's exercise of constitutionally protected freedom."[48]

The Court then examined the necessity of keeping physically unfit teachers out of the classroom. It said:

> There can be no doubt that such an objective is perfectly legitimate, both on educational and safety grounds. And, despite the plethora of conflicting medical testimony in these cases, we can assume, *arguendo*, that at least some teachers become physically disabled from effectively performing their duties during the latter stages of pregnancy.
>
> The mandatory termination provisions of the Cleveland and Chesterfield County rules surely operate to insulate the classroom from the presence of potentially incapacitated pregnant teachers. But the question is whether the rules sweep too broadly. That question must be answered in the affirmative, for the provisions amount to a conclusive presumption that every pregnant teacher who reaches the fifth or sixth month of pregnancy is physically incapable of continuing. . . . The rules contain an irrebuttable presumption of physical incompetency, and that presumption applies even when the medical evidence as to an individual woman's physical status might be wholly to the contrary.[49]

The testimony of the medical experts in the cases, although in disagreement on several points, was unanimous that the ability of a given pregnant woman to work beyond any fixed time in her pregnancy was an individual matter. The Court cautioned, however:

This is not to say that the only means for providing appropriate protection for the rights of pregnant teachers is an individualized determination in each case and in every circumstance. We are not dealing in these cases with maternity leave regulations requiring a termination of employment at some firm date during the last few weeks of pregnancy. We therefore have no occasion to decide whether such regulations might be justified by considerations not presented in these records. . . . [50]

On the question of eligibility to return to work after giving birth, the Court disapproved of the Cleveland provision that a teacher would not be eligible until the beginning of the next regular school semester following the time her child attained the age of three months. As with the invalidated pre-birth requirement, the irrebuttable presumption that no mother is fit to resume teaching for at least three months following the birth was held to be unconstitutional as not rationally related to continuity of instruction while unnecessarily burdening the right to bear children.

The Court, however, found it constitutionally sound to require a physician's certificate of fitness before a teacher who has recently borne a child may return to the classroom. It also approved of Cleveland's requirement of an additional physical examination at the option of the board. Further, the Court sustained the validity of the provision setting the eligibility to return date at the beginning of the semester following delivery. This would be a "precisely drawn means of serving the school board's interest in avoiding unnecessary changes in classroom personnel during any one school term."[51]

The Court spoke as follows in relation to Chesterfield County's return-to-work provision:

We perceive no . . . constitutional infirmities in the Chesterfield County rule. In that school system, the teacher becomes eligible for re-employment upon submission of a medical certificate from her physician; return to work is guaranteed no later than the beginning of the next school year following the eligibility determination. The medical certificate is both a reasonable and narrow method of protecting the school board's interest in teacher fitness, while the possible deferring of return until the next school year serves the goal of preserving continuity of instruction. In short, the Chesterfield County rule manages to serve the legitimate state interests here without employing unnecessary presumptions that broadly burden the exercise of protected constitutional liberty.[52]

Five months later, by a vote of six-to-three, the Court upheld against a fourteenth amendment challenge the California disability insurance system which excluded from benefits those disabled by normal pregnancy and childbirth.[53] The Court found that the state rationally could establish a self-supporting insurance program for those in private employment who were temporarily unable to work because of disabilities not covered by workers' compensation. That the program did not cover all risks did not violate the equal protection clause. In order to cover normal pregnancy and childbirth, the required contributions of all participants would have to be increased. Further, prior Supreme Court decisions established that in the social welfare area states are not required to choose between attacking every aspect of a problem or not attacking the problem at all. The Court said that this was not a gender-based classification because there was no risk that only one sex was protected against. "The program divides potential recipients into two groups—pregnant women and nonpregnant persons. While the first group is exclusively female, the second includes members of both sexes. The fiscal and actuarial benefits of the program thus accrue to members of both sexes."[54] The Court specifically recognized that if there were evidence that the exclusion was a pretext for discrimination, the dispute would be decided differently. As a matter of fact, women had contributed twenty-eight percent of the fund and had benefited from thirty-eight percent of it.

TITLE VII REQUIREMENTS. In 1976, a six-Justice majority extended the above reasoning to a Title VII claim concerning a "strikingly similar" benefit plan of a private company.[55] Since such a plan had been found not discriminatory per se on the basis of sex, the Title VII bar to gender discrimination was held not to be applicable to the General Electric Company plan. In this case, as in *Geduldig*, costs of the existing plan per female employee compared favorably with costs per male employee. (In response to this decision, Congress in 1978 amended Title VII to proscribe exclusion of pregnancy from coverage under disability benefit plans.)

The Justices unanimously agreed in 1977, however, that a policy of denying accumulated seniority to female employees returning from pregnancy leave did violate Title VII.[56] *Nashville Gas Company v. Satty* was distinguished from the two preceding cases in that here the employer "has not merely refused to extend to women a benefit that men cannot and do not receive, but has imposed on women a substantial burden that men need not suffer."[57] Title VII, said the Court, does not "permit an employer to burden female employees in such a way as to deprive them of employment opportunities because of their different role ['in the scheme of human existence']."[58]

Retirement Policies

Another case involving sex discrimination in employment policies was decided by the Court in 1978.[59] Challenged was the almost universal practice of using gender-based actuarial tables to determine retirement benefits. Since women as a class live longer than men as a class, common practice in insurance plans had been either to require higher payments from women for the same benefits or to grant them lesser benefits for the same payments made by males. The particular case was brought against a city department of Los Angeles under Title VII of the Civil Rights Act of 1964.

This arrangement was found to violate the statute by a majority of five Justices, with two Justices in dissent, one Justice not reaching the merits, and one Justice not participating. The opinion of the Court emphasized that Title VII used the word "individual" to indicate the object of the protection against discrimination. This focus precluded the use of group characteristics for generalizations under the statute. Since any individual's life expectancy is based on a number of factors, of which sex is only one, actuarial tables based solely on sex discriminate against individual women. The Court distinguished this case from *Geduldig* and *General Electric Co.* in that "[o]n its face this plan discriminates on the basis of sex . . . [rather than] on the basis of a special physical disability."[60] Furthermore, in those two pregnancy-exclusion cases, the evidence was that women as a group had received benefits from the plans equal to or greater than those received by men as a group relative to contributions.

The Court recognized the financial implications of its decision by holding that its ruling would have only prospective applicability. It summarized as follows:

> Although we conclude that the Department's practice violated Title VII, we do not suggest that the statute was intended to revolutionize the insurance and pension industries. All that is at issue today is a requirement that men and women make unequal contributions to an employer-operated pension fund. Nothing in our holding implies that it would be unlawful for an employer to set aside equal retirement contributions for each employee and let each retiree purchase the largest benefit which his or her accumulated contributions could command in the open market. Nor does it call into question the insurance industry practice of considering the composition of an employer's work force in determining the probable cost of a retirement or death benefit plan. Finally, we recognize that in a case of this kind it may be necessary to take special care in fashioning appropriate relief.[61]

1. 42 U.S.C. § 2000e (1976). *See* Appendix C.
2. Griggs v. Duke Power Co., 401 U.S. 424, 91 S. Ct. 849 (1971).
3. *Id.* at 431, 91 S. Ct. at 853.
4. *Id.*

5. *Id.*
6. *Id.*
7. *Id.* at 431-432, 91 S. Ct. at 853-854.
8. *Id.* at 436, 91 S. Ct. at 856.
9. *Id.*
10. Albemarle Paper Co. v. Moody, 422 U.S. 405, 95 S. Ct. 2362 (1975).
11. *Id.* at 425, 95 S. Ct. at 2375.
12. McDonnell Douglas Corp. v. Green, 411 U.S. 792, 93 S. Ct. 1817 (1973).
13. *Id.* at 802, 93 S. Ct. at 1824.
14. *Id.*
15. *Id.* at 804, 93 S. Ct. at 1825.
16. Furnco Construction Co. v. Waters, 438 U.S. 567, 98 S. Ct. 2943 (1978).
17. *Id.* at 577, 98 S. Ct. at 2949-2950.
18. *Id.* at 577-578, 98 S. Ct. at 2950.
19. Texas Dep't of Community Affairs v. Burdine, 450 U.S. 248, 101 S. Ct. 1089 (1981).
20. *Id.* at 257-260, 101 S. Ct. at 1096-1097.
21. International Bhd. of Teamsters v. United States, 431 U.S. 324, 97 S. Ct. 1843 (1977).
22. Hazelwood School Dist. v. United States, 433 U.S. 299, 97 S. Ct. 2736 (1977).
23. International Bhd. of Teamsters v. United States, 431 U.S. at 360, 97 S. Ct. at 1867.
24. *Id.*
25. *Id.*
26. *Id.* at 352, 97 S. Ct. at 1863.
27. *Id.* at 353-354, 97 S. Ct. at 1864.
28. Hazelwood School Dist. v. United States, 433 U.S. at 308, 97 S. Ct. at 2742.
29. *Id.*
30. McDonald v. Santa Fe Trail Transportation Co., 427 U.S. 273, 96 S. Ct. 2574 (1976).
31. *Id.* at 283-284, 96 S. Ct. at 2580.
32. Trans World Airlines, Inc. v. Hardison, 432 U.S. 63, 97 S. Ct. 2264 (1977).
33. *Id.* at 81, 97 S. Ct. at 2275.
34. Delaware State College v. Ricks, 449 U.S. 250, 101 S. Ct. 498 (1980).
35. *Id.* at 258, 101 S. Ct. at 504.
36. *Id.* at 261, 101 S. Ct. at 505-506.
37. Chardon v. Fernandez, ___ U.S. ___, 102 S. Ct. 28 (1981).
38. Washington v. Davis, 426 U.S. 229, 96 S. Ct. 2040 (1976).
39. *Id.* at 242, 96 S. Ct. at 2048-2049.
40. *Id.*
41. *Id.* at 251, 96 S. Ct. at 2053.
42. United States v. State of S.C., 445 F. Supp. 1094 (D.S.C. 1977), *aff'd*, 434 U.S. 1026, 98 S. Ct. 756 (1978).
43. Personnel Administrator of Mass. v. Feeney, 442 U.S. 256, 99 S. Ct. 2282 (1979).
44. *Id.* at 277, 99 S. Ct. at 2295.
45. *Id.* at 279, 99 S. Ct. at 2296.
46. Cleveland Bd. of Educ. v. LaFleur, 414 U.S. 632, 94 S. Ct. 791 (1974). The companion case was captioned *Cohen v. Chesterfield Cty. School Bd.*
47. *Id.* at 640, 94 S. Ct. at 796
48. *Id.* at 643, 94 S. Ct. at 798.
49. *Id.*
50. *Id.* at 647 n.13, 94 S. Ct. at 799-800 n.13.
51. *Id.* at 649, 94 S. Ct. at 800.
52. *Id.* at 650, 94 S. Ct. at 801.
53. Geduldig v. Aiello, 417 U.S. 484, 94 S. Ct. 2485 (1974).
54. *Id.* at 496-497, 94 S. Ct. at 2492 n.20.
55. General Electric Co. v. Gilbert, 429 U.S. 125, 97 S. Ct. 401 (1976).
56. Nashville Gas Co. v. Satty, 434 U.S. 136, 98 S. Ct. 347 (1977).
57. *Id.* at 142, 98 S. Ct. at 351.
58. *Id.*
59. City of Los Angeles, Dep't of Water and Power v. Manhart, 435 U.S. 702, 98 S. Ct. 1370 (1978).
60. *Id.* at 715, 98 S. Ct. at 1379.
61. *Id.* at 717-718, 98 S. Ct. at 1380.

CHAPTER 14

Student Rights

The Key Case

It was in February 1969 that the United States Supreme Court issued the only opinion in its history dealing directly with the validity of a pre-college public school disciplinary rule that did not implicate religious values.[1] The case of *Tinker v. Des Moines Independent Community School District* established some guidelines by which to reconcile the constitutional rights of students and the legitimate powers of school authorities. It seems safe to say that in the ensuing years, no public school case has been referred to more frequently in legal or educational circles.

Some facts of the case are crucial to an understanding of the phraseology of the opinion. The principals of the Des Moines, Iowa schools, having been made aware that certain students were planning to wear armbands to protest hostilities in Vietnam and to support a truce, adopted a policy that any student wearing an armband would be asked to remove it, and if he refused, he would be suspended until he returned without the armband. A handful of students wore the armbands, refused to remove them, and were suspended solely on that ground. The position of the school authorities was supported by the district court and by a four-to-four vote of the Eighth Circuit Court of Appeals. By a seven-to-two vote, the Supreme Court reversed. (It is interesting to note that the two dissenters were Justice Harlan, generally characterized judicially as very conservative, and Justice Black, generally characterized as very liberal.)

In its opinion, the Supreme Court observed that "the wearing of armbands in the circumstances of this case was entirely divorced from actually or potentially disruptive conduct by those participating in it. It was closely akin to 'pure speech' which, we have repeatedly held, is entitled to comprehensive protection under the First Amendment."[2] To emphasize the unique nature of the right being threatened by school authorities, the Court pointed out what was *not* involved:

> The problem posed by the present case does not relate to regulation of the length of skirts or the type of clothing, to hair style, or deportment. It does not concern aggressive, disruptive

action or even group demonstrations. Our problem involves direct, primary First Amendment rights akin to "pure speech."[3]

In this opinion, the Court enunciated the general bounds to be observed between first amendment rights of students in public schools and the authority of school officials. In the tumult evoked by the Vietnam War during the years immediately following this decision, the first of the following summary statements was to receive much more attention in the rash of suits brought on behalf of students than was the second. On behalf of student rights, the Court said:

> First Amendment rights, applied in light of the special characteristics of the school environment, are available to teachers and students. It can hardly be argued that either students or teachers shed their constitutional rights to freedom of speech or expression at the schoolhouse gate.[4]

The counterbalancing view was expressed in the following words:

> On the other hand, the Court has repeatedly emphasized the need for affirming the comprehensive authority of the States and of school officials, consistent with fundamental constitutional safeguards, to prescribe and control conduct in the schools.[5]

The Court noted that the few students with armbands were silent, made no attempt to force other students to wear armbands, and took no action disruptive to the operation of the school or in conflict with the rights of other students. Not only had no disturbance or disorder occurred, but there were no facts that might reasonably have led school authorities to "forecast substantial disruption of or material interference with school activities...."[6]

Another fact cited by the Court was that the principals did not ban the wearing of all symbols of political or controversial significance, but selected only the particular symbol of the black armband worn to exhibit opposition to involvement of the United States in Vietnam. Thus, the content of this message was the target of the rule, and it is content that lies at the heart of the first amendment protection of speech. "Clearly, the prohibition of expression of one particular opinion, at least without evidence that it is necessary to avoid material and substantial interference with schoolwork or discipline, is not constitutionally permissible."[7]

Students in public schools, explained the Court, may not be confined to the expression of those sentiments that are officially approved. Personal intercommunication among students is not only an inevitable part of the process of attending school; it is also an important part of the educational process. That school authorities may "desire to avoid the discomfort and unpleasantness that always accompany an un-popular viewpoint"[8] is not sufficient reason for prohibiting a particular expression of opinion. For a ban on speech there must be evidence of actual or imminent disruption of a substantial nature traceable to the communication. "But conduct by the student, in class or out of it, which for any reason—whether it stems from time, place, or type of behavior—materially disrupts classwork or involves substantial disorder or invasion of the rights of others is, of course, not immunized by the constitutional guarantee of freedom of speech."[9]

Three College Cases

Three cases have been decided by the Supreme Court in the area of student conduct rules in public higher education. The earliest case, decided in 1915, upheld the implementation of a statute barring students from membership in Greek letter secret societies in the state's institutions of higher education.[10] A University of Mississippi rule requiring that students admitted after a certain date disavow allegiance to any such group was challenged on various grounds. The Supreme Court held that the fourteenth amendment did not prevent a state from establishing a rule governing its higher educational institutions when state courts said the legislature had the power and there was a basis for the rule, *i.e.*, preventing students from being "distracted from that singleness of purpose which the State desired to exist in its public educational institutions."[11] The Court stated that the wisdom or necessity of such a regulation was not for federal judicial determination. It also dismissed as irrelevant the asserted merits of secret societies and what was done in universities in other states.

The second case developed during the days of protests against the Vietnam War and involved the denial by Central Connecticut State College of recognition for campus privileges to a local chapter of a group known as Students for a Democratic Society (SDS).[12] Some SDS chapters on other campuses had been associated with disruptive campus activities. The Supreme Court set out the principles of law to be applied by the lower courts in such situations. The Court stated that because denial of recognition is a form of prior restraint, first amendment freedoms of speech and assembly must be considered. Citing *Tinker*, the Court said that properly the burden rested on the college to show the appropriateness of denial of recognition, rather than on the students to show entitlement to recognition.

The record compiled in the lower courts was ambiguous as to precisely why recognition had been denied. For that reason, the Supreme Court discussed four possible justifications which could be derived from the record. It found three to be unconstitutional and one to be valid. The three unconstitutional reasons were: (1) association of the local group with the national SDS (invalid because one cannot be penalized merely for an ill-defined association with a group that has not been outlawed), (2) the college president's disagreement with the philosophy of the local group (invalid because government "may not restrict speech or association simply because it finds the views expressed by any group to be abhorrent"),[13] and (3) concern that the local group would be a disruptive influence on the campus (invalid under the *Tinker* rationale because there was no substantial basis for that conclusion). The reason that would be constitutional was that the group was unwilling to be bound by reasonable rules governing conduct. The Court said that members of the group "may, if they so choose, preach the propriety of amending or even doing away with any or all campus regulations. They may not, however, undertake to flout these rules."[14] The Court continued:

> Just as in the community at large, reasonable regulations with respect to the time, the place, and the manner in which student groups conduct their speech-related activities must be respected. A college administration may impose a requirement, such as may have been imposed in this case, that a group seeking official recognition affirm in advance its willingness to adhere to reasonable campus law.[15]

In the third case concerning student conduct rules in public higher education, a graduate journalism student at the University of Missouri had been expelled in the middle of a semester for the on-campus distribution of a newspaper containing what university authorities called "forms of indecent speech" in violation of a bylaw of the Board of Curators [Trustees].[16] The student had been allowed to remain on campus until the end of the term, but she was not given credit for the one course in which she received a passing grade.

The lower courts had upheld the university authorities in decisions made prior to *Healy*. The Supreme Court, reversing with a per curiam opinion, said that *Healy* made it clear "that the mere dissemination of ideas—no matter how offensive to good taste—on a state university campus may not be shut off in the name alone of "conventions of decency.""[17] According to the Court, the political cartoon and the story that prompted the University's action were not constitutionally obscene. The Court further observed that it was solely the *content* of the newspaper that prompted the expulsion. There was no disruption caused by the process of distribution, nor were any "time, place, or manner" rules violated.

Procedural Due Process for Short Suspensions

The Supreme Court rendered its first opinion on procedural due process for students subject to punishment by public school authorities in 1975.[18] The punishment involved in the case was a suspension of up to ten days. Many students in several schools in Columbus, Ohio, received such punishment for misconduct following a period of widespread student unrest and demonstrations. It had been found that the plaintiffs in the case had received no hearings in connection with their suspensions.

As the due process clause of the fourteenth amendment is triggered only by a deprivation of life, liberty, or property, school officials argued that it did not apply because none of these elements was present. The Court by a vote of five-to-four disagreed, pointing out that Ohio law provided qualified persons with a right to public education and that this state-granted right was indeed a property right. In addition, the fact that the suspensions would be entered on the students' records amounted to a liberty interest because the charges of misconduct could damage their reputations with their teachers and fellow students as well as interfere with later opportunities for higher education and employment.

The Court also rejected the argument that the punishment here was too slight to bring the due process clause into play. It observed that the severity of a deprivation is not decisive of the basic right to some type of hearing. Further, it found the ten-day suspension not to be so insignificant as to except its imposition from due process considerations. It said:

> [T]he total exclusion from the educational process for more than a trivial period, and certainly if the suspension is for 10 days, is a serious event in the life of the suspended child. Neither the property interest in educational benefits temporarily denied nor the liberty interest in reputation, which is also implicated, is so insubstantial that suspensions may constitutionally be imposed by any procedure the school chooses, no matter how arbitrary.[19]

Having decided that due process applies, the Court discussed what procedures were required. It reviewed prior interpretations of the due process clause in other contexts and concluded that "[a]t the very minimum ... students facing suspension and the consequent interference with a protected property interest must be given *some* kind of notice and afforded *some* kind of hearing."[20] It continued:

> It also appears from our cases that the timing and content of the notice and the nature of the hearing will depend on appropriate accommodation of the competing interests involved. The student's interest is to avoid unfair or mistaken exclusion

from the educational process, with all of its unfortunate consequences. The Due Process Clause will not shield him from suspensions properly imposed, but it disserves both his interest and the interest of the State if his suspension is in fact unwarranted.... Disciplinarians, although proceeding in utmost good faith, frequently act on the reports and advice of others; and the controlling facts and the nature of the conduct under challenge are often disputed. The risk of error is not at all trivial, and it should be guarded against if that may be done without prohibitive cost or interference with the educational process.[21]

The Court then pronounced that, in connection with a suspension of ten days or less, the due process clause requires that "the student be given oral or written notice of the charges against him and, if he denies them, an explanation of the evidence the authorities have and an opportunity to present his side of the story."[22]

The Court said that the notice could be given orally, and that "there need be no delay between the time 'notice' is given and the time of the hearing."[23] It amplified the point by adding:

In the great majority of cases the disciplinarian may informally discuss the alleged misconduct with the student minutes after it has occurred. We hold only that, in being given an opportunity to explain his version of the facts at this discussion, the student first be told what he is accused of doing and what the basis of the accusation is.[24]

What was *not* required (and why) was explained as follows:

We stop short of construing the Due Process Clause to require, countrywide, that hearings in connection with short suspensions must afford the student the opportunity to secure counsel, to confront and cross-examine witnesses supporting the charge, or to call his own witnesses to verify his version of the incident. Brief disciplinary suspensions are almost countless. To impose in each such case even truncated trial-type procedures might well overwhelm administrative facilities in many places and, by diverting resources, cost more than it would save in educational effectiveness. Moreover, further formalizing the suspension process and escalating its formality and adversary nature may not only make it too costly as a regular disciplinary tool but also destroy its effectiveness as part of the teaching process.[25]

Taking cognizance of the reality of some situations in which prior notice and hearing might be infeasible, the Court said that students "whose presence poses a continuing danger to persons or property or an ongoing threat of disrupting the academic process may be immediately removed from school. In such cases, the necessary notice and rudimentary hearing should follow as soon as practicable."[26]

The opinion concluded with an emphasis on the fact that the case involved a short suspension, not exceeding ten days. "Longer suspensions or expulsions for the remainder of the school term, or permanently, may require more formal procedures."[27]

Corporal Punishment: Penalty and Process

In 1977, the Supreme Court treated the relationship of the due process clause to the imposition of corporal punishment on public school students.[28] By a five-to-four vote, the Court said, "[W]e find that corporal punishment in public schools implicates a constitutionally protected liberty interest, but we hold that the traditional common-law remedies are fully adequate to afford due process."[29] In *Ingraham v. Wright*, the Court also held that corporal punishment of students was not per se a violation of the eighth amendment's prohibition of "cruel and unusual punishments."

In addressing both questions, the Court began by examining history. It observed:

> The use of corporal punishment in this country as a means of disciplining school children dates back to the colonial period. It has survived the transformation of primary and secondary education from the colonials' reliance on optional private arrangements to our present system of compulsory education and dependence on public schools. . . . Professional and public opinion is sharply divided on the practice, and has been for more than a century. Yet we can discern no trend toward its elimination. [Statutes of twenty-one states expressly authorize it, whereas two bar it.]

> At common law a single principle has governed the use of corporal punishment since before the American Revolution: Teachers may impose reasonable but not excessive force to discipline a child. . . . The basic doctrine has not changed. . . . To the extent that the force is excessive or unreasonable, the educator in virtually all States is subject to possible civil and criminal liability.

> . . . All of the circumstances are to be taken into account in determining whether the punishment is reasonable in a particular case. Among the most important considerations are the seriousness of the offense, the attitude and past behavior of the child, the nature and severity of the punishment, the age and strength of the child, and the availability of less severe but equally effective means of discipline.[30]

The Court examined the history of the eighth amendment's cruel and unusual punishments clause and interpretations of it through the years. The conclusion was that the provision was meant to apply to criminal punishment, and that the milieu of the public school was not analogous to that of prisoners. Children who may be subjected to "paddling" leave school daily, and in school, a child is rarely out of sight of teachers and other students who would witness and expose any mistreatment. Further, there is a general supervision of schools by the community. "As long as the schools are open to public scrutiny, there is no reason to believe that the common-law constraints will not effectively remedy and deter excesses such as those alleged in this case."[31]

On the point of fourteenth amendment due process, the Court spoke as follows:

> Were it not for the common-law privilege permitting teachers to inflict reasonable corporal punishment on children in their care, and the availability of the traditional remedies for abuse, the case for requiring advance procedural safeguards would be strong indeed. But here we deal with a punishment—paddling—within that tradition, and the question is whether the common-law remedies are adequate to afford due process.
>
> . . . Whether in this case the common law remedies for excessive corporal punishment constitute due process of law must turn on an analysis of the competing interests at stake, viewed against the background of "history, reason, [and] the past course of decisions." The analysis requires consideration of three distinct factors: "first, the private interest that will be affected . . . ; second, the risk of an erroneous deprivation of such interest . . . and the probable value, if any, of additional or substitute procedural safeguards; and, finally, the [state] interest, including the function involved and the fiscal and administrative burdens that the additional or substitute procedural requirement would entail."[32]

The Court noted that the liberty interest of the child in avoiding corporal punishment while in the care of public school authorities was subject to the historical limitation that as long as it was "reasonable," the punishment was legally permissible. It then observed that Florida "has continued to recognize, and indeed has strengthened by statute, the common-law right of a child not to be subjected to excessive corporal punishment in school. . . . The uncontradicted evidence suggests that corporal punishment in the Dade County schools was, '[w]ith the exception of a few cases, . . . unremarkable in physical severity.'"[33] The Court further reasoned:

Moreover, because paddlings are usually inflicted in response to conduct directly observed by teachers in their presence, the risk that a child will be paddled without cause is typically insignificant. In the ordinary case, a disciplinary paddling neither threatens seriously to violate any substantive rights nor condemns the child "to suffer grievous loss of any kind."

In those cases where severe punishment is contemplated, the available civil and criminal sanctions for abuse—considered in light of the openness of the school environment—afford significant protection against unjustified corporal punishment.... Teachers and school authorities are unlikely to inflict corporal punishment unnecessarily or excessively when a possible consequence of doing so is the institution of civil or criminal proceedings against them.[34]

The Court expressed doubt that even if the need for advance procedural safeguards were clear the incremental benefits could justify the costs. Even informal hearings would require time, personnel, and a diversion of attention from normal school pursuits. Also, the effectiveness of corporal punishment in many instances would be reduced if it were not swiftly administered without notice. Teachers might be forced to rely on disciplinary measures they believed less effective rather than confront possible disruption from a notice-and-hearing requirement. The Court cited "societal costs" of such a choice "result[ing] from this Court's determination of an asserted right to due process, rather than from the normal processes of community debate and legislative action."[35]

The Court summarized its opinion in the following words:

In view of the low incidence of abuse, the openness of our schools, and the common-law safeguards that already exist, the risk of error that may result in violation of a schoolchild's substantive rights can only be regarded as minimal. Imposing additional administrative safeguards as a constitutional requirement might reduce that risk marginally, but would also entail a significant intrusion into an area of primary educational responsibility. We conclude that the Due Process Clause does not require notice and a hearing prior to the imposition of corporal punishment in the public schools, as that practice is authorized and limited by the common law.[36]

Academic Penalties

In 1978 the Supreme Court decided a higher education case in which the question of due process in academic, as distinguished from disciplinary, matters was involved.[37] The narrow question was whether a medical school student could be dismissed during her final year of study for failure to meet academic standards. One of the student's claims was that she had not received procedural due process.

All nine Justices agreed that her receipt of warnings and chances to demonstrate improvement had afforded her "at least as much due process as the Fourteenth Amendment requires."[38] Four Justices saw no need to discuss what due process requirements must be met in cases of exclusion for academic reasons. The five-Justice opinion of the Court, however, distinguished academic decisions from disciplinary decisions by school officials, and it expressly overruled the Court of Appeals' interpretation that *Goss* required some type of hearing at which the student could defend her academic ability and performance. The opinion included the following:

> A school is an academic institution, not a courtroom or administrative hearing room. . . .
>
> Academic evaluations of a student, in contrast to disciplinary determinations, bear little resemblance to the judicial and administrative factfinding proceedings to which we have traditionally attached a full hearing requirement. . . . Like the decision of an individual professor as to the proper grade for a student in his course, the determination whether to dismiss a student for academic reasons requires an expert evaluation of cumulative information and is not readily adapted to the procedural tools of judicial or administrative decisionmaking.
>
> Under such circumstances, we decline to ignore the historic judgment of educators and thereby formalize the academic dismissal process by requiring a hearing. The educational process is not by nature adversarial; instead it centers around a continuing relationship between faculty and students, "one in which the teacher must occupy many roles—educator, adviser, friend, and, at times, parent-substitute." This is especially true as one advances through the varying regimes of the educational system, and the instruction becomes both more individualized and more specialized. . . . We decline to further enlarge the judicial presence in the academic community and thereby risk deterioration of many beneficial aspects of the faculty-student relationship.[39]

"Undocumented" Alien Children

In 1982, by a vote of five-to-four, the Supreme Court answered in the negative the question "whether, consistent with the Equal Protection Clause of the Fourteenth Amendment, Texas may deny to undocumented school-age children the free public education that it provides to children who are citizens of the United States or legally admitted aliens."[40] Challenged successfully was a 1975 revision of the education law of Texas that withheld from local school districts any state funds for the education of children not "legally admitted" into the United States and authorized local school districts to refuse to enroll such children in the public schools.

The Court, after holding that the equal protection clause applies to undocumented aliens, said that the constitutionality of the classification depended on "whether it may fairly be viewed as furthering a substantial interest of the State."[41] The view of the Court was that the uniqueness of education distinguishes it from general forms of social welfare, and triggers the necessity for a state to support withholding it by more substantial justification than that required by the usual rational-relationship-to-a-legitimate-state-interest criterion. "Both the importance of education in maintaining our basic institutions, and the lasting impact of its deprivation on the life of the child, mark the distinction. . . . In addition, education provides the basic tools by which individuals might lead economically productive lives to the benefit of us all."[42]

The Court emphasized that although the children were innocent of the unlawful conduct of their parents, the impact of the Texas law was to severely punish the children while they were in this country. (Any illegal entrants can, of course, be deported under federal law.) The Court also stated that the evidence did not support contentions that there was a significant burden on the state's economy by reason of educating undocumented children, that the exclusion of such children would likely improve the overall quality of education in the state, and that such children are less likely than others to remain within the state and put their education to productive use there.

Access to Books in School Library

In 1982, the Court decided a case brought by students against a school board that had removed from the school library some books it described as "anti-American, anti-Christian, anti-Semitic, and just plain filthy."[43] By a vote of five-to-four, but with no opinion accepted by a majority of the Justices, the Court remanded the case to the district court to determine with more specificity why the board removed the books. Five Justices believed that when the district court granted summary judgment for the board, the circumstances surrounding the removal had not been clearly enough established to enable them to assess fully the first amendment implications of the action. The other four Justices, in separate dissenting opinions, would have upheld the board without further judicial inquiry.

Four of the five Justices voting for remand (Justices Brennan, Marshall, Blackmun, and Stevens) subscribed to the following view:

> [W]hether petitioners' removal of books from their school libraries denied respondents their First Amendment rights depends upon the motivation behind petitioners' actions. If petitioners *intended* by their removal decision to deny respondents access to ideas with which petitioners disagreed, and if this intent was a decisive factor in petitioners' decision, then petitioners have exercised their discretion in violation of the Constitution. On the other hand, . . . an unconstitutional motivation would *not* be demonstrated if it were shown that petitioners had decided to remove the books at issue because those books were pervasively vulgar. . . . And again, . . . if it were demonstrated that the removal decision was based solely upon the "educational suitability" of the books in question, then their removal would be "perfectly permissible."[44]

Justice White voted for remand solely on the belief that the Court should have a "factual refinement" before it decided such complex constitutional questions as were implicit in the case. He saw no justification for the Court "to go further and issue a dissertation on the extent to which the First Amendment limits the discretion of the school board to remove books from the school library."[45] Thus, this widely publicized case, the bellwether of many on the subject of removal of books from school libraries, stands only for the general principle of constitutional law that school authorities do not have absolute discretion to remove any book from a school library for any or no reason. Also, it may be inferred from the seven opinions in the case that proof of an unconstitutional removal will be difficult unless a school board acts outrageously.

---

1. Tinker v. Des Moines Indep. Commun. School Dist., 393 U.S. 503, 89 S. Ct. 733 (1969).
2. *Id*. at 505-506, 89 S. Ct. at 736.
3. *Id*. at 507-508, 89 S. Ct. at 737.
4. *Id*. at 506, 89 S. Ct. at 736.
5. *Id*. at 507, 89 S. Ct. at 737.
6. *Id*. at 514, 89 S. Ct. at 740.
7. *Id*. at 511, 89 S. Ct. at 739.
8. *Id*. at 509, 89 S. Ct. at 738.
9. *Id*. at 513, 89 S. Ct. at 740.
10. Waugh v. Board of Trustees, 237 U.S. 589, 35 S. Ct. 720 (1915).
11. *Id*. at 597, 35 S. Ct. at 723.
12. Healy v. James, 408 U.S. 169, 92 S. Ct. 2338 (1972).
13. *Id*. at 187-188, 92 S. Ct. at 2349.
14. *Id*. at 192, 92 S. Ct. at 2351-2352.
15. *Id*. at 192-193, 92 S. Ct. at 2352.
16. Papish v. Board of Curators of Univ. of Mo., 410 U.S. 667, 93 S. Ct. 1197 (1973).
17. *Id*. at 670, 93 S. Ct. at 1199.

18. Goss v. Lopez, 419 U.S. 565, 95 S. Ct. 729 (1975).
19. *Id.* at 576, 95 S. Ct. at 737.
20. *Id.* at 579, 95 S. Ct. at 738.
21. *Id.* at 579-580, 95 S. Ct. at 738-739.
22. *Id.* at 581, 95 S. Ct. at 740.
23. *Id.*
24. *Id.*
25. *Id.* at 583, 95 S. Ct. at 740-741.
26. *Id.* at 582-583, 95 S. Ct. at 740.
27. *Id.* at 584, 95 S. Ct. at 741.
28. Ingraham v. Wright, 430 U.S. 651, 97 S. Ct. 1401 (1977).
29. *Id.* at 672, 97 S. Ct. at 1413.
30. *Id.* at 660-662, 97 S. Ct. at 1406-1408.
31. *Id.* at 670, 97 S. Ct. at 1412.
32. *Id.* at 674-675, 97 S. Ct. at 1414.
33. *Id.* at 676-677, 97 S. Ct. at 1415-1416.
34. *Id.* at 677-678, 97 S. Ct. at 1416.
35. *Id.* at 681, 97 S. Ct. at 1417.
36. *Id.* at 682, 97 S. Ct. at 1418.
37. Board of Curators of Univ. of Mo. v. Horowitz, 435 U.S. 78, 98 S. Ct. 948 (1978).
38. *Id.* at 85, 98 S. Ct. at 952.
39. *Id.* at 88-90, 98 S. Ct. at 954-955.
40. Plyler v. Doe, 50 U.S.L.W. 4651 (U.S. June 15, 1982).
41. *Id.* at 4654.
42. *Id.* at 4655.
43. Board of Educ., Island Trees Union Free School Dist. No. 26 v. Pico, 50 U.S.L.W. 4831, 4832 (U.S. June 25, 1982).
44. *Id.* at 4836.
45. *Id.* at 4839.

CHAPTER 15

Liability for Civil Rights Violations

Personal Liability of School Authorities

Since 1871 those whose civil rights have been violated by actions carried out by persons purporting to act officially on behalf of government have had a right to redress through the federal courts under a statute known popularly as "Section 1983" (§ 1983).[1] Over a century later the Supreme Court addressed the question of personal liability of school board members under § 1983 for violation of student rights in a case that had become procedurally complex because of the way it had been handled in the lower federal courts.[2]

The case is significant primarily because of the Court's abstract discussion of liability. (Whether liability actually existed under the facts was not determined.) The Court also made the important points that (1) "[i]t is not the role of the federal courts to set aside decisions of school administrators which the Court may view as lacking a basis in wisdom or compassion,"[3] (2) "Section 1983 does not extend the right to relitigate in federal court evidentiary questions arising in school disciplinary proceedings or the proper construction of school regulations,"[4] and (3) "Section 1983 was not intended to be a vehicle for federal court correction of errors in the exercise of that discretion which do not rise to the level of violations of specific constitutional guarantees."[5]

On the liability question, the vote of the Court was five-to-four. The Court observed that as of that date

> [t]he nature of the immunity from awards of damages under Section 1983 available to school administrators and school board members is not a question which the lower federal courts have answered with a single voice. There is general agreement on the existence of a 'good faith' immunity, but the courts have either emphasized different factors as elements of good faith or have not given specific content to the good-faith standard.[6]

The Court summarized the common-law situation as follows:

> Common-law tradition, recognized in our prior decisions, and strong public-policy reasons also lead to a construction of Section 1983 extending a qualified good-faith immunity to

school board members from liability for damages under that section. Although there have been differing emphases and formulations of the common-law immunity of public school officials in cases of student expulsion or suspension, state courts have generally recognized that such officers should be protected from tort liability under state law for all good-faith, nonmalicious action taken to fulfill their official duties.[7]

Clearly recognized was the fact that "imposition of monetary costs for mistakes which were not unreasonable in the light of all the circumstances would undoubtedly deter even the most conscientious school decisionmaker from exercising his judgment independently, forcefully, and in a manner best serving the long-term interest of the school and the students."[8] Implicit, however, in the common-law development of a qualified immunity protecting school officials from liability for damages in lawsuits alleging improper suspensions or expulsions was the conclusion that absolute immunity "would not be justified since it would not sufficiently increase the ability of school officials to exercise their discretion in a forthright manner to warrant the absence of a remedy for students subjected to intentional or otherwise inexcusable deprivations."[9]

Noting that Congress had offered no "legislative guidance" on the matter, the Court proceeded to establish the following test for determining liability of individual school board members:

> To be entitled to a special exemption from the categorical remedial language of Section 1983 in a case in which his action violated a student's constitutional rights, a school board member, who has voluntarily undertaken the task of supervising the operation of the school and the activities of the students, must be held to a standard of conduct based not only on permissible intentions, but also on knowledge of the basic, unquestioned constitutional rights of his charges. ...
> Therefore, in the specific context of school discipline, we hold that a school board member is not immune from liability for damages under Section 1983 if he knew or reasonably should have known that the action he took within his sphere of official responsibility would violate the constitutional rights of the student affected, or if he took the action with the malicious intention to cause a deprivation of constitutional rights or other injury to the student.[10]

The Court said that such a standard was warranted "in light of the value which civil rights have in our legal system. Any lesser standard would deny much of the promise of Section 1983."[11]

The Court emphasized that it was not saying that school board members are charged with predicting the future course of constitutional law. It concluded the portion of its opinion relating to liability with the following mandate: "A compensatory award will be appropriate only if the school board member has acted with such an impermissible motivation or with such disregard of the student's clearly established constitutional rights that his action cannot reasonably be characterized as being in good faith."[12]

Violations Solely of Procedural Due Process

Three years later the Court considered the question of liability under § 1983 for the denial of procedural due process in connection with the suspension of a student when the punishment was ultimately found to be justified.[13] The Court unanimously held that under such circumstances, there could be no award of compensatory damages without proof that an injury had occurred. Stated another way, damages may not be presumed solely from the fact that procedural due process was not afforded. "Procedural due process rules are meant to protect persons not from the deprivation, but from the mistaken or unjustified deprivation of life, liberty, or property."[14] The Court said that any mental or emotional distress actually caused by the denial of due process (as distinguished from the justified deprivation itself) could be proved in the usual manner by showing the circumstances of the wrong and its effects on the plaintiff as observed by others.

Aware, however, that "a purpose of procedural due process is to convey to the individual a feeling that the government has dealt with him fairly, as well as to minimize the risk of mistaken deprivation of protected interests,"[15] the Court held that nominal damages not to exceed one dollar must be awarded when procedural due process was not followed but the penalty was justified. The Court observed that the potential liability of defendants for attorney's fees (authorized expressly in 1976 by the Civil Rights Attorney's Fees Awards Act[16]) as well as the possibility of punitive damage awards to deter or punish violators of constitutional rights would tend to assure that government agents would not deliberately ignore procedural due process rights.

Liability of School Districts

School Districts Are "Persons"

In 1978, the Court answered in the affirmative the question whether local governmental units (including school districts) were to be considered "persons" for purposes of application of § 1983.[17] In 1961, the Court had held that they were not "persons" and also that they were not liable under § 1983 for the constitutional torts of their employees.[18] Some inconsistencies implicit in rulings over the years since 1961 had been developing. In *Monell*, the Court, after reexamining the history of the adoption of § 1983 in 1871, by a seven-to-two vote, overruled the first prong of the *Monroe v. Pape* holding, thus permitting damage suits against school boards under § 1983. The Court in concluding that Congress had not intended to grant absolute immunity to local governmental bodies declined to treat the question of whether local governments could be afforded some degree of immunity short of absolute immunity.

It stated, however, that a local government may not be sued under the statute "for an injury inflicted solely by its employees or agents. Instead, it is when execution of a government's policy or custom, whether made by its lawmakers or by those whose edicts or acts may fairly be said to represent official policy, inflicts the injury that the government as an entity is responsible under Section 1983."[19] The Court, noticing that school boards differ in some legal respects from municipalities, observed that for purposes of § 1983 there was no intent of Congress to treat them differently.

> In the wake of our decisions [in desegregation cases brought against school boards for equitable relief under Section 1983], Congress not only has shown no hostility to federal-court decisions against school boards, but it has indeed rejected efforts to strip the federal courts of jurisdiction over school boards. Moreover, recognizing that school boards are often defendants in school desegregation suits, which have almost without exception been Section 1983 suits, Congress has twice passed legislation authorizing grants to school boards to assist them in complying with federal-court decrees.[20]

No Immunity for "Good Faith"

Less than two years later the Court answered the question reserved in the *Monell* case, namely, whether local governments were to be afforded some form of official immunity short of absolute immunity.[21] By a one-vote margin, the Court answered "no," and held that a municipality is not permitted to assert the good faith of its officers or agents as a defense to liability under § 1983. The Court said that its "rejection of a construction of Section 1983 that would accord municipalities a qualified immunity for their good-faith constitutional violations is compelled both by the legislative purpose in enacting the statute and by considerations of public policy."[22] The purpose of the statute was to provide protection to persons wronged by misuse of power possessed by virtue of state law and made possible by the wrongdoer's having the authority of state law. A damages remedy was deemed by the Court to be a vital component of any arrangement for vindicating the Constitution's guarantees, but under *Wood v. Strickland*, there could be damages assessed against individuals only for violations of clearly established constitutional rights. By holding the governmental entity liable for damages not only would those illegally treated be compensated, but officials would likely be more careful in conducting the affairs of government and would supervise the conduct of their subordinates more carefully. Also, reasoned the Court, constitutional development would not be impeded by the discouragement of suits because of difficulties of recovering damages. Furthermore, said the Court, "even where some constitutional development could not have been foreseen by municipal officials, it is fairer to allocate any resulting financial loss to the inevitable costs of government borne by all the taxpayers, than to allow its impact to be felt solely by those whose rights, albeit newly recognized, have been violated."[23]

The Court said that doctrines of tort law had changed significantly over the past century and that views of governmental responsibility should properly reflect that evolution. It observed that the principle of "equitable loss-spreading" had joined "fault" as another factor to be considered in connection with award of damages. It concluded:

> We believe that today's decision, together with prior precedents in the area, properly allocates these costs among the three principals in the scenario of the Section 1983 cause of action: the victim of the constitutional deprivation; the officer whose conduct caused the injury; and the public, as represented by the municipal entity. The innocent individual who is harmed by an abuse of governmental authority is assured that he will be compensated for his injury. The offending official, so long as he conducts himself in good faith, may go about his business secure in the knowledge that a qualified immunity will protect him from personal liability for damages that are more appropriately chargeable to the populace as a whole. And the public will be forced to bear only the costs of injury inflicted by the "execution of a government's policy or custom, whether made by its lawmakers or by those whose edicts or acts may fairly be said to represent official policy."[24]

Coverage of Section 1983

Two months later, the Court decided two other cases pertaining to the use of § 1983 as a basis for suits against government authorities. In one, the Court held by a six-to-three vote that the words "and laws" in the § 1983 phrase "secured by the Constitution and laws" encompassed all federal statutes, not only civil rights or equal rights law.[25] Recognizing that "one conclusion which emerges clearly is that the legislative history does not permit a definitive answer,"[26] the majority elected to follow "the plain language" and not limit the scope of "laws." The case involved an application of the Social Security Act by a state agency which had been challenged successfully in the state courts of Maine.

In *Maine v. Thiboutot,* the Court also held that attorneys' fees properly were awarded to the plaintiffs under the federal legislation providing that such could be granted by a court to the prevailing party (other than the federal government) in a proceeding to enforce certain civil rights statutes, including § 1983. The Court said that, as § 1983 was listed in the fees statute along with substantive civil rights statutes, the provision covered any § 1983 action whether brought in federal or state courts.

In the second case pertaining to the use of § 1983 as a basis for suits against government authorities, the Court unanimously held that "prevailing party" could include those who accepted a remedy through settlement rather than litigation.[27]

---

1. 42 U.S.C. § 1983 (1976). *See infra* Appendix C.
2. Wood v. Strickland, 420 U.S. 308, 95 S. Ct. 992 (1975).
3. *Id.* at 326, 95 S. Ct. at 1003.
4. *Id.*
5. *Id.*
6. *Id.* at 315, 95 S. Ct. at 997.
7. *Id.* at 318, 95 S. Ct. at 999.
8. *Id.* at 319-320, 95 S. Ct. at 999-1000.
9. *Id.* at 320, 95 S. Ct. at 1000.
10. *Id.* at 322, 95 S. Ct. at 1000-1001.
11. *Id.*, 95 S. Ct. at 1001.
12. *Id.*
13. Carey v. Piphus, 435 U.S. 247, 98 S. Ct. 1042 (1978).
14. *Id.* at 259, 98 S. Ct. at 1050.
15. *Id.* at 262, 98 S. Ct. at 1051.
16. 42 U.S.C. § 1988 (1976).
17. Monell v. Department of Social Services of City of N.Y., 436 U.S. 658, 98 S. Ct. 2018 (1978).
18. Monroe v. Pape, 365 U.S. 167, 81 S. Ct. 473 (1961).
19. Monell, 436 U.S. at 694, 98 S. Ct. at 2037-2038.
20. *Id.* at 696-697, 98 S. Ct. at 2039.
21. Owen v. City of Independence, Mo., 445 U.S. 622, 100 S. Ct. 1398 (1980).
22. *Id.* at 650, 100 S. Ct. at 1415.
23. *Id.* at 655, 100 S. Ct. at 1417.
24. *Id.* at 657, 100 S. Ct. at 1419.
25. Maine v. Thiboutot, 448 U.S. 1, 100 S. Ct. 2502 (1980).
26. *Id.* at 7, 100 S. Ct. at 2505.
27. Maher v. Gagne, 448 U.S. 122, 100 S. Ct. 2570 (1980).

CHAPTER 16

Structure and Finance of School Districts

Legal Status of School Districts

As education is a state (rather than federal) function, it is left to each state to organize and finance education as it sees fit, subject only to federal constitutional restrictions such as those discussed in the preceding chapters. Since school districts are subdivisions of a state, they are in most respects subject to the constitutional and common law applicable to municipal corporations in matters of operation and finance. A major general exception, however, is that school districts are considered to be direct agencies of the state rather than purely local governmental entities. Also, any implied powers of school districts are restricted to educational matters, rather than extended to general health, safety, and welfare matters that are within the purview of municipalities.

The right of a state to alter boundaries of school districts and to provide for the reallocation of their assets and liabilities has been specifically upheld by the Supreme Court.[1] The major federal contention raised in that 1905 case was that the particular act violated the impairment of contracts clause of the Constitution. The Court tersely disposed of that argument by referring to a decision of 1875 in which the Court had held that it was within a state's power to distribute debt burdens and property among subdivisions it had created when it altered county lines.[2] Subdivisions have no contractual rights against the state to assets or to boundaries.

School Finance and Equal Protection

In 1973, by a five-to-four vote, the Supreme Court held that the basic method used in forty-nine states for financing education through a combination of state and local funds did not violate the equal protection clause of the Constitution.[3] (Hawaii has only one school district.) The idea of trying a fourteenth amendment assault on existing finance systems, which tolerated (or encouraged) uneven per pupil expenditures among the school districts in a state, developed in the mid-1960's after the Supreme Court for a decade had been interpreting the equal protection clause in an expanded way to grant certain rights to blacks excluded from facilities and services because of race, to voters whose votes were diluted because of boundaries of voting districts, and to criminal defendants who were unable to take full advantage of legal safeguards because of indigence.

Citing such cases, the Supreme Court of California in 1971 had rendered a decision that in the year and a half before its federal constitutional theory was repudiated by the Supreme Court of the United States had probably generated more reaction in both educational and political circles than any other decision of a single state court.[4] The California court's opinion, however, remained controlling in California because a footnote stated that the California Constitution mandated what the court erroneously had thought the federal Constitution did. The decision was not rendered after an evidentiary trial, but set forth the view that if the facts were proved, a revamping of school financing would be required to prevent discrepancies in expenditures based on property values in local districts. When, after remand, the merits were before the Supreme Court of California, that court reaffirmed its position, but by a vote of four-to-three rather than the original six-to-one.[5]

A three-judge federal district court in Texas followed the California court's reasoning and ordered that the taxing and financing system for public schools in Texas be altered within a period of two years so that the educational opportunities afforded Texas public school students would not be a function of wealth other than the wealth of the state as a whole.[6] The Texas system of financing public schools did not differ in essence from plans in most other states. A statewide minimum foundation program was established and financed by state and local revenue. The amount of the contribution of a local school district to the program reflected the relative taxpaying ability of the district measured by assessable property. Local districts could supplement the foundation program by additionally levied local property taxes.

The Supreme Court, in *San Antonio Independent School District v. Rodriguez*, set out its framework for analysis as follows:

> We must decide, first, whether the Texas system of financing public education operates to the disadvantage of some suspect class or impinges upon a fundamental right explicitly or implicitly protected by the Constitution, thereby requiring strict judicial scrutiny. If so, the judgment of the District Court should be affirmed. If not, the Texas scheme must still be examined to determine whether it rationally furthers some legitimate, articulated state purpose and therefore does not constitute an invidious discrimination in violation of the Equal Protection Clause of the Fourteenth Amendment.[7]

Its first conclusion was that the proper test to be applied was the usual rational basis test, not the exceptional strict scrutiny test. The opinion stated that the form of wealth discrimination discovered by the lower court and by several other courts that had recently struck down school financing laws in other states was unlike any of the forms of wealth discrimination previously reviewed by the Court. It said:

> Rather than focusing on the unique features of the alleged discrimination, the courts in these cases have virtually assumed their findings of a suspect classification through a simplistic process of analysis: since, under the traditional systems of financing public schools, some poorer people receive less expensive educations than other more affluent people, these systems discriminate on the basis of wealth. This approach largely ignores the hard threshold questions, including whether it makes a difference for purposes of consideration under the Constitution that the class of disadvantaged "poor" cannot be identified or defined in customary equal protection terms, and whether the relative—rather than absolute— nature of the asserted deprivation is of significant consequence. Before a State's laws and the justifications for the classifications they create are subjected to strict judicial scrutiny, we think these threshold considerations must be analyzed more closely than they were in the court below.[8]

The Court observed that plaintiffs presented "no definitive description of the classifying facts or delineation of the disfavored class."[9] The Court pointed out that in prior cases the "individuals, or groups of individuals, who constituted the class discriminated against . . . shared two distinguishing characteristics: because of their impecunity they were completely unable to pay for some desired benefit, and as a consequence, they sustained an absolute deprivation of a meaningful opportunity to enjoy that benefit."[10] In the Texas situation, no one was completely deprived of educational opportunity, for there was a minimum foundation program. The Court observed that in cases of wealth classifications, it previously granted relief only on the basis of lack of access to a meaningful quality of a service, not to a desirable quality. When an indigent is entitled to an attorney at public expense, it is not to the best attorney, nor to an attorney whose services can be purchased only with a particular sum of money.

A serious flaw in the presentation of the original plaintiffs was the absence of a showing that the poorest families, in fact, resided in the districts with the least property values. The Supreme Court cited this gap, and, referring to a Connecticut study, stated that there is reason to believe that the poorest families are not necessarily clustered in the poorest property districts. Also, it was alleged that the system was discriminatory because expenditures per child showed an inverse variation with the wealth of the child's family. The evidence, however, did not support such a conclusion. The affidavit submitted by the plaintiffs did show that the ten wealthiest-in-property districts in the sample had the highest median family incomes and spent the most on education, and also that the four poorest districts had the lowest family incomes and devoted the least amount of money to education. However, the correlation was inverted for the remaining ninety-six districts, that is, the districts that spent next to the most money on education were populated by families having next to the lowest median family incomes while the districts spending next to the least had next to the highest median family incomes. The Court commented, "It is evident that, even if the conceptual questions were answered favorably to appellees, no factual basis exists upon which to found a claim of comparative wealth discrimination."[11]

In summary on the point, the Court said:

> However described, it is clear that appellees' suit asks this Court to extend its most exacting scrutiny to review a system that allegedly discriminates against a large, diverse, and amorphous class, unified only by the common factor of residence in districts that happen to have less taxable wealth than other districts. The system of alleged discrimination and the class it defines have none of the traditional indicia of suspectness: the class is not saddled with such disabilities, or subjected to such a history of purposeful unequal treatment, or relegated to such a position of political powerlessness as to command extraordinary protection from the majoritarian political process.[12]

On the question of whether education is a "fundamental" right in the constitutional sense, the Court, after reviewing a number of its prior cases, stated:

> The lesson of these cases in addressing the question now before the Court is plain. It is not the province of this Court to create substantive constitutional rights in the name of guaranteeing equal protection of the laws. Thus the key to discovering whether education is "fundamental" is not to be found in comparisons of the relative societal significance of education as opposed to subsistence or housing. Nor is it to be found by weighing whether education is as important as the right to travel. Rather, the answer lies in assessing whether there is a right to education explicitly or implicitly guaranteed by the Constitution.[13]

The Court further commented that "the undisputed importance of education will not alone cause this Court to depart from the usual standard for reviewing a State's social and economic legislation."[14] The Court expressly declined to accept the argument that because education is crucial to the exercise of freedom of speech and the exercise of the vote, it should be declared fundamental in the constitutional sense, particularly since no evidence was presented to indicate that the present levels of educational expenditure in Texas provided an education falling short of minimum considerations.

Having found neither a suspect class nor a fundamental right, the Court then examined the Texas system of finance under the traditional standard of review for the equal protection clause (the standard that the state's system must bear some rational relationship to legitimate state purposes). The Court found to be rational the state's desire to maintain a degree of local autonomy in connection with education. Although recognizing that reliance on local property taxation for school revenues provides less freedom of choice with respect to expenditures for some districts than for others, the Court said the existence of some inequalities in the manner in which a state's rationale is achieved is not alone a sufficient basis for striking down an entire system. Nor is it fatal that the state's interest may be achieved by other methods resulting in less drastic disparities in expenditures. "Only where state action impinges on the exercise of fundamental constitutional rights or liberties must it be found to have chosen the least restrictive alternative."[15]

The Court emphasized its concern about intruding in an area left to the states by the Constitution, especially when massive change was at issue in forty-nine states, the present system of state-local financing had been carefully developed over many years, alternative finance methods had not been tested, and experts disagreed on the effects of many factors related to finance plans. The Court said that although "practical considerations, of course, play no role in the adjudication of the constitutional issues presented . . . they serve to highlight the wisdom of the traditional limitations on this Court's function."[16]

The Court's opinion closed with the following:

> We hardly need add that this Court's action today is not to be viewed as placing its judicial imprimatur on the status quo. The need is apparent for reform in tax systems which may well have relied too long and too heavily on the local property tax. And certainly innovative thinking as to public education, its methods, and its funding is necessary to assure both a higher level of quality and greater uniformity of opportunity. These matters merit the continued attention of the scholars who

already have contributed much by their challenges. But the ultimate solutions must come from the lawmakers and from the democratic pressures of those who elect them.[17]

Voting Rights

One Person-One Vote Principle

The Supreme Court rendered five of its many decisions in the voting rights area in cases directly involving school districts. The first was in 1967 in a case in which the question was whether the one person-one vote principle applied to the selection of county school boards in Michigan, the members of which were elected by delegates from local boards.[18] Each local board had one vote, regardless of population. The Court unanimously upheld the system. It said that the arrangement was basically appointive, rather than elective, and that, therefore, one person-one vote did not apply. Although school district electors could vote for the members of the local boards, they were given no statutory voice in deciding whom the delegates from the local boards would choose for membership on the county board. The Court said that the Constitution does not bar the state from making the county board appointive, either by an elected official or as was done here. There was no challenge to the election system for local board members.

Three years later, the Court decided a case involving a statute that provided for members of a consolidated junior college district board to be elected by the electors of the constituent school districts on the basis of the number of persons between the ages of six and twenty years residing in each district.[19] The Court, by a five-to-three vote, held that "the Fourteenth Amendment requires that the trustees of this junior college district be apportioned in a manner which does not deprive any voter of his right to have his own vote given as much weight, as far as is practicable, as that of any other voter in the junior college district."[20] As applied to the present situation, the Court said that "when members of an elected body are chosen from separate districts, each district must be established on a basis that will insure, as far as is practicable, that equal numbers of voters can vote for proportionally equal numbers of officials."[21] The Court found that the challenged statutory system failed to pass constitutional muster primarily because of a built-in bias in favor of small districts.

A third one person-one vote case was decided by a seven-to-two vote in 1971.[22] The question was the constitutionality of a state provision that required any bonded indebtedness or any increase of tax rate beyond certain limits to be approved by sixty percent of the voters in a referendum election. Obviously, such an arrangement gives more weight mathematically to a vote cast in the negative. However, in upholding the constitutionality of the provision, the Court said that it does not deny or dilute the voting power of an elector on the basis of a group characteristic such as that of geographic location, the factor in the preceding *Hadley* case, and the Constitution, itself, provides that certain matters be decided by more than a simple majority vote. As for the issuance of bonds, the Court found that it is not irrational for a state to have a requirement of more than a majority because the commitment is partially that of minors and of those yet unborn. The Court said:

> Wisely or not, the people of the State of West Virginia have long since resolved to remove from a simple majority vote the choice on certain decisions as to what indebtedness may be incurred and what taxes their children will bear.
>
> We conclude that so long as such provisions do not discriminate against or authorize discrimination against any identifiable class they do not violate the Equal Protection Clause.[23]

Qualifications to Vote in School Elections

A key case related to qualifications of voters was decided within the context of public education. A six-to-three decision in 1969 invalidated certain prescriptions in New York for voting in school district elections.[24] In essence, the statutory requirement was that an elector must own or lease taxable property within the district, be the spouse of one who owns or leases property, or be a parent or guardian of a child enrolled in a local public school. The challenge was brought by a bachelor who lived rent-free with his parents.

The Court said that a compelling state interest must be shown if a statute grants the right to vote to some bona fide residents of requisite age and citizenship and denies the franchise to others. Although not rejecting outright the possibility that the right to vote in an election could be limited to fewer than all persons voting in general elections, the Court concluded that the New York provision did not, in fact, accomplish the purpose of limiting the franchise to those primarily interested in and/or primarily affected by the results of the election "with sufficient precision to justify denying appellant the franchise."[25] The classifications, the Court observed, "permit inclusion of many persons who have, at best, a remote and indirect interest in school affairs and, on the other hand, exclude others who have a distinct and direct interest in the school meeting decisions."[26]

In 1970, a unanimous court rejected the requirement of ownership of real property in the district as a qualification for membership on a board of education.[27] The Court declared that although those challenging the arrangement had no right to be public office holders, the state "may not deny to some the privilege of holding public office that it extends to others on the basis of distinctions that violate federal constitutional guarantees."[28] The Court found that the Georgia requirement did not meet even the traditional test for application of substantive due process in that it was not rationally related to achieving a valid state objective. It thus declined to say whether a compelling interest must be shown on an office-holding, as distinguished from a voting, qualification. Indeed, the state's argument that anyone who seriously aspired to county school-board membership "would be able to obtain a conveyance of the single square inch of land" required was taken by the Court as an "indication of the insubstantiality of [Georgia's] interest in preserving"[29] the requirement.

Federal-State Relations

In 1976, the Supreme Court declared a provision of the Fair Labor Standards Act applicable to states and their political subdivisions unconstitutional in a case of great import in the area of federal-state relations.[30] The five-to-four vote invalidated a 1974 amendment that had extended the minimum-wage and maximum-hours-before-overtime provisions of the Act to all employees of state and local government units. The key reasoning of the Court was that the commerce clause of the Constitution does not enable Congress "to directly displace the States' freedom to structure integral operations in areas of traditional governmental functions."[31] In holding that the sovereignty of the states would be impaired if Congress could dictate in the area of wages and hours of employees, the Court expressly overruled a 1968 opinion[32] which had allowed Congress to extend the Act beyond private employees to employees of state hospitals, institutions, and schools.

The rationale supporting the 1976 decision would seem to prevent Congress from either placing all public employees under the National Labor Relations Act or enacting a separate statute requiring and regulating collective bargaining for state and local government employees. "Congress may not exercise [commerce clause] power so as to force directly upon the States its choices as to how essential decisions regarding the conduct of integral governmental functions are to be made."[33]

1. Attorney General of State of Mich *ex rel.* Kies v. Lowrey, 199 U.S. 233, 26 S. Ct. 27 (1905).
2. Laramie County v. Albany County, 92 U.S. 307 (1875).
3. San Antonio Indep. School Dist. v. Rodriguez, 411 U.S. 1, 93 S. Ct. 1278 (1973).
4. Serrano v. Priest, 5 Cal.3d 584, 96 Cal. Rptr. 601, 487 P.2d 1241 (Cal. 1971) [hereinafter cited as Serrano I].
5. Serrano v. Priest, 18 Cal.3d 728, 135 Cal. Rptr. 345, 557 P.2d 929 (Cal. 1976), *cert. denied* 432 U.S. 907, 97 S. Ct. 2951 (1977) [hereinafter cited as Serrano II].
6. Rodriguez v. San Antonio Indep. School Dist., 337 F. Supp. 280 (W.D. Tex. 1971).
7. San Antonio Indep. School Dist. v. Rodriguez, 411 U.S. at 17, 93 S. Ct. at 1288.
8. *Id.* at 19, 93 S. Ct. at 1289.
9. *Id.*
10. *Id.* at 20, 93 S. Ct. at 1290.
11. *Id.* at 27, 93 S. Ct. at 1293.
12. *Id.* at 28, 93 S. Ct. at 1294.
13. *Id.* at 33, 93 S. Ct. at 1297.
14. *Id.* at 35, 93 S. Ct. at 1297-1298.
15. *Id.* at 51, 93 S. Ct. at 1306.
16. *Id.* at 58, 93 S. Ct. at 1309.
17. *Id.* at 58-59, 93 S. Ct. at 1309-1310.
18. Sailors v. Board of Educ. of County of Kent, 387 U.S. 105, 87 S. Ct. 1549 (1967).
19. Hadley v. Junior College Dist. of Metropolitan K.C., Mo., 379 U.S. 50, 90 S. Ct. 791 (1970).
20. *Id.* at 52, 90 S. Ct. at 793.
21. *Id.* at 56, 90 S. Ct. at 795.
22. Gordon v. Lance, 403 U.S. 1, 91 S. Ct. 1889 (1971).
23. *Id.* at 7, 91 S. Ct. at 1892.
24. Kramer v. Union Free School Dist. No. 15, 395 U.S. 621, 89 S. Ct. 1886 (1969).
25. *Id.* at 632, 89 S. Ct. at 1892.
26. *Id.*
27. Turner v. Fouche, 396 U.S. 346, 90 S. Ct. 532 (1970).
28. *Id.* at 362-363, 90 S. Ct. at 541.
29. *Id.* at 363, 90 S. Ct. at 542.
30. National League of Cities v. Usery, 426 U.S. 833, 96 S. Ct. 2465 (1976).
31. *Id.* at 852, 96 S. Ct. at 2474.
32. Maryland v. Wirtz, 392 U.S. 183, 88 S. Ct. 2017 (1968).
33. National League of Cities v. Usery, 426 U.S. at 855, 96 S. Ct. at 2476.

CHAPTER 17

Federal Legislation Affecting Education

The Supreme Court, as the highest federal court, has the responsibility for determining the meaning and scope of federal legislation as well as its constitutionality. The exercise of this function as applied to employment discrimination legislation is treated in chapter 13 and as applied to liability for violations of civil rights in chapter 15. Additional statutory construction of importance to education is presented in this chapter.

Elementary and Secondary Education Act of 1965

Title I of the Elementary and Secondary Education Act of 1965[1] makes federal funds available to local public education agencies for the purpose of better serving the educational needs of "educationally deprived children" in both public and nonpublic schools. In 1974, the Supreme Court, in a case with a complex procedural history, decided two points of substantive consequence by a vote of eight-to-one.[2] The first point was that the Act did not preempt state constitutional spending proscriptions as a condition for receipt of federal funds. The Court said that if state-level prohibitions prevent a particular use of the funds in nonpublic schools, services should be utilized that are not banned under state law. The second holding was that the Act required "comparable" services for nonpublic school children, not "identical" services.

Those instituting the suit had sought instructors, paid with federal funds, to teach remedial courses on the premises of private schools. The Court said that the substantive matter was not properly before it for review. (The next year, however, the Court ruled that the state of Pennsylvania was prevented by the first amendment from furnishing on-the-premises remedial instruction in parochial schools.[3]) In *Wheeler v. Barrera*, the Court added:

> [I]f the State is unwilling or unable to develop a plan which is comparable, while using Title I teachers in public but not in private schools, it may develop and submit an acceptable plan which eliminates the use of on-the-premises instruction in the public schools, and instead, resorts to other means, such as neutral sites or summer programs....[4]

Of course, as an alternative, the state could decline to participate in the federally funded program.

Title VI of Civil Rights Act of 1964

Title VI of the Civil Rights Act of 1964[5] bars discrimination based on "race, color, or national origin" in activities receiving federal financial assistance. In 1974, the Court unanimously held that the provision was violated by the failure of the school board in San Francisco to take any significant steps to deal with crippling language deficiencies of some 1,800 of the 2,800 students of Chinese ancestry.[6] Although the equal protection clause was invoked by the plaintiffs, the Court specifically refused to discuss its application because the case could be decided on the basis of Title VI. Compliance with the implementing regulations of the Department of Health, Education and Welfare (HEW) was part of a contract signed by the board as a condition for receiving federal funds. The regulations required that school districts receiving funds take steps to eliminate language deficiencies that prevented students of a particular race, color, or national origin from obtaining the education generally available to other students in the school system.

The Court took no position on what educational techniques were called for. It said:

> No specific remedy [was] urged upon us. Teaching English to the students of Chinese ancestry who do not speak the language is one choice. Giving instructions to this group in Chinese is another. There may be others. Petitioners ask only that the Board of Education be directed to apply its expertise to the problem and rectify the situation.[7]

Referring to an HEW regulation, the Court said, "Discrimination [on the basis of national origin] is barred which has that *effect* [emphasis in original] even though no purposeful design is present...."[8] That sentence, written by Justice Douglas, was destined to trouble the Court. In 1978, Justices Brennan, White, Marshall, and Blackmun said:

> We recognize that *Lau*, especially when read in light of our subsequent decision in *Washington v. Davis*, which rejected the general proposition that governmental action is unconstitutional solely because it has a racially disproportionate impact, may be read as being predicated upon the view that, at least under some circumstances, Title VI proscribes conduct which might not be prohibited by the Constitution. Since we are now of the opinion ... that Title VI's standard, applicable alike to

public and private recipients of federal funds, is no broader than the Constitution's, we have serious doubts concerning the correctness of what appears to be the premise of that decision.[9]

Justice Powell, in the *Bakke* case, wrote, "In view of the clear legislative intent, Title VI must be held to proscribe only those racial classifications that would violate the Equal Protection Clause or the Fifth Amendment."[10] The other four Justices said that there was no need for a ruling on the point. Justice Stewart, however, during the next year said flatly, "Title VI prohibits only purposeful discrimination."[11] Thus, by 1979, six sitting Justices had repudiated the apparent acceptance in *Lau* of an *effects* test (rather than a *purpose* test) for discrimination under Title VI. The other three Justices (Burger, Rehnquist, and Stevens) had not commented on the point.

Emergency School Aid Act of 1972

In 1979, the Court construed an aspect of the eligibility requirements for local school districts to receive federal financial assistance under the Emergency School Aid Act of 1972.[12] The Act provides funds to school districts for eliminating "minority group isolation." Funds are limited and school districts compete for the funds. The specific question in the case of the *Board of Education of City School District of City of New York v. Harris*[13] was whether the Department of Health, Education and Welfare (HEW) could declare a school district ineligible for funds if there were some schools in the district that were identifiable as existing for either minority or nonminority students solely based upon the race of faculty with the situation not resulting from any intentional discriminatory practices by the board. In other words, can ineligibility be predicated on a showing of discriminatory impact of policies, or must discriminatory intent be proven?

New York City's application for funds had been rejected by HEW because of the existing pattern of teacher assignments. The board contended that the statistical disparaties resulted from a combination of factors including state statutes, the local collective bargaining contract, wishes of individual black principals, desires of individual parent associations, and powers of the state-mandated community school boards. HEW found that these reasons were not adequate to rebut the statistical evidence, but made no findings of intentional discriminatory acts by the board.

By a vote of six-to-three, the Supreme Court held that, although the statutory language regarding ineligibility "suffers from imprecision of expression and less-than-careful draftsmanship,"[14] the overall approach of Congress in the Act indicated that funds were not to be made available to districts having policies that had a discriminatory impact regardless of the motivation for the policies. As the HEW regulation required only that schools not be racially identifiable by faculty assignments, it was held to be consistent with the statute. The justifications offered by the board expressly were not considered by the Court because the board had not contested the conclusion of HEW that they were insufficient, a conclusion that had been supported by the lower courts.

The Court summarized as follows:

> In sum, we hold that discriminatory impact is the standard by which ineligibility under ESAA is to be measured . . . , that a prima facie case of discriminatory impact may be made by a proper statistical study . . . , and that the burden of rebutting that case [is] on the Board.[15]

Title IX of Education Amendments of 1972

Title IX of the Education Amendments of 1972,[16] which prohibits discrimination on the basis of sex in education programs or activities receiving federal financial assistance, was first construed by the Supreme Court a decade after its enactment.[17] The basic issue in the 1982 case was whether the statute covered employment. Lower federal courts were not in agreement as to the validity of the regulations governing employment that had been promulgated by the Department of Health, Education and Welfare (HEW).[18]

By a vote of six-to-three, the Court held that Congress intended the provision to encompass employees in federally funded education programs, as well as students. The Court based its decision on the use in the statute of the word "person," the legislative history of the provision, and several post-enactment events. The Court, however, emphasized that the statute was "program-specific," that is, federal funds may be withheld from an activity only if discrimination is found in connection with that program.

As there had been no trials on the merits because the two defendant school boards had challenged the authority of HEW to adopt *any* rules affecting employees, it was necessary for the Court to remand the cases for trial. The Court expressly declined to "undertake to define 'program' in this opinion."[19] It observed:

> Neither school board opposed HEW's investigation into its employment practices on the grounds that the complaining employees' salaries were not funded by federal money, that the

employees did not work in an education program that received federal assistance, or that the discrimination they allegedly suffered did not affect a federally funded program.[20]

Education for All Handicapped Children Act of 1975

In 1982, the Court rendered its first opinion on the Education for All Handicapped Children Act of 1975 (widely known as "P.L. 94-142")[21] in a case in which, by a vote of six-to-three, it held the act does not require a school district to furnish a sign-language interpreter for a deaf elementary school student "who is receiving substantial specialized instruction and related services, and who is performing above average in the regular classrooms of a public school system."[22]

In essence, the substantive parts of the act provide that as a condition for receipt of federal funds, a state must establish a detailed plan for assuring all handicapped children the right to a "free appropriate public education," tailored to each child's needs through an "individualized educational program" (IEP) developed with the participation of the child's parents. The Court said that the act did not require a state "to maximize the potential of each handicapped child commensurate with the opportunity provided nonhandicapped children.... Rather, Congress sought primarily to identify and evaluate handicapped children and to provide them with access to a free public education."[23] The Court summarized as follows:

> Insofar as a State is required to provide a handicapped child with a "free appropriate public education," we hold that it satisfies this requirement by providing personalized instruction with sufficient support services to permit the child to benefit educationally from that instruction. Such instruction and services must be provided at public expense, must meet the State's educational standards, must approximate the grade levels used in the State's regular education, and must comport with the child's IEP. In addition, the IEP, and therefore the personalized instruction, should be formulated in accordance with the requirements of the Act and, if the child is being educated in the regular classrooms of the public education system, should be reasonably calculated to enable the child to achieve passing marks and advance from grade to grade.[24]

---

1. 20 U.S.C. § 2701 (1976).
2. Wheeler v. Barrera, 417 U.S. 402, 94 S. Ct. 2274 (1974).
3. Meek v. Pittenger, 421 U.S. 349, 95 S. Ct. 1753 (1975). *See* Chapter 5.
4. Wheeler v. Barrera, 417 U.S. at 425, 94 S. Ct. at 2287.
5. 42 U.S.C. § 2000d (1976). *See* Appendix C.

6. Lau v. Nichols, 414 U.S. 563, 94 S. Ct. 786 (1974).

7. *Id.* at 564-565, 94 S. Ct. at 787.

8. *Id.* at 568, 94 S. Ct. at 789.

9. Regents of University of Cal. v. Bakke, 438 U.S. 265, 352, 98 S. Ct. 2733, 2779 (1978). In this case the Court invalidated an admissions program at a state medical school (without a history of segregation) that allowed "minority" students to have sixteen seats exclusively and also to be eligible to compete for the remaining eighty-four seats. No opinion was supported by a majority of Justices. Five Justices said, however, that consideration of race as *one* factor in a university admissions program was not unconstitutional. The other four said that they believed the plan in California was barred by Title VI because race was the *only* factor for the sixteen seats. They made no comment on "race as *one* factor."

10. *Id.* at 287, 98 S. Ct. at 2746.

11. Board of Educ. of City School Dist. of City of N.Y. v. Harris, 444 U.S. 130, 160, 100 S. Ct. 363, 379 (1979) (Stewart, J., dissenting).

12. 20 U.S.C. § 1601 (1976).

13. 444 U.S. 130, 100 S. Ct. 363 (1979).

14. *Id.* at 138, 100 S. Ct. at 368.

15. *Id.* at 151-152, 100 S. Ct. at 375.

16. 20 U.S.C. § 1681 (1976). *See* Appendix C.

17. North Haven Bd. of Educ. v. Bell, 102 S. Ct. 1912 (1982).

18. As of 1980, the regulations are administered by the Department of Education.

19. North Haven Bd. of Educ., 102 S. Ct. at 1927.

20. *Id.*

21. 20 U.S.C. § 1401 (1976).

22. Board of Educ. of Hendrick Hudson Central School Dist. v. Rowley, 50 U.S.L.W. 4925, 4932 (U.S. June 28, 1982).

23. *Id.*

24. *Id.* at 4932-4933.

CHAPTER 18

Some Observations

The preceding chapters have dealt objectively and in some depth with decisions of the Supreme Court of the United States directly affecting public education. It is intended that the presentation will serve the reader as a foundation for understanding exactly what the Court has ruled and for contemplating the impact of the cases on education and society.

One perusing contemporary discussions of specific Supreme Court cases in both popular and professional media must be struck by the uneven nature of the coverage as to accuracy regarding the Court's holding, the quality of analysis of the Court's reasoning, and the place of the case in the expanse of constitutional law. Also, in many instances, it would appear that attention by writers to possible or favored implications of a decision is allowed to obscure its true parameters as actually set out in the opinion of the Court. Unfortunately, such observations sometimes also apply to historic as well as contemporary treatment of cases.

There is simply no substitute for reading the full opinion of the Court on matters of considerable concern to an individual. Even correct quotations and competent analyses may not be fully comprehended by the reader of a secondary source. In reality, most decisions of the Supreme Court on constitutional questions do not require extensive legal training for an understanding of the substantive, as distinguished from the technical, aspects. Part of the effectiveness of the Supreme Court as an instrument of government has been its ability to communicate to people of ordinary intelligence and experience about that document which frames the societal part of their lives.

It is the firm conclusion of the author that the Supreme Court not only has been very faithful to its role of constitutional interpreter, but has done so in a remarkably responsible manner. It has maintained stability and a wholesome degree of predictability while concurrently expanding the scope of the Constitution to encompass changing knowledge and changing attitudes. Development of constitutional law has been steady rather than spasmodic.

To be sure there have been key decisions that were critical in the literal sense of being turning points that established new directions. Inevitably, there are "cases of first impression" in which the Court enters new fields of decisionmaking. Since World War II, the emphasis on rights and liberties of individuals and classes of persons has led the Court to answer constitutional questions in domains not theretofore addressed. In such areas, the initial decisions tend to establish broad contours and to present broad principles which subsequently must be applied to many emerging situations. As more of the latter are brought through lower courts and as the issues raised comport with the criteria for Supreme Court review noted in chapter 1, the Court refines the general principles, establishes limitations, and makes distinctions between differing sets of facts. The preceding chapters were structured to help make this process evident for the various major themes.

The sphere of race and education offers perhaps the best example of a long procession of cases in which the questions before the Court not only became increasingly specific after 1954, but became progressively more difficult to decide. Thus, votes of the Justices on cases eroded from nine-to-zero on the 1954 to 1971 cases to five-to-four on some later ones as competing considerations became more evenly balanced. The same phenomenon is observable in the series of cases concerning teacher loyalty oaths. Differences in wording of the oaths led from unanimous invalidations to divided votes to invalidate, to divided votes to uphold, and finally to the unanimous acceptance of language patterned after the presidential oath in the Constitution.

In the area of church and pre-college education, no decision has been unanimous. Yet there has been a development and articulation by the Court of criteria by which to judge the constitutionality of any arrangement. This formulation, presented in *Lemon v. Kurtzman*[1] in 1971 and derived from opinions of the Court rendered over the preceding twenty-four years, can be utilized by anyone. The subsequent applications by the Court are of assistance in assessing legal nuances of new fact situations. Sometimes, however, the equities are almost evenly balanced, and as the Court recognized in 1980, there is no "litmus-paper test to distinguish permissible from impermissible aid to religiously oriented schools."[2]

Due to the nature of the federal questions that may arise in education cases and that warrant Supreme Court resolution, it should not be surprising that frequently the Justices are not of one mind as to proper outcomes. Indeed, the complexity of constitutional questions, in general, is probably the reason for the size of the Supreme Court bench. When competing considerations are relatively strong, consensus on the ultimate outcome would be an unrealistic expectation. If society itself finds a balance delicate, the Court is likely to reflect this situation on questions that permit reasonable people to differ on whether the Constitution is violated and precisely why it is or is not.

On the latter point, the appropriateness of the writing of concurring opinions is a subject of theoretical dispute. Probably there is no general answer as to whether they help or hinder the development and understanding of case law. Tradition leaves it to each Justice who agrees with the majority vote on the answer to a question to determine whether he will put into the record anything not included to his satisfaction in the majority opinion of the Court on the particular question.

Concurring opinions have been particularly frequent in the church and education area. A most remarkable fact is their omission on substantive points for almost two decades of desegregation cases beginning with *Brown I.*[3] Evidently, the Justices realized the necessity of having only one semantic presentation of this body of constitutional law. Presumably that which could not be unanimously accepted was left out of the opinion in each of these cases.

Sometimes a concurring opinion has been used to signal that a Justice thinks a prior case's holding or rationale should be restricted as to precedential weight. Most dramatic in the education area is the concurring opinion of Justice Douglas in *Engel v. Vitale*[4] (nondenominational prayer) in which in 1962 he stated that in retrospect he believed that the four dissenting Justices in 1947 in *Everson v. Board of Education*[5] (transportation to parochial schools) had been correct. If Justice Douglas had believed in 1947 as he did in 1962 that first decision to uphold the constitutionality of certain aids to parochial schools would have "gone the other way."

Separate concurring opinions by Justices Powell and Stevens in *Runyon v. McCrary*[6] (racial segregation in private schools) indicated that they felt bound by a prior Supreme Court interpretation of a statute even though they disagreed with it. Separate concurring opinions by Justices Black and Harlan in *Epperson v. Arkansas*[7] (ban on teaching evolution) contained criticisms of some of the passages written for the unanimous Court by Justice Fortas. He had included extensive comments on academic freedom and on vagueness of the statute before making the *ratio decidendi* a violation of the establishment of religion clause. Justice Harlan said, "In the process of *not* deciding [the contentions that the statute was unconstitutionally vague and that it interfered with free speech], the Court obscures its otherwise straightforward holding, and opens its opinion to possible implications from which I am constrained to disassociate myself."[8]

A concurring opinion may be a vehicle for a Justice to stress facts essential to understanding his acceptance of a judgment. In *Lau v. Nichols*[9] (non-English speaking students), it was through a concurring opinion that Justice Blackmun, joined by Justice Burger, emphasized that in a case where the number of children was "very few," the Court's unanimous decision would not be viewed by them "as conclusive upon the issue whether [Title VI] and the guidelines require the funded school district to provide special instruction. For me, numbers are at the heart of this case and my concurrence is to be understood accordingly."[10]

The use of a concurring opinion to stress points *not* to be inferred from a vote for a judgment is illustrated by Justice Stewart's concurrence in *City of Madison, Joint School District No. 8 v. Wisconsin Employment Relations Commission*[11] (nonunion teacher speaking at board meeting). He commented that under the Constitution, a public body was not required to allow anybody to speak on any topic. "I write simply to emphasize that we are not called upon in this case to consider what constitutional limitations there may be upon a governmental body's authority to structure discussion at public meetings."[12]

Occasionally a "trial balloon" is floated in a concurring opinion. Justice Powell, in 1973, in *Keyes v. School District No. 1, Denver, Colorado*[13] (de jure segregation in Denver) concurred only in the order of remand and expressed the view that the de jure/de facto distinction in approaching racial segregation cases was inappropriate. He said that "we must recognize that the evil of operating separate schools is no less in Denver than in Atlanta ... [and] should abandon a distinction which long since has outlived its time, and formulate constitutional principles of national rather than merely regional application."[14] Justice Douglas joined the opinion of the Court in the case, but expressed the view that "there is, for the purpose of the Equal Protection Clause of the Fourteenth Amendment as applied to the school cases, no difference between *de facto* and *de jure* segregation."[15] This view has never been accepted by any other Justice, and the de jure/de facto distinction has been reinforced and extended by the Court to areas other than education in years subsequent to 1973.

It must be remembered, however, that it is the "opinion of the Court" that authoritatively states the law in each case, and that the views accepted by a majority of the Justices comprise the precedents. Each opinion of the Court must be a vehicle for rationalizing the conclusions reached by the Court in that case based upon background facts of the case and prior opinions. Personal value judgments are to be avoided. In *Zorach v. Clauson*,[16] although the Court upheld the constitutionality of the arrangement for released time for religious instruction off school premises, the opinion pointedly observed, "This program may be unwise and improvident from an educational or a community viewpoint.... Our individual preferences, however, are not the constitutional standard."[17]

In *San Antonio Independent School District v. Rodriguez,*[18] wherein the Court found the Texas system of school finance to be constitutional, it commented, "We hardly need add that this Court's action today is not to be viewed as placing its judicial imprimatur on the status quo. The need is apparent for reform in tax systems [to support public schools]."[19]

Nor are the preferences of the president or of other high officials a valid consideration for the Court. This was dramatically illustrated in 1971 when the Court twice ruled contrary to views publicly expressed by President Nixon—unanimously in *Swann v. Charlotte-Mecklenburg Board of Education*[20] to uphold busing as a tool to correct de jure segregation and eight-to-one in *Lemon v. Kurtzman*[21] to invalidate forms of financial aid to parochial schools. The dissenter in the latter case was neither of President Nixon's appointees, Justices Burger and Blackmun. It was Justice White, an appointee of President Kennedy, who had politically opposed the type of financial arrangement Justice White, alone, voted to support in terms of its constitutionality.

Although the Court must be aware of the changing social, economic, and political environment, its continuing role is to apply the Constitution as it was intended by the framers and as it has been interpreted by Court decisions over the years. One of the most eloquent statements of the necessity for the Court not to be swayed by political majorities of the moment was written in *West Virginia State Board of Education v. Barnette*[22] (flag salute):

> The very purpose of a Bill of Rights was to withdraw certain subjects from the vicissitudes of political controversy, to place them beyond the reach of majorities and officials and to establish them as legal principles to be applied by the courts. One's right to life, liberty, and property, to free speech, a free press, freedom of worship and assembly, and other fundamental rights may not be submitted to vote; they depend on the outcome of no elections.[23]

Many public education cases were decided in a way diametrically contrary to prevailing public opinion. Sometimes that attitude was nationwide, as was support of loyalty oaths for teachers. Sometimes it was regional, as for racial segregation. Sometimes it was in one state, as indicated in *Pierce v. Society of Sisters of the Holy Names of Jesus and Mary*[24] by the Oregon legislation enacted directly by the voters to require attendance of all children of certain ages at public schools only.

The Court has cautioned the judicial branch to be wary of intruding unnecessarily into the education process. In *Epperson v. Arkansas*[25] (ban on teaching evolution) it was said, "Judicial interposition in the operation of the public school system of the Nation raises problems requiring care and restraint.... Courts do not and cannot intervene in the resolution of conflicts which arise in the daily operation of school systems and which do not directly and sharply implicate basic constitutional values."[26] In *Tinker v. Des Moines Independent Community School District*[27] (student armbands), the Court stated that it "has repeatedly emphasized the need for affirming the comprehensive authority of the States and of school authorities, consistent with fundamental constitutional safeguards, to prescribe and control conduct in the schools."[28]

Yet, as the preceding chapters illustrate, courts increasingly *are* deciding education cases, for in the words of the Supreme Court in *Tinker*, "It can hardly be argued that either students or teachers shed their constitutional rights to freedom of speech or expression at the schoolhouse gate."[29] This was a quarter century after the Court had said in *West Virginia State Board of Education v. Barnette* (flag salute):

> [O]ur duty to apply the Bill of Rights to assertions of official authority [does not] depend upon [the Justices'] possession of marked competence in the field where the invasion of rights occurs.... We cannot, because of modest estimates of our competence in such specialities as public education, withhold the judgment that history authenticates as the function of this Court when liberty is infringed.[30]

Many times arguments presented to the Court appear weak, if not frivolous, but the Court usually has responded to them with perhaps more respect than some deserve. In *Meyer v. Nebraska*[31] (ban on teaching German), one reason offered to support the statute was to protect the child's health by limiting his mental activities. In *Cleveland Board of Education v. La Fleur*[32] (mandatory maternity leave), the school authorities advanced the argument that the required leave five months before the expected date of birth of the child was to serve the objective of continuity of instruction. One of the teachers, however, was required to leave in mid-December rather than the end of the semester in January, and two others could well have finished the school year and still have been about two months from their expected times for giving birth. In *Hazelwood School District v. United States*[33] (pattern of employment discrimination), it was contended that for statistical purposes black teachers in the city of St. Louis should not be counted in the relevant labor market area of the suburbs because the city had actively recruited black teachers from other parts of the country. In *Committee for Public Education and Religious Liberty v. Nyquist*[34] (financial aid for parochial schools), it was argued that since parents were reimbursed for money already spent, the situation differed significantly from circumstances previously declared unconstitutional (where the money had been directly routed to the parochial schools through parents) because the dollars given the parents were not the dollars that had been given to the schools and might never reach the schools. In *Murray v. Curlett*[35] (Lord's Prayer and Bible in public schools), school authorities testified that acknowledgment of the existence of God as symbolized in the opening exercise had a nonreligious purpose in that it established a "discipline tone" that caused students to conform to accepted standards of behavior in school. In *Stone v. Graham*[36] (posting of the Ten Commandments) it was claimed that the purpose was not religious despite the focus of such admonitions as not to "take the name of the Lord, thy God, in vain."

Despite the fact that the Constitution expressly prescribes that certain actions can be taken only by a vote of more than a simple majority, the requirement of a sixty percent vote for passage of a school bond referendum was attacked as being unconstitutional in *Gordon v. Lance*.[37] A comparable situation arose regarding loyalty oaths. The Constitution contains an oath obliging the president to swear, "I will faithfully execute the Office of President of the United States, and will to the best of my Ability, preserve, protect and defend the Constitution of the United States."[38] A similar phrase in an oath for teachers was attacked in *Cole v. Richardson*[39] as unconstitutional.

Even though a question appears to have been judicially settled by an opinion of the Court, a change in material facts or a new argument may cause the Court to accept a similar case for review and take another look at the subject. This also gives the Court a chance to elaborate on principles it may wish to clarify in light of reactions to the prior case and/or apparent misconstructions of it by lower courts.

An example of reconsideration of a precedent in light of a new argument is to be found in connection with the furnishing of textbooks to students in parochial schools. In 1968, in *Board of Education v. Allen*,[40] the Court considered the effect of the establishment of religion clause on the practice, which it had upheld in 1930 in *Cochran v. Louisiana State Board of Education*[41] without arguments based on that clause presented. The outcome was not changed: nonsectarian textbooks may be furnished to children in parochial schools if a state so desires.

Reconsideration because of a changed material fact is illustrated in relation to released time for public school enrollees for religious instruction. The Court, in 1952, in *Zorach v. Clauson*[42] upheld the practice of granting students released time for religious instruction off school premises, whereas the practice in 1948 had been forbidden within school buildings in *People of State of Illinois ex rel. McCollum v. Board of Education*.[43] The change of location of the religious instruction changed the answer to the question of constitutionality.

Using a subsequent opinion to clarify reasoning behind a prior decision is illustrated by the Court's 1962 and 1963 school prayer cases. Surely if use of a nondenominational prayer as part of opening exercises was unconstitutional, as had been held in *Engel v. Vitale*,[44] so would be the patently sectarian Lord's Prayer and Bible involved in *School District of Abington Township, Pa. v. Schempp*.[45] There had been, however, a tremendous public controversy following the *Engel* decision. In the *Abington* opinion, the Court took the opportunity to address many of the criticisms and attempted to allay some extremist projections of the *Engel* opinion.

Occasionally, the highest court of a state or a federal court of appeals simply fails correctly to apply established federal case law, and the Supreme Court is obliged to review a case in order to rectify the error and to reinforce the precedent established previously. Unanimous votes to reverse lower appellate court decisions have been cast since 1968 in such diverse education cases as *Epperson v. Arkansas*[46] (ban on teaching evolution), *Healy v. James*[47] (restricting a student organization), *City of Madison, Joint School District No. 8 v. Wisconsin Employment Relations Commission*[48] (nonunion teacher speaking at board meeting), *Mt. Healthy City School District v. Doyle*[49] (nonrenewal of teacher's contract), *Givhan v. Western Line Consolidated School District*[50] (private criticism of principal), *Harrah Independent School District v. Martin*[51] (inservice requirement for teachers), and *Texas Department of Community Affairs v. Burdine*[52] (burdens of proof in employment discrimination cases).

The Court has directly or in effect overruled itself on five points of law in cases treated in this volume. The first took fifty-eight years to transpire. Although, because the Court never had expressly upheld the practice, it was not a direct overruling that rejected "separate but equal" arrangements for educating black children, the Court in its 1954 opinion in *Brown I*[53] repudiated the language that had appeared in some earlier decisions that had implicitly upheld the doctrine for public schools. The Court said that it could not "turn the clock back" to 1868 when the fourteenth amendment was adopted or even to 1896 when the expression appeared in the case upholding separate railroad cars for blacks and whites in Louisiana. "We must consider public education in the light of its full development and its present place in American life throughout the Nation."[54] In *Brown I*, which was the first case to challenge the "separate but equal" doctrine for public schools, it is important to note that the Court could rely on psychological evidence to establish that separate facilities had a detrimental effect on black children and, therefore, were "inherently unequal." Thus, this ruling was in accord with uncontradicted evidence. It was not a holding based on the personal social views of the Justices, as has been claimed by many critics.

The second change of course, by contrast, was abrupt. In 1940, against a religious claim, the Court upheld the requirement that students recite the Pledge of Allegiance. Three years later in *West Virginia State Board of Education v. Barnette*,[55] the Court not only ruled to the contrary, but its opinion barring the requirement was not limited to those who asserted religious reasons for nonparticipation. That this decision came in the darker days of World War II makes it all the more impressive.

The third change occurred in 1967 when the Court in *Keyishian v. Board of Regents of University of State of New York*[56] invalidated the regulatory scheme developed in New York State to implement the Feinberg Law, a statute designed to assure that subversive teachers were not employed in the schools and colleges of the state. In 1952, the Court found the statute not to be unconstitutional on its face. In the intervening fifteen years, there developed what the Court called a "regulatory maze" that made the statute, as it was implemented, constitutionally unacceptable. The Court expressly said, however, that "to the extent that [the 1952 opinion] sustained the provision of the Feinberg Law constituting membership in an organization advocating forceful overthrow of government a ground for disqualification, pertinent constitutional doctrines have since rejected the premises upon which that conclusion rested."[57]

The fourth and fifth changes affected local government units in general as well as school districts. In 1968, the Court approved an amendment to the Fair Labor Standards Act that extended the Act beyond the private sector to include employees of state hospitals, institutions, and schools. In 1976 in *National League of Cities v. Usery*,[58] the Court expressly overruled that holding. In the latter case, it held unconstitutional another amendment that would have made all state and local governments comply with federal minimum wage and maximum hours requirements. The Court said that this provision would intrude on the right of states to structure their integral governmental functions, and thus was not authorized under the Constitution's grant to Congress of the power to regulate commerce among the several states.

The most recent reversal of direction came in 1978 in *Monell v. Department of Social Services of City of New York*[59] when the Court repudiated a contrary conclusion of 1961 and held that for purposes of § 1983, local governments *were* to be considered as "persons." A reassessment of the legislative history behind § 1983 and some inconsistencies implicit in some of its decisions between 1961 and 1978 led to the Court's change that had the effect of making school boards liable for monetary damages for violations of civil rights. School boards, prior to 1978, had been subject to suit under § 1983, but plaintiffs could obtain only injunctive relief.

Recognition of the importance of education to our nation frequently is expressed in Court opinions. The unanimous opinion in *Brown I* (racial desegregation) succinctly stated, "Today, education is perhaps the most important function of state and local governments;"[60] and no Justice dissented from the statement in *Wisconsin v. Yoder* (Amish exemption), "Providing public schools ranks at the very apex of the function of a State."[61]

Another theme inherent in many cases is that of respect for and sensitivity to the role of the teacher. In 1979, in *Ambach v. Norwick*[62] (citizenship requirement for teachers), the Court expressed it as clearly as in any preceding decision when it said:

> [A] teacher serves as a role model for his students, exerting a subtle but important influence over their perceptions and values. Thus, through both the presentation of course materials and the example he sets, a teacher has an opportunity to influence the attitudes of students toward government, the political process, and a citizen's social responsibilities. The influence is crucial to the continued good health of a democracy.[63]

In several contexts the Court has stressed the need for keeping classrooms free from thought control. In *Shelton v. Tucker* (preconditions for teacher employment), it said, "The vigilant protection of constitutional freedoms is nowhere more vital than in the community of American schools."[64] In *Keyishian v. Board of Regents of University of State of New York* (teacher loyalty program), it stated emphatically, "Our Nation is deeply committed to safeguarding academic freedom, which is of transcendent value to all of us and not merely to the teachers concerned. That freedom is therefore a special concern of the First Amendment, which does not tolerate laws that cast a pall of orthodoxy over the classroom."[65] In *Pickering v. Board of Education of Township High School District No. 205*[66] (public criticism of policy by teacher) and in *Givhan v. Western Line Consolidated School District*[67] (private criticism of policy by teacher), the Court unanimously supported the right of a teacher to participate in the formulation of broad school policy by commenting critically on matters of public concern. Teachers may not "constitutionally be compelled to relinquish the First Amendment rights they would otherwise enjoy as citizens to comment on matters of public interest in connection with the operation of the public schools in which they work."[68]

Another general emphasis of the Court is the recognition not only of the constitutional power of states in education matters but of the long history of local operation of schools within individual states. In *Milliken I*[69] (multidistrict remedies for racial segregation), the Court commented, "No single tradition in public education is more deeply rooted than local control over the operation of schools; local autonomy has long been thought essential both to the maintenance of community concern and support for public schools and to quality of the educational process."[70] In *San Antonio Independent School District v. Rodriguez* (financing of education) the Court observed that "local control means . . . the freedom to devote more money to the education of one's children . . . [and] the opportunity . . . for participation in the decision-making process that determines how those local tax dollars will be spent."[71] Also to be noted is that the Court in *Brown II*[72] (implementation of racial desegregation) relied on a program for racial desegregation that provided for local school boards to be the initiators of desegregation plans to be submitted for approval by the courts. In *Ingraham v. Wright* (corporal punishment), "[t]he openness of the public school and its supervision by the community"[73] were key factors in persuading the Court that there were checks on the excessive corporal punishment of students that were not present in the case of prisoners, thereby making the eighth amendment bar to cruel and unusual punishments inapplicable to the school setting.

The quality of evidence offered in support of assertions about education matters has been consistently examined with care by the Court. In *Wisconsin v. Yoder*[74] (Amish exemption), the Court accepted the goals of compulsory education as advanced by the state, but observed that the evidence showed the Amish to be "productive and very law-abiding members of society; they reject public welfare in any of its usual modern forms."[75] Further, the Court concluded that the Amish had "carried the even more difficult burden of demonstrating the adequacy of their alternative mode of continuing informal vocational education [for youth fourteen to sixteen years old] in terms of precisely those overall interests that the State advances in support of its program of compulsory high school education."[76]

In *San Antonio Independent School District v. Rodriguez*[77] (financing of education), the Court exposed an egregious error in the principal statistical evidence that the lower federal court had accepted to support a claim that in Texas expenditures per pupil and wealth of school districts and residents thereof were positively correlated. The "evidence" had been submitted by a professor at Syracuse University's Educational Finance Policy Institute. The Court summarized, "It is evident that, even if the conceptual questions were answered favorably to [those challenging the finance system], no factual basis exists upon which to found a claim of comparative wealth discrimination."[78]

It is highly unlikely that anyone could *favor* the results reached by the Supreme Court in all of the cases discussed. It is highly unlikely that anyone could *agree* that the holdings were constitutionally inevitable in all of the cases. Nevertheless, it is highly unlikely that anyone of intelligence and industry could fail to *understand* the logic set forth in the opinions of the Court and the incremental development of case law under the Constitution. Such understanding is essential for all who have interest in education policy. To help the reader accomplish that goal has been the purpose of this volume.

1. 403 U.S. 602, 91 S. Ct. 2105 (1971).
2. Committee for Pub. Educ. and Religious Liberty v. Regan, 444 U.S. 646, 662, 100 S. Ct. 840, 851 (1980).
3. 347 U.S. 483, 74 S. Ct. 686 (1954).
4. 370 U.S. 421, 82 S. Ct. 1261 (1962).
5. 330 U.S. 1, 67 S. Ct. 504 (1947).
6. 427 U.S. 160, 96 S. Ct. 2586 (1976).
7. 393 U.S. 97, 89 S. Ct. 266 (1968).
8. *Id.* at 115, 89 S. Ct. at 276.
9. 414 U.S. 563, 94 S. Ct. 786 (1974).
10. *Id.* at 572, 94 S. Ct. at 791.
11. 429 U.S. 167, 97 S. Ct. 421 (1976).
12. *Id.* at 177, 97 S. Ct. at 428.
13. 413 U.S. 189, 93 S. Ct. 2686 (1973).
14. *Id.* at 219, 93 S. Ct. at 2703.
15. *Id.* at 215, 93 S. Ct. at 2700.
16. 343 U.S. 306, 72 S. Ct. 679 (1952).
17. *Id.* at 314, 72 S. Ct. at 684.
18. 411 U.S. 1, 93 S. Ct. 1278 (1973).
19. *Id.* at 58, 93 S. Ct. at 1309.
20. 402 U.S. 1, 91 S. Ct. 1267 (1971).
21. 403 U.S. 602, 91 S. Ct. 2105 (1971).
22. 319 U.S. 624, 63 S. Ct. 1178 (1943).
23. *Id.* at 638, 63 S. Ct. at 1185.
24. 268 U.S. 510, 45 S. Ct. 571 (1925).
25. 393 U.S. 97, 89 S. Ct. 266 (1968).
26. *Id.* at 104, 89 S. Ct. at 270.
27. 393 U.S. 503, 89 S. Ct. 733 (1969).
28. *Id.* at 507, 89 S. Ct. at 737.
29. *Id.* at 506, 89 S. Ct. at 736.
30. 319 U.S. at 639-640, 63 S. Ct. at 1186.
31. 262 U.S. 390, 43 S. Ct. 625 (1923).
32. 414 U.S. 632, 94 S. Ct. 791 (1974).
33. 433 U.S. 299, 97 S. Ct. 2736 (1977).
34. 413 U.S. 756, 93 S. Ct. 2955 (1973).
35. 374 U.S. 203, 83 S. Ct. 1560 (1963).
36. 449 U.S. 39, 101 S. Ct. 192 (1980).
37. 403 U.S. 1, 91 S. Ct. 1889 (1971).
38. U.S. CONST. art. II, § 1.
39. 405 U.S. 676, 92 S. Ct. 1332 (1972).
40. 392 U.S. 236, 88 S. Ct. 1923 (1968).
41. 281 U.S. 370, 50 S. Ct. 335 (1930).
42. 343 U.S. 306, 72 S. Ct. 679 (1952).

43. 333 U.S. 203, 68 S. Ct. 461 (1948).
44. 370 U.S. 421, 82 S. Ct. 1261 (1962).
45. 374 U.S. 203, 83 S. Ct. 1560 (1963).
46. 393 U.S. 97, 89 S. Ct. 266 (1968).
47. 408 U.S. 169, 92 S. Ct. 2338 (1972).
48. 429 U.S. 167, 97 S. Ct. 421 (1976).
49. 429 U.S. 274, 97 S. Ct. 568 (1977).
50. 439 U.S. 410, 99 S. Ct. 693 (1979).
51. 440 U.S. 194, 99 C. Ct. 1062 (1979).
52. 450 U.S. 248, 101 S. Ct. 1089 (1981).
53. 347 U.S. 483, 74 S. Ct. 686 (1954).
54. *Id.* at 492-493, 74 S. Ct. at 691.
55. 319 U.S. 624, 63 S. Ct. 1178 (1943).
56. 385 U.S. 589, 87 S. Ct. 675 (1967).
57. *Id.* at 595, 87 S. Ct. at 679.
58. 426 U.S. 833, 96 S. Ct. 2465 (1976).
59. 436 U.S. 658, 98 S. Ct. 2018 (1978).
60. 347 U.S. 483, 493, 74 S. Ct. 686, 691 (1954).
61. 406 U.S. 205, 213, 92 S. Ct. 1526, 1532 (1972).
62. 441 U.S. 68, 99 S. Ct. 1589 (1979).
63. *Id.* at 78-79, 99 S. Ct. at 1595-1596.
64. 364 U.S. 479, 487, 81 S. Ct. 247, 251 (1960).
65. 385 U.S. 589, 603, 87 S. Ct. 675, 683 (1967).
66. 391 U.S. 563, 88 S. Ct. 1731 (1968).
67. 439 U.S. 410, 99 S. Ct. 693 (1979).
68. Pickering, 391 U.S. at 568, 88 S. Ct. at 1734.
69. 418 U.S. 717, 94 S. Ct. 3112 (1974).
70. *Id.* at 741-742, 94 S. Ct. at 3125-3126.
71. 411 U.S. 1, 49-50, 93 S. Ct. 1278, 1305 (1973).
72. 349 U.S. 294, 75 S. Ct. 753 (1955).
73. 430 U.S. 651, 670, 97 S. Ct. 1401, 1412 (1977).
74. 406 U.S. 205, 92 S. Ct. 1526 (1972).
75. *Id.* at 222, 92 S. Ct. at 1537.
76. *Id.* at 235, 92 S. Ct. at 1543.
77. 411 U.S. 1, 93 S. Ct. 1278 (1973).
78. *Id.* at 27, 93 S. Ct. at 1293.

APPENDIX A

Glossary

Action: Lawsuit.

Amicus curiae: Friend of the court, applied to a brief submitted by one not a party to the suit; requires court's permission.

Appellant: Party who brings an action in a higher court.

Appellee: Party against whom an action is brought in a higher court.

Arguendo: For the sake of argument.

Case at bar: The case presently being decided by the court.

Caveat: Let him or her beware; a warning.

Certiorari: Proceeding in which a higher court reviews a decision of an inferior court.

Class action: A lawsuit brought by one or more persons on behalf of all persons similarly situated as to complaint and remedy sought.

De facto: In fact; in reality.

Defendant: Party against whom an action is brought.

De jure: By action of law.

De minimis: Something so insignificant as to be unworthy of judicial attention.

Dicta: Statements in a judicial opinion not necessary to the decision of the case.

Enjoin: Command to maintain the status quo either by doing or refraining from doing a specific act; the writ is called an injunction.

Et al.: And others.

Et seq.: And those following.

Express: Directly set forth in words.

Ex rel.: On the information supplied by.

Holding: A ruling by the court; court's decision on a question properly raised in a case.

In loco parentis: In place of the parent, having some of the rights and duties of a parent.

Infra: Below; following.

Injunction: *See* "enjoin."

Instant case: The case presently being decided by the court.

Judgment: Final determination by the court of the rights of parties in a case.

Liable: Legally responsible.

Malice: Improper motive; intentionally committing a wrongful act without justification or excuse.

Mandamus: Writ ordering the execution of a non-discretionary duty by one charged with responsibility therefor.

Material: Important.

Merits: The factual issues raised, as distinguished from procedural issues; substance of a case, rather than technicalities.

Ministerial: Not involving discretion as to whether or how an act is to be performed.

Moot case: A case in which the factual controversy no longer exists and in which a judgment would be abstract with no practical effect.

On its face: Based on wording alone, without waiting to see the application of the language.

Opinion: Reasoning offered by a court to explain why it has decided a case as it has. The "opinion of the court" is that reasoning accepted by a majority of the participating judges. A "concurring opinion" contains the views of a judge who agrees with the court's judgment but desires to express some views not contained to his satisfaction in the opinion of the court. A "dissenting opinion" expresses the reasons a judge would decide the case differently from the majority of the judges. When several questions arise in one case, there may be partial concurrences or dissents.

Parens patriae: Concept of the state's guardianship over persons unable to direct their own affairs, *e.g.*, minors.

Per curiam: By the court; an opinion with no identification of the author.

Per se: In and of itself.

Petitioner: Party bringing a case before a court; the appellant in a case appealed.

Plaintiff: Party instituting a legal action.

Police power: The inherent power of government to impose restrictions in order to provide for health, safety, and welfare of its constituents.

Prima facie: On its face; evidence supporting a conclusion unless it is rebutted.

Quasi: As if; almost.

Ratio decidendi: Reasoning applied by a court to crucial facts of a case in process of determining the judgment; basic reason for a holding.

Reductio ad absurdum: Interpretation which would lead to results clearly illogical or not intended.

Remand: Send back a case to the court from which it was appealed for further action by the lower court.

Res judicata: A matter finally decided by the highest court of competent jurisdiction.

Respondent: Party against whom a legal action is brought; the appellee in a case appealed.

Scienter: Knowledge of a set of facts.

Stare decisis: Doctrine of precedents whereby prior decisions of courts are followed under similar facts.

Sub judice: Being considered by a court.

Summary: Immediate; without a full proceeding.

Supra: Above; preceding.

Ultra vires: Outside the legal power of an individual or body.

Vacate: Annul.

Vel non.: Or not.

Vested: Fixed; accrued; not subject to any contingency.

Void: Having no legal force or effect.

APPENDIX B

Key Provisions of the United States Constitution

Article I, Section 10

No State Shall . . . pass any . . . Law impairing the Obligation of Contracts. . . .

Amendment 1

Congress shall make no law respecting an establishment of religion, or prohibiting the free exercise thereof; or abridging the freedom of speech, or of the press; or the right of the people peaceably to assemble, and to petition the Government for a redress of grievances.

Amendment 5

No person . . . shall be compelled in any criminal case to be a witness against himself, nor be deprived of life, liberty, or property, without due process of law; nor shall private property be taken for public use, without just compensation.

Amendment 8

Excessive bail shall not be required, nor excessive fines imposed, nor cruel and unusual punishments inflicted.

Amendment 10

The powers not delegated to the United States by the Constitution, nor prohibited by it to the States, are reserved to the States respectively, or to the people.

Amendment 14

All persons born or naturalized in the United States, and subject to the jurisdiction thereof, are citizens of the United States and of the State wherein they reside. No State shall make or enforce any law which shall abridge the privileges or immunities of citizens of the United States; nor shall any State deprive any person of life, liberty, or property, without due process of law; nor deny to any person within its jurisdiction the equal protection of the laws.

See also first page of chapter 1.

APPENDIX C

Key Federal Statutory Provisions

Title VI of Civil Rights Act of 1964
[42 U.S.C. § 2000d (1976)]

No person in the United States shall, on the ground of race, color or national origin, be excluded from participation in, be denied the benefits of, or be subjected to discrimination under any program or activity receiving Federal financial assistance.

Title VII of Civil Rights Act of 1964
[42 U.S.C. § 2000e-2(a)(1976)]

It shall be an unlawful employment practice for an employer (1) to fail or refuse to hire or to discharge any individual, or otherwise to discriminate against any individual with respect to his compensation, terms, conditions, or privileges of employment, because of such individual's race, color, religion, sex, or national origin; or (2) to limit, segregate, or classify his employees or applicants for employment in any way which would deprive or tend to deprive any individual of employment opportunities or otherwise adversely affect his status as an employee, because of such individual's race, color, religion, sex, or national origin.

Title IX of Education Amendments of 1972
[20 U.S.C. § 1681 (1976)]

No person in the United States shall, on the basis of sex, be excluded from participation in, be denied the benefits of, or be subjected to discrimination under any education program or activity receiving Federal financial assistance.

Section 1981
[42 U.S.C. § 1981 (1976)]

All persons within the jurisdiction of the United States shall have the same right in every State and Territory to make and enforce contracts . . . as is enjoyed by white citizens, ...

Section 1983
[42 U.S.C. § 1983 (1976)]

Every person who, under color of any statute, ordinance, regulation, custom, or usage, of any State or Territory, subjects, or causes to be subjected, any citizen of the United States or other person within the jurisdiction thereof to the deprivation of any rights, privileges, or immunities secured by the Constitution and laws, shall be liable to the party injured in an action at law, suit in equity, or other proper proceeding for redress.

See also chapter 17.

TABLE OF CASES

INDEX

ABOUT THE AUTHOR

E. Edmund Reutter, Jr. is Professor of Education in the Division of Educational Institutions and Programs at Teachers College, Columbia University. He is the author or coauthor of sixteen editions of nine books on education law, including *The Law of Public Education* (with Robert R. Hamilton), *The Yearbook of School Law* for 1967 through 1970 (with Lee O. Garber), and *The Courts and Student Conduct.* Dr. Reutter is past president of NOLPE, regional editor of the *NOLPE School Law Reporter,* and a lecturer nationwide in the fields of education and law.